READING DOSTOEVSKY

READING DOSTOEVSKY

Victor Terras

The University of Wisconsin Press

The University of Wisconsin Press
2537 Daniels Street
Madison, Wisconsin 53718

3 Henrietta Street
London WC2E 8LU, England

5   4   3   2   1

Printed in the United States of America

Library of Congress Cataloging-in-Publication Data
Terras, Victor.
    Reading Dostoevsky / Victor Terras.
    184 pp.   cm.
    Includes bibliographical references and index.
    ISBN 0-299-16050-5 (cloth: alk. paper).
  ISBN 0-299-16054-8 (pbk.: alk. paper)
    1. Dostoyevsky, Fyodor, 1821–1881 — Criticism and
interpretation.   I. Title.
    PG3328.Z6T397   1998
    891.73'3 — dc21   98-23342

To Rita

CONTENTS

PREFACE

A book on Dostoevsky requires justification. I do not find it in a claim to have discovered a new approach or model of interpretation. Rather, I find it in recognizing that it is precisely the wealth of diverse and even contradictory readings allowed by a Dostoevskian text that accounts for the greatness of his art. The following brief survey of various approaches taken to Dostoevsky's works will show how the semantic range of their interpretation has expanded and how new meanings have been attributed to them.

Early in his career, Dostoevsky was recognized primarily as the author of *Poor Folk* (1846), his first novel, and hence as a leading exponent of "sentimental naturalism" (a term of Apollon Grigoriev's coinage) and a champion of the misfits and victims of society. This is how N. A. Dobroliubov presented him in his review article "Downtrodden People" (1861), written in response to Dostoevsky's novel *The Insulted and Injured* (1861).

After the appearance of *Notes from Underground* (1864), critics began to suspect that Dostoevsky's concern with the insulted and injured was motivated not so much by compassion as by an unhealthy (in their view) curiosity about the darker recesses of the human psyche (Ivan Turgenev, for one, thought so), by a perverse attraction to the diseased states of the human mind (V. G. Belinsky was the first to come up with this notion in his review of *The Double*), or, worse yet, by sadistic pleasure in observing human suffering (N. K. Mikhailovsky made this charge in the celebrated essay "A Cruel Talent," 1882).

Dostoevsky's penetrating psychology caught the attention of critics, as well as of the psychiatric profession, even in his lifetime.[1] Subsequently,

---

1. See, for example, Vladimir F. Chizh, *Dostoevskii kak psikhopatolog* (Moscow, 1885). The author, a professor of psychiatry, recommends Dostoevsky's novels as useful reading to his students.

many psychological studies, by Freudian psychologists and others, have been devoted to his works.

As editor of *Vremia* (1861–63) and *Epokha* (1864–65), Dostoevsky was a party to unceasing ideological controversy. The journals of the Dostoevsky brothers steered a precarious course between the Slavophile Right and the Nihilist Left, yet with little sympathy with westernizing Liberals. The result was a predominantly negative response to Dostoevsky's fiction by critics of these camps. His journalistic writings, gathered in *A Writer's Diary* after 1873, made him the leading voice of the conservative nationalist *pochva* ("the soil") movement. While there exist many connections between Dostoevsky's journalism and his fiction, there is a fundamental difference between the logic of a work of fiction and that of a newspaper article. Nevertheless, the value — or absence of it — seen in Dostoevsky's fiction by his contemporaries of the 1860s and 1870s depended largely on the reader's ideological position. This continued after Dostoevsky's death and through the entire twentieth century. His thought is not without a political extension even in today's Russia.

Only after his death was Dostoevsky recognized as an important thinker. The philosopher Vladimir Soloviev was the first to assert this in "Three Talks in Memory of Dostoevsky" (1881–83). He was followed by V. V. Rozanov, whose study *The Legend of the Grand Inquisitor by F. M. Dostoevsky* (1894) recognized the power of the questions raised by Dostoevsky's antihero in *Notes from Underground* and by Ivan Karamazov in *The Brothers Karamazov*. Lev Shestov's study *Dostoevsky and Nietzsche: The Philosophy of Tragedy* (1903) linked Dostoevsky's thought to that of Stirner, Kierkegaard, and Nietzsche, making him one of the forerunners of twentieth-century Existentialism. The writings of D. S. Merezhkovsky (1865–1941), such as *L. Tolstoi and Dostoevsky* (1901–2) and "Dostoevsky: Prophet of the Russian Revolution" (1906) made Dostoevsky's ideas widely known, in Russia and in the West.

The Russian symbolist Viacheslav Ivanov (1866–1949) discovered a mythical subtext in Dostoevsky's novels, and archetypes in their plots and characters. Ivanov termed Dostoevsky's novels "novel-tragedies" (*roman-tragedii*) and analyzed them in terms of classical drama.[2]

Since Ivanov, several scholars have suggested that Dostoevsky's texts proceed simultaneously on several semantic levels — empirical, psychological,

2.   First in "Dostoevskii i roman-tragediia," in *Borozdy i mezhi: Opyty esteticheskie i kriticheskie* (Moscow: Musaget, 1916), pp. 5–60.

and symbolic. "Symbolic" may be variously understood as political, moral, metaphysical, allegoric, or anagogic.

The Russian scholar Boris Engelhardt, in a study entitled "Dostoevsky's Ideological Novel" (1925), saw the main characters of Dostoevsky's novels as ideas incarnate. This conception has been subsequently much elaborated on, in Russia as well as in the West.

In the 1920s, scholars like Iu. N. Tynianov, V. V. Vinogradov, and V. L. Komarovich were richly rewarded when they turned their attention to intertextual connections in Dostoevsky's works.[3] Dostoevsky's fiction is teeming with quotations, parodies, allusions, polemical sorties, and other references to a large number of Russian and foreign works. Scholars have compiled a long list of authors and works with which Dostoevsky enters into some kind of dialogue, either explicitly or implicitly. Literary comparatists are still finding more instances of "another voice" in Dostoevsky's texts.

Then, in 1929, M. M. Bakhtin's now famous study *Problems of Dostoevsky's Poetics* created a synthesis of all previous observations. Its thesis was that Dostoevsky's fiction is dialogic or polyphonic as a matter of principle, with the dialogue assuming various forms: intertextual, as in parody, quotation, allusion, or debate; and intratextual, as in the inner dialogue of a character or narrator, or in irony, travesty, and ambiguity. This left Dostoevsky's works open to different ways of reading, since the meaning of any given passage depended on the reader's alertness, erudition, imagination, *Weltanschauung,* and emotional slant. A scholar will recognize many allusions and hear "another voice" where today's general reader will miss them. To Bakhtin, Dostoevsky's art is quintessentially "novelistic," taking maximal advantage of the novel as an "open form."

Yet, on the other side, structuralist critics have made a case for a well-integrated, and hence "closed," structure, based on a recognizable code in Dostoevsky's major works. For that matter, partisan readers, pro and contra, have always recognized that code. The archconservative K. P. Pobedonostsev did not hesitate to recommend Dostoevsky's works to the Tsar's family. The radical M. E. Saltykov-Shchedrin recognized the Christian subtext even in *Notes from Underground,* where no mention is ever made of religion. Recently, Peeter Torop, a follower of Iu. M. Lotman's school of

---

3. Iurii N. Tynianov, *Dostoevskii i Gogol': K teorii parodii* (Petrograd: Opoiaz, 1921); V. V. Vinogradov, *Evoliutsiia russkogo naturalizma: Gogol' i Dostoevskii* (Moscow: Academia, 1929); W. Komarowitsch, *F. M. Dostojewski—Die Urgestalt der Brüder Karamasoff* (Munich: R. Piper, 1928).

Tartu structuralists, has made a convincing demonstration of a detailed and cohesive "Christocentric" subplot in *Crime and Punishment,* pointing out a large number of details that may be plausibly read as Christian symbols relating to death and resurrection, and specifically to the raising of Lazarus.[4]

Dostoevsky's challenging personality and eventful biography have invited readers to look for projections of both in his works. Correspondence and extant notebooks help one to recognize the author's intent and to identify prototypes of his characters and the intended function of significant details. An approach that sees Dostoevsky's works as a function of his personality was first introduced by N. N. Strakhov in his *Biography* of 1883[5] and has been successfully practiced by L. P. Grossman, L. M. Rozenblium, and most recently by S. V. Belov, L. L. Volgin, Robert Belknap, and Joseph Frank.

I believe that all of the above-mentioned approaches are essential to an understanding and appreciation of Dostoevsky's art. I also believe that the only generalization that fits Dostoevsky's art is that his texts have a semiotic quality of consistent and intense markedness, achieved by every conceivable device.

The chapters of my book are arranged chronologically and cover much of Dostoevsky's fiction, yet the emphasis in each chapter is on a particular aspect of Dostoevsky's art and hence on a particular approach to it.[6]

It remains for me to thank those to whom I owe, either directly or indirectly, everything that is said in this book. Their names are found in the bibliography or index, and it would be unfair to single out any names in particular. But I must thank Jane Barry, my copy editor, for having converted my text, almost all of which was written for casual oral delivery, into what I hope is good scholarly prose.

4.   Peeter Torop, "Perevoploshchenie personazhei v romane F. Dostoevskogo *Prestuplenie i nakazanie,*" in *Dostoevskii: Istoriia i ideologiia* (Tartu: Tartu Ülikooli Kirjastus, 1997), pp. 104–15.

5.   Strakhov's "Reminiscences about Fiodor Mikhailovich Dostoevsky" are a part of the volume *Biografiia, pis'ma i zametki iz zapisnoi knizhki F. M. Dostoevskogo* (St. Petersburg: Tipografiia A. S. Suvorina, 1883).

6.   I use conventional English spelling for Russian names in the text (Dostoevsky, Gogol, Soloviev, Grigoriev); in bibliographical references in the notes as well as in the Bibliography I use an exact transcription according to the Library of Congress system (Dostoevskii, Gogol', Solov'ev, Grigor'ev).

READING DOSTOEVSKY

Detractors and Defenders
of Dostoevsky's Art

IN HIS lifetime, Dostoevsky was not blessed with laudatory reviews.
With time, he became defensive about the artistic quality of his work and
made the excuse that he had had to write hurriedly, with no time to pay attention to stylistic niceties. Anybody familiar with Dostoevsky's notebooks,
drafts, and galley proofs knows that this was hardly true. But generations of
critics have used Dostoevsky's remarks to corroborate their negative assessment of his art.

Most negative opinions about Dostoevsky's art boil down to an assertion
that, while his works are of some interest psychologically or philosophically,
their artistic quality is low. Thus, N. A. Dobroliubov, in an otherwise positive review of Dostoevsky's novel *The Insulted and Injured,* "Downtrodden
People" (*Zabitye liudi,* 1861), said in fact that it was "artistically below criticism." Some more recent critics, such as Ivan Bunin and Vladimir Nabokov,
concur. To be sure, much negative criticism was and still is caused by the
critics' disagreement with Dostoevsky's ideological positions or his general
ethos ("good, but pretentious," said Chekhov).

As regards novelistic structure, some critics have seen Dostoevsky's plots
as chaotic and disorganized, while others have found them "Gothic" and
aimed at cheap effects. Still others have charged Dostoevsky with excessive psychologizing (his rival Turgenev found it intolerable) and with overly
pronounced naturalism ("copying court records").[1] Many critics have found

---

1. P. N. Tkachev, "Bol'nye liudi," *Delo* 3/4 (1873). Quoted from F. M. Dostoevskii, *Polnoe*

Dostoevsky's characters unrealistic, schematic, and contrived. The observation that they all talk alike—like the author—is heard often.

Even more intense is the criticism leveled at Dostoevsky's stylistic craftsmanship. From the very beginning, critics found his style prolix, repetitious, and lacking in polish. Often enough Dostoevsky was also found to be obscure, artificial, and sentimental. Finally, he has been found to lack balance, restraint, and good taste. In a word, whatever the merits of his oeuvre as a whole, its aesthetic value was found to be slight or nonexistent.

Great moral flaws have also been found in Dostoevsky's works. The charge heard most often is that of pessimism. Almost as often, the *outré,* hysterical, and morbid nature of Dostoevsky's works is held up to censure. The label of a "cruel talent" has stuck to him ever since N. K. Mikhailovsky's essay of that title (*Zhestokii talant*) appeared in 1882. Dostoevsky's fascination with the extremes of the human condition is condemned by many critics. Less common are charges of insincerity, unctuousness, and "rosy Christianity."[2]

The truth content of Dostoevsky's works has been often challenged as well. In particular, he is said to have pursued the exceptional instead of the typical. Tendentious distortion of reality is a common charge.[3] In an age of realism, Dostoevsky's penchant for the fantastic, the paradoxical, and the mystical met with much disapproval.[4]

These opinions, each voiced by critics of note, may be assumed to be representative of a substantial body of readers and deserve attention not only as a record of *Rezeptionsgeschichte,* but also as an avenue to an analysis of Dostoevsky's works.

As regards the structure of Dostoevsky's novels, the critics' dissatisfaction is well founded. If the ideal is a well-spaced and economically developed linear plot, a Dostoevskian novel with its multitude of minor characters and subplots, inserted anecdotes, philosophical dialogues, and the narra-

sobranie sochinenii v tridtsati tomakh (Leningrad: Nauka, 1972–90), 12:262. Hereafter abbreviated as *PSS.*

2. K. N. Leont'ev, "Nashi novye khristiane," *Sobranie sochinenii,* 9 vols. (Moscow, 1912), 8:183.

3. For example, N. K. Mikhailovskii, "Literaturnye i zhurnal'nye zametki," *Otechestvennye zapiski* (1873), no. 2/II, calls the nihilists of *The Possessed* "puppets."

4. M. A. Antonovich's review of *The Brothers Karamazov,* entitled "A Mystic-Ascetic Novel" (1881), concentrates on this issue.

tor's essayistic and other digressions is hardly "well structured." It must be considered, though, that this linear — or syntagmatic — view ignores the wealth of paradigmatic structures that may do quite as much to integrate the text as an elegant linear plot would: leitmotifs, situation rhyme, recurrent imagery, mirroring and doubling, symbolic foreshadowing, parallelism, literary echoes and outright quotations, and other such devices are all plentiful in Dostoevsky's novels. Their effect tends to be subliminal, and their presence has been demonstrated only through the efforts of generations of literary scholars.[5]

Claims for Dostoevsky's greatness as a novelist must be staked in connection with the Bakhtinian sense of the novel as an all-inclusive, wide-open expression of the fullness of life in a world in flux. The pattern of a tightly structured tragic plot may be discerned within this loose texture.[6] Isaiah Berlin was, I believe, deeply wrong when he called Dostoevsky a monist "hedgehog" whose art is all about a single issue, rather than a "fox" with a bagful of tricks.[7] A great novelist in this Bakhtinian sense must be a pluralist. Dostoevsky is a pluralist in a variety of ways. He has been aptly called a "romantic realist."[8] He has been thought, certainly in the West, to be the most Russian of novelists; yet his greatest impact has been on Western readers. Dobroliubov considered Dostoevsky a champion of the "downtrodden," and his art is decidedly demotic, yet it came to be appreciated by the intellectual elite of the twentieth century, the Prousts, Gides, and Hermann Hesses.

All these contradictions are enhanced by what Bakhtin called the polyphonic quality of Dostoevsky's art: the presence in his texts of a persistent "other voice," generated by devices such as an ironic narrator, often himself the unwary butt of the implied author's irony, frequent "inner dialogue," multiple ambiguities, and an incessant stream of literary and journalistic quotations, echoes, and allusions.

5. Some key titles on these topics: Robert Belknap, *The Structure of* The Brothers Karamazov (The Hague: Mouton, 1967); Ralph E. Matlaw, "Recurrent Imagery in Dostoevskii," *Harvard Slavic Studies* 3:201–25; Dmitri Chizhevsky, "The Theme of the Double in Dostoevsky," in *Dostoevsky: A Collection of Critical Essays,* ed. René Wellek (Englewood Cliffs, N.J.: Prentice-Hall, 1962); Vyacheslav Ivanov, *Freedom and the Tragic Life: A Study of Dostoevsky,* trans. Norman Cameron (New York: Noonday, 1952); Nina Perlina, *Varieties of Poetic Utterance: Quotation in* The Brothers Karamazov (Lanham, Md.: University Presses of America, 1985).

6. See Chapter 5 for details.

7. Isaiah Berlin, *The Hedgehog and the Fox* (London: Weidenfeld & Nicolson, 1953).

8. Donald Fanger, *Dostoevsky and Romantic Realism: A Study of Dostoevsky in Relation to Balzac, Dickens and Gogol* (Cambridge: Harvard University Press, 1965).

Dostoevsky's texts contain many semantic levels. Their narrative level, itself many-faceted, is synchronized with a moral or political argument, such as the antinomy of human and divine justice in *The Brothers Karamazov;* an allegorical message, say, the prophetic anticipation of the Russian Revolution in *The Possessed;* and metaphysical symbolism, such as the theme of resurrection in *Crime and Punishment.*

Dostoevsky's novels encompass antagonistic philosophies and value systems. He is an excellent "devil's advocate." Sophisticated readers have mistaken for his own ideas what Dostoevsky was in fact trying to refute.[9] Dostoevsky's negative characters, his losers, scoundrels, and villains, are presented with as much empathy as his tragic heroes. Bakhtin drew attention to the carnivalistic strain in Dostoevsky's novels, where a tragic plot may develop from what was initially a scandalous incident or a bad joke. Burlesque comedy is interspersed with tragic action. Serious ideas are advanced by disreputable types, buffoons, or characters who are clearly wrong about things that are dear to the writer's heart. Often Dostoevsky's most cherished thoughts appear in travesty: Lebedev, a disreputable character, praying for the soul of the Countess Du Barry is in fact living up to Father Zosima's principle of universal guilt and responsibility.[10]

Dostoevsky's novels have been called ideological.[11] His heroes may be perceived as ideas incarnate and his plots as conflicts of ideas. But then, too, Dostoevsky "aimed at concreteness all his life," as Viktor Shklovsky put it.[12] A wealth of concrete detail, both incidental and significant, is to be found in his novels. Mundane concerns appear throughout in the most concrete terms. Dostoevsky is a master of the realistic *detail évocateur.* Sonia's

---

9.   This is particularly true of the Grand Inquisitor chapter of *The Brothers Karamazov.* V. V. Rozanov felt that Dostoevsky's attempts at a theodicy reflected his incapacity for true religious feeling: *Dostoevsky and the Legend of the Grand Inquisitor,* trans. Spencer E. Roberts (Ithaca: Cornell University Press, 1972), pp. 174–75, 189–90. Nikolai Berdiaev was not sure whose side Dostoevsky was on, God's or the Devil's: *Mirosozertsanie Dostoevskogo* (Prague: YMCA, 1923), p. 195. D. H. Lawrence found in the Grand Inquisitor chapter an irritating "cynical-satanical" pose, failing to realize that Dostoevsky had set up Ivan Karamazov in that pose: see Edward Wasiolek, *Dostoevsky: the Major Fiction* (Cambridge: MIT Press, 1964), p. 164.

10.   L. P. Grossman has pointed out that Dostoevsky likes to develop high tragedy from what initially appears to be merely a scandalous occurrence. He is also fond of introducing strident dissonances; see my essay "Dissonance and False Notes in a Literary Text," in *The Structural Analysis of Narrative Texts* (Columbus: Slavica, 1980), pp. 82–95.

11.   B. M. Engel'hardt, "Ideologicheskii roman Dostoevskogo," in *F. M. Dostoevskii: Stat'i i materialy,* ed. A. S. Dolinin (Moscow and Leningrad: Academia, 1924), 2:79–109.

12.   Viktor Shklovskii, *Za i protiv: Zametki o Dostoevskom* (Moscow: Sovetskii pisatel', 1957), p. 15.

plaid shawl, Stavrogin's little red spider, Arkady's white-and-blue check-
ered handkerchief, Iliusha's toy cannon, Aliosha's sausage sandwich, and
hundreds of such details are remembered by the reader.

Dostoevsky's novels are ambiguous even structurally. On the one hand,
they leave openings to "real life" in a variety of ways (including allusions to
contemporary events and concerns, and especially to contemporary literature). On the other, they are structured artefacts by virtue of the presence in
them of abstract ideas that are brought home through various artful devices.
A tragic plot in which ancient mythical themes have been detected may be
embedded in what is recognizably an old-fashioned family novel with many
feuilletonistic digressions, as is the case in *The Idiot* and *The Brothers Karamazov.*

The charge that Dostoevsky's novels have Gothic traits and feature high
or perverse passions, intrigue, murder, and suicide is of course valid. Dostoevsky's main characters are exceptional human beings in extreme situations. Yet it must be understood that they live in a world populated by
crowds of ordinary people leading ordinary lives. The saints, fanatics, murderers, and tragic sufferers of Dostoevsky's novels live among men and
women who pursue their mundane concerns in familiar ways. This does
not invalidate the charge, however, and Dostoevsky's answer to it was that
extreme types and situations were more revealing of the human condition
than the so-called "average."[13] This is a fundamental question on which
Dostoevsky disagreed with most of his contemporaries. Maximilian Braun
has wisely suggested that the crises, rare but still real, of human life were
precisely Dostoevsky's forte, while he had less of an eye and ear for everyday life: courtship and marriage, making a living, raising a family, and such.
Which area one considers more important depends on one's *Weltanschauung.*[14]

The charge of "naturalism" is also justified. This goes both for Dostoevsky's use of topics and details of current journalistic interest and for his
frequent depictions of the seamy side of life and distasteful aspects of personal appearance and behavior. Dostoevsky offended not only Victorian
sensibilities in this respect.[15]

---

13. See the author's prefatory note in *The Brothers Karamazov, PSS* 14:5.

14. Maximilian Braun, *Dostojewskij: Das Gesamtwerk als Vielfalt und Einheit* (Göttingen:
Vandenhoeck & Ruprecht, 1976), pp. 274–75.

15. This is a point emphasized by K. N. Leont'ev, "Novye Khristiane," who finds fault not
only with Dostoevsky but also with Tolstoi for dwelling on characters' unaesthetic bodily functions.

As for Dostoevsky's characters, it is true that many of them are based on identifiable real-life prototypes. It is also true that these, as well as some other, apparently imaginary characters, are readily perceived as "types," which was Dostoevsky's intent. The portraits of, say, Turgenev in *The Possessed* or of G. Z. Eliseev in *The Brothers Karamazov* are indiscreetly recognizable and quite cruel. They are also drawn satirically, as social types. But this can hardly be considered an aesthetic blemish, unless one clings to a narrow conception of realist art that excludes satire on the grounds that it distorts reality.

More serious is M. E. Saltykov-Shchedrin's charge that *The Idiot* contains, "on the one side, characters full of life and truth, but on the other, some mysterious puppets whirling madly as though in a dream, made by hands trembling with rage."[16] Similar impressions come from other reputable critics who were at odds with Dostoevsky's political views. They tended to find Dostoevsky's characters contrived and carelessly executed. For instance, Mikhailovsky calls the nihilist figures in *The Possessed,* including Stavrogin, Piotr Verkhovensky, Shatov, and Kirillov, "puppets" and "pale, pretentious, and artificial."[17] Tolstoi's identical charge refers to *The Brothers Karamazov* as a whole.[18] These opinions are to be explained by the fact that the characters perceived as artificial and contrived were in fact created as ideas incarnate. They owe their existence to the ideas that possess them.[19] Their social and psychological Gestalt is a function of these ideas. The disagreement between Dostoevsky and critics who would rather see ideas as a function of a character's social identity is of a basic nature. It is a disagreement between a positivist social determinism and Dostoevsky's idealist belief in the freedom of the human spirit.

Another violation of strict realism may be seen in Dostoevsky's tendency to give many of his characters the gift of imaginative expression. Too many of them talk and think well, or at least interestingly, to be altogether believ-

---

16.   M. E. Saltykov-Shchedrin, review of Omulevsky's novel *Shag za shagom, Otechestvennye zapiski* (1871): 300–308.

17.   See Mikhailovskii, "Literaturnye i zhurnal'nye Zametki."

18.   A. V. Chicherin, "Poeticheskii stroi iazyka v romanakh Dostoevskogo," in *Tvorchestvo F. M. Dostoevskogo* (Moscow: AN SSSR, 1959), draws attention to this passage in Tolstoi's diary (it refers to *The Brothers Karamazov*): "His dialogues are impossible and entirely unnatural. . . . I was surprised by his sloppiness, artificiality, the fabricated quality . . . so awkward . . . how unartistic: outright unartistic . . . everybody speaking the same language" (p. 444).

19.   Engel'hardt, "Ideologicheskii roman Dostoevskogo."

able. Homer, Dante, and Shakespeare, to name only the greatest, take the same risk. The gain is in expressiveness. It is this form of poetic license that energizes Dostoevsky's texts and makes them so memorable.

The most damaging of the charges, that all Dostoevsky's characters talk like the author, has been heard often since V. G. Belinsky first leveled it, and from as authoritative a reader as Tolstoi.[20] It clashes with Bakhtin's polyphonic conception of the Dostoevskian novel.[21] How is this patent contradiction to be resolved? It is a fact that Dostoevsky, never a writer "from the notebook" (in the literal sense, that is), is not a very careful stylist when it comes to creating a social, regional, or occupational idiolect for his characters. He also lets some of his characters express thoughts which appear to be "over their heads" and which may be a part of the author's ideological argument. Furthermore, more than most novelists, Dostoevsky likes to introduce a literary subtext into his dialogue, a trait that runs the danger of deconstructing its realism, as the reader's mind is directed to the text quoted or alluded to and away from the situation at hand. The justification for this practice is that Dostoevsky's novels are not primarily novels of manners, or even realistic social novels, but are rather in many ways close to the tradition that began with the Platonic dialogue. They are novels about ideas as much as about people.

Dostoevsky's texts are alive, rather than lucid, well written, or elegant. They present the narrator's and the characters' speech in living flux, rather than as a finished product. An undercurrent of emotion or thought-in-progress is constantly present. The text is energized by an ever-active "inner form," by which I mean any kind of verbal content beyond direct routine communication, or, in other words, any active ingredient added to the message by its medium. Metaphoric expression, such as *podpol'e*, "underground," *nadryv*, "rupture," or *besy*, "demons," is the most obvious example. "Inner form" may be generated also by rhythm, dialogic expression (as in irony, ambiguity, allusion, innuendo), over- and understatement, poignancy, solemnity, strangeness (through quirkiness, buffoonery, slang, idiolect, catachresis), challenging the reader by open partisanship, provocation, suspense, or novelty, and the narrator's and everybody else's unflagging personal interest in the action. "Inner form" makes the reader see things by making them concrete. For instance, the first chapter subtitle in

20.   See n. 18 above.
21.   M. M. Bakhtin, *Problemy tvorchestva Dostoevskogo* (Leningrad: Priboi, 1929).

The Brothers Karamazov might have been "The Story of a Family," which would have been routine communication without inner form. Instead, it is *Istoriia Odnoi Semeiki* — "The (Hi)Story of One Nice Little Family."

A reputation as a poor stylist has accompanied Dostoevsky since the publication of his first works. The critics' opinion is the result of a misunderstanding that has been removed by Bakhtin's insights. Bakhtin showed that Dostoevsky's text creates a polyphonic concert of living voices, one of which is the narrator's (which itself may well be dialogic!), rather than a homophonic narrative dominated by the narrator's voice. Hence a controlled, economical, and well-integrated narrative style is not what Dostoevsky pursues. He will write elegantly only when the voice in question demands it. If one disregards the "polyphony" argument, Dostoevsky's highly uneven narrative style, often distinctly colloquial, often journalistic, sometimes chatty, then again lyrical, solemn, or pathetic, places his work with the *roman-feuilleton* and may be legitimately seen as an aesthetic flaw. Today it is commonly seen as an innovative trait, adopted by Céline, Faulkner, Grass, and other leading novelists of the twentieth century.

The alleged moral flaws of Dostoevsky's works are a function of the critic's *Weltanschauung*. I believe that a Christian view close to Dostoevsky's lets these flaws disappear. This is also true of Dostoevsky's alleged pessimism. Thus, it is often said of *The Idiot* that the Good, personified in Prince Myshkin, is wholly ineffectual, and the ideal that the Prince stands for quite incompatible with life. Such criticism is invalid from Dostoevsky's Christian viewpoint, for a Christian's hope and joy are nurtured not by any earthly "and they lived happily ever after," but by faith in resurrection. A similar defense may be advanced against the charge that the atmosphere Dostoevsky created is sickly, hysterical, or *outré* (as he said himself). Nietzsche once called the evangelic world a mixture of the sickly, the childlike, and the sublime. The fervent excitement that permeates Dostoevsky's world is shared with every ambience of religious or political ferment.

Dostoevsky's religious thought is concerned with the ways in which men live and die *with* or *without* God. The solipsist antihero of *Notes from Underground,* the would-be Nietzschean *Übermensch* Raskolnikov, *l'homme revolté* Kirillov of *The Possessed,* burnt-out Byronic heroes like Svidrigailov and Stavrogin, sensualists like Fiodor Pavlovich Karamazov, crude cynics like Smerdiakov, and even god-builders like Ivan Karamazov or Versilov of *A Raw Youth* — they are all humanists who believe that man can stand alone, without God — or against God. Dostoevsky's peculiar approach to existence without God made him a forerunner of Existentialism. He asked not whether or not there is a God, but what living with or without God means for the existence of modern man.[22] Despite his efforts to discredit atheist humanism, Dostoevsky became a prophet of the "death of God." He certainly defined the condition of man without God with great power, though this achievement may have lost some of its provocative edge in our godless age.

Those of Dostoevsky's characters who are with God, holy men like Tikhon, Makar Dolgoruky, or Zosima, simple souls like Sonia Marmeladov, Prince Myshkin, or Aliosha Karamazov, humble sinners like Marmeladov or Dmitry Karamazov, are no less memorable. Their state of grace is not determined by good deeds, or even by the fruits of their striving, but entirely by their unquestioning acceptance of God's fatherhood. This position is complemented by a doctrine, stated most clearly by Father Zosima, of human solidarity in sonhood, which lets every human bear guilt and responsibility for every sin of humanity.[23]

Dostoevsky believed that a Christian's progress is a struggle *against* human nature.[24] Man is sustained in this struggle by epiphanies of divine grace, Father Zosima's "contacts with other worlds," which intrude upon man's mundane existence. This position, and Dostoevsky's rejection of ethical rationalism, are in accord not only with Orthodox doctrine, but also with some strains of romantic idealism. Dostoevsky's religious philosophy is generally in tune with Russian Slavophile thought. Important as Dostoevsky's religious ideas and *Kulturkritik* may be, to see his greatness mainly in these terms may divert us from an appreciation of his genius, simply because today, as in the writer's lifetime, many readers will reject these ideas out of hand.

As for the cruelty of Dostoevsky's talent, a charge raised by V. P. Burenin[25] even before Mikhailovsky's celebrated article, and reiterated by Nabokov, who speaks of Dostoevsky's "wallowing in the tragic misadventures of human dignity," this too depends on the critic's point of view. A remark by Saltykov-Shchedrin, rather to the same effect, may put this trait in the right context. Speaking of *Notes from Underground,* Saltykov-Shchedrin

22.   For an analysis of this conception, see Ina Fuchs, "Homo Apostata," *die Entfremdung des Menschen: Philosophische Analysen zur Geistmetaphysik F. M. Dostojewskijs* (Munich: Otto Sagner, 1987).

23.   *PSS* 14:290–92.

24.   Stated clearly in the notebook passage *Masha lezhit na stole* ("Masha is laid out") of 1864, *PSS* 20:172–74.

25.   V. P. Burenin's review of *The Possessed* in *Sankt-Peterburgskie vedomosti,* no. 250, October 11, 1871, quoted in *PSS* 12:260.

suggests that the point of this work is to show that every man is trash; nor will he ever become a good man until he is convinced that he is indeed trash. He then adds: "In the end, he moves on to the real subject of his musings. He draws his proofs mostly from St. Thomas Aquinas, but since he fails to reveal this, his readers may think that these thoughts are the narrator's own." [26] The meaning of this Aesopian comment is that Dostoevsky has taken his hero to the depths of abjection only in order to lead him thereafter to faith and salvation. From a Christian viewpoint there is nothing wrong with this. But it is difficult for a reader who does not share Dostoevsky's Christian convictions to see it this way, or, for another example, to see Marmeladov, that image of abjection and degradation, as an edifying example and perhaps the most positive character of *Crime and Punishment,* discounting Sonia, who is a saint.

Other charges related to the moral aspect of Dostoevsky's works are also a matter of ideology. Such are the charges of unctuousness and "rosy Christianity." The former is a matter of faith: a nonbeliever like Nabokov will find the reading of the Gospel that brings together "the murderer and the harlot" to be simply in bad taste. The believer will find it moving and edifying. Leontiev's charge of "rosy Christianity," shared with some conservative Orthodox churchmen, may well be valid for some of Dostoevsky's writings, though not for his total oeuvre.

Turning now to the truth content of Dostoevsky's works, the foremost charge is that he deals with the exceptional, rather than with the typical: a serious charge, considering Dostoevsky's insistence that he was a realist, albeit "in a higher sense." V. G. Belinsky said that madmen — Dostoevsky's Goliadkin, hero of *The Double* (1846), is the case in point — being atypical, "belong in lunatic asylums, not in novels." [27] Dostoevsky, in commenting on his novel years later, said that he had heralded, precisely in this character, a new social type of importance. So Goliadkin's madness was typical after all. Analogous disagreements between author and critics were repeated in connection with almost every work. Dostoevsky was confident that the future would prove him right: his "exceptional" characters would one day be recognized as prophetic of Russia's future, while those of Goncharov, Turgenev, and Tolstoi would appear as what they were, even at their appearance: representations of Russia's past.[28] The last word may not yet have been said about Dostoevsky the prophet and religious thinker. His analysis of the

26.   M. E. Saltykov-Shchedrin's feuilleton "Strizhi" (1864), quoted in *PSS* 5:312.
27.   V. G. Belinskii, *Polnoe sobranie sochinenii,* 13 vols. (Moscow: AN SSSR, 1953–59), 10:41.
28.   See notebooks for *The Possessed, PSS* 16:329.

mentality that caused the Russian Revolution was profoundly correct, yet he was wrong, judging from the present point in history, in assuming that Russian spirituality would prevail over the demons of godless humanism and nihilism.

The charges of outright distortion of reality relate mostly to Dostoevsky's understanding of the mood and moral attitude of the young generation of the Russian intelligentsia. It would seem that he was overly optimistic when he hoped that Kolia Krasotkin would follow the example of Aliosha Karamazov, rather than that of Rakitin.

Since the 1840s, Dostoevsky has had a reputation as a keen psychologist. Even then some critics found his psychologism excessive. In the 1860s and 1870s, such charges were heard frequently, and it was suggested that Dostoevsky's morbidly self-conscious and self-lacerating characters were unrepresentative of Russian society, but were, rather, projections of the author's own diseased mind. Unquestionably, Dostoevsky had a deep understanding of humans under conditions of great stress caused by want, suffering, frustration, rejection, and despair. He understood the psychology of poverty, humiliation, resentment, jealousy, cynicism, and cruelty better than most. Whether he had a balanced view of the Russian men and women of his age is a different question. Excellence as a psychologist is hardly the measure of his greatness, however, especially because Dostoevsky himself often spoke disparagingly of "scientific" psychology.[29]

As for the charge that Dostoevsky developed his psychological dramas in a vacuum, neglecting to give them a natural and social background, I believe that it is unfounded. A careful reader will find that each scene of a Dostoevskian novel is provided with ample and aptly chosen detail that acts as a proper setting for the scene. Some critics have said that mundane details, such as food and drink, clothing and land- or city-scape, are missing from Dostoevsky's novels. This is simply not true. There is ample material for an article on "Food and Drink in *The Brothers Karamazov*," for example, or on "The Topography of St. Petersburg in *Crime and Punishment*."

29. See Chapter 3 for details.

2

The Early Dostoevsky

STYLE is the young Dostoevsky's forte. His plots are quite tenuous and abound in all-too-obvious echoes from Russian as well as foreign authors. Some contemporaries charged him with plagiarism.[1] The young Dostoevsky is largely an "adapter," to use Charles Passage's term.[2]

In the 1920s Komarovich, Vinogradov, and A. L. Bem,[3] among others, identified many instances in which Pushkin, Gogol, E. T. A. Hoffmann, and other authors were present in Dostoevsky's texts, while Tynianov and Bakhtin created a model that allowed one to dispense with the pursuit of "influences" and perceive quotations, reminiscences, echoes, and allusions as integral elements of these texts.[4] Tynianov's observations on the theory of parody may be viewed as a preliminary stage of Bakhtin's concept of the

1.   Several critics pointed out Gogol's influence on Dostoevsky, especially in *The Double*. See V. V. Vinogradov, *Evoliutsiia russkogo naturalizma: Gogol' i Dostoevskii* (Moscow: Academia, 1929), pp. 207–9. P. V. Annenkov, "Zametki o russkoi literature proshlogo goda," *Sovremennik* (January 1849), claimed that Dostoevsky's story "An Honest Thief" was an imitation of George Sand's *François le champi*. Other critics said that the children in *Netochka Nezvanova* bore a strong resemblance to those of *Dombey and Son* by Charles Dickens.

2.   Charles E. Passage, *Dostoevski the Adapter* University of North Carolina Studies in Comparative Literature, vol. 10 (Chapel Hill: University of North Carolina Press, 1954).

3.   For Vinogradov, see *Evoliutsiia;* for Bem, see A. L. Bem, " '*Skupoi rytsar*'' v tvorchestve Dostoevskogo," in *O Dostoevskom: Sbornik statei,* ed. A. L. Bem, 3 vols. (Prague: Petropolis, 1929–36), 3:82–123, and other articles in this collection. For Komarovich, see W. Komarowitsch, *F. M. Dostojewski—Die Urgestalt der Brüder Karamasoff* (Munich: R. Piper, 1928), pp. 177–81. Komarovich points out a number of parallels between *Poor Folk* and J.-J. Rousseau's *Julie.*

4.   See Iurii N. Tynianov, *Dostoevskii i Gogol': K teorii parodii* (Petrograd: Opoiaz, 1921); M. M. Bakhtin, *Problemy tvorchestva Dostoevskogo* (Leningrad: Priboi, 1929).

"alien voice" (*chuzhoi golos*), where parody is but one of its various forms. More recently, D. D. Blagoi, V. S. Nechaeva, Gary Rosenshield, and others have adduced more evidence linking the early Dostoevsky to the Russian literary scene of the 1840s and making it plausible that the basic tendency of his art was to give the idealist or metaphysical themes of romantic literature a realistic social context.[5] Blagoi takes Devushkin's reading of "The Stationmaster" in *Poor Folk* to be Dostoevsky's own, interprets "Mr. Prokharchin" as a direct response to "The Covetous Knight," and develops a direct analogy between Arkadii's epiphany at the conclusion of "A Faint Heart" and Evgenii's poignant illumination in "The Bronze Horseman."[6] Rosenshield interprets *The Double* as "the depoetization of the myth of Petersburg." W. J. Leatherbarrow has developed an interpretation of Dostoevsky's early works that is quite close to Blagoi's. He suggests that Pushkin was Dostoevsky's model in a "struggle to resist the influence of Gogol" and to overcome "the caustic superficiality of Gogol's embittered view of his fellow man."[7] Dostoevsky's Devushkin is then a "correction" of Gogol's Akakii Akak'evich,[8] and Goliadkin and Prokharchin are likewise revisions of Gogolian characters, produced by adding an individual dimension to Gogol's types.

Dostoevsky, "a reader of genius,"[9] was also a literary critic all his life. It is possible that in his early years he was not fully convinced of his own creative faculty, yet firmly believed in the correctness of his critical judgment.[10] His early works are, in a way, critical variations on literary themes rather than original conceptions. In particular, the "alien voice" of Gogol keeps intruding into Dostoevsky's texts, turning them into polemic-parodic dialogues with Gogol. This dialogic quality appears most clearly in *Poor Folk*.

Echoes of a host of famous and not-so-famous works of Russian and foreign literature are heard in *Poor Folk*.[11] But first and foremost, it is a variation

5. D. D. Blagoi, "Dostoevskii i Pushkin," in *Dusha v zavetnoi lire: Ocherki zhizni i tvorchestva Pushkina* (Moscow: Sov. pis., 1977), pp. 453–525; V. S. Nechaeva, *Rannii Dostoevskii, 1821–1849* (Moscow: Nauka, 1979). Gary Rosenshield, "*The Bronze Horseman* and *The Double*: The Depoeticization of the Myth of Petersburg in the Young Dostoevskii," *Slavic Review* 55 (1996): 399–428.

6. Blagoi, "Dostoevskii i Pushkin," pp. 481–87, 472–73.

7. W. J. Leatherbarrow, "Idealism and Utopian Socialism in Dostoyevsky's *Gospodin Prokharchin* and *Slaboe serdtse*," *Slavonic and East European Review* 58 (1980): 524–40.

8. Blagoi, "Dostoevskii i Pushkin," pp. 466–67.

9. "Dostoevskii, genial'nyi chitatel'," the title of an article by A. L. Bem.

10. See p. 28 below.

11. In addition to Pushkin, Gogol, and Lermontov, we also recognize J.-J. Rousseau,

on the theme of Gogol's "The Overcoat." The image of its hero, Makar Alek-seevich Devushkin, is a polemical antiparody (*parodie sérieuse*) of Gogol's antihero Akakii Akak'evich Bashmachkin.

In his letter of July 8, Devushkin, having read "The Overcoat," recognizes in its hero an accurate description of a poor clerk, that is, of himself, and indignantly declares that "this is an ill-intentioned booklet." To what extent is Devushkin's reaction Dostoevsky's? It becomes immediately clear that behind Devushkin's naive judgment there is concealed Dostoevsky's own opinion, which was hardly naive.

Devushkin admits that some external details of the poor clerk's life "are correctly observed": walking on tiptoes to save the heels of his shoes, re-nouncing tea with his meals for the sake of economy, the "voluptuousness" of the poor clerk's pleasure in a new piece of clothing. Nor can Devushkin fail to recognize, in Gogol's "important personage," his own superior, Fio-dor Fiodorovich, who, "still a young dignitary, likes to shout at you on occa-sion." When it comes to these and some other external details, Dostoevsky must be of one mind with his hero. Devushkin does not protest against any of the facts presented by Gogol. On the contrary, he sees in Gogol's tale "a trivial example from lowly day-to-day life."

But he is indignant that somebody has "concocted a lampoon" and ex-posed his private life to a jeering public. This charge targets the entire Natural School, which was precisely dealing with trivial examples from day-to-day life. Being himself an exponent of this school, Dostoevsky could not criticize Gogol for excessive naturalism. He presents his hero's indigna-tion with obvious authorial irony. Thus, he agrees with Gogol. Further on, Devushkin considers the position of "the important personage" and de-fends a superior's right to dish out "tonguelashings according to rank." Of course we see authorial irony here as well, and Dostoevsky is still in agree-ment with Gogol. There remains Devushkin's final objection, which derives from his dissatisfaction with the sad conclusion of "The Overcoat":

> Alright then, why couldn't he make some amends for it in the end, for example, at least he could have, after that point when they were strewing little pieces of paper on his head; that, anyway, in spite of it all, he was a virtuous man, a good citizen, and did not deserve such treatment by his fellow workers, that he obeyed his elders, (here, an example might be given), had no ill feelings toward anybody, believed in God and died (if he absolutely wants him to die) mourned

---

Francois-Guillaume Ducray-Duminil, Nicolas Léonard, and Samuel Richardson, to name but a few.

by all. But it would have been best not to let him die at all, the poor soul, but make it so that his overcoat was found, that the general, having learned about his virtues, summoned him to his office, gave him a promotion in rank and a nice increase in salary, so that you see how it would be: evil would be punished, virtue would have triumphed, and his fellow office staff would be left with nothing. (*PSS* 1:63)

Devushkin suggests a happy ending to the story, and Dostoevsky seemingly agrees with him, giving his own story a mock dénouement with a happy ending: in *Poor Folk,* "the important personage" turns out to be a humane and generous superior, who extends to his hapless and browbeaten subordinate, who is, moreover, guilty of a negligent error, not only a hundred rubles (more than Akakii Akak'evich's overcoat cost!), but also a handshake. Here, the author's irony is not as obvious, at least not in the definitive version of the text. However, reading the original version as it appeared in *Peterburgskii Sbornik* leaves no doubt that this passage, too, has an ironic subtext.[12]

So then, Devushkin's complaint does not contain any substantial criticism of Gogol's story that might be attributed to Dostoevsky. All of Devushkin's protestations are cut down by authorial irony, and Gogol's image of the poor clerk is thus confirmed. Dostoevsky's criticism of "The Overcoat" must be sought not here but in the general plan of *Poor Folk.* The point is that Devushkin credits Gogol's speechless and mindless hero with all kinds of thoughts and feelings, which are of course his own. And this is not refuted by the author: there is no irony on this score anywhere in the novel. Significantly, Devushkin — and hence his creator, Dostoevsky — singles out precisely "that point when they were strewing little pieces of paper on his head."[13] It is at this point that Gogol actually lets us know that Akakii Akak'evich is a human being with feelings, when he says: "Leave me alone! Why are you hurting me?" In short, through the words and actions of his own hero, Dostoevsky endows Gogol's hero with a psychology that is almost entirely absent in "The Overcoat."

12. Devushkin's words regarding "his excellency" in the original version: "They are themselves not wealthy. They admitted it all to me themselves. Of course, they have a small house, in fact they have two small houses, and a village or two in the country, but what do you want, my dear, what do you want to do about it, for they must after all live in a style that is different from ours" (*PSS* 1:450). Note that he is referring to his superior in a *plurale maiestatis* all the way and trying to minimize his wealth, calling his house a "little house" (*domik*). "A village or two" (*dereven'ka drugaia*) means that the man owns hundreds of serfs. All quotations are from the thirty-volume Academy edition of Dostoevsky's *Collected Works* (Leningrad, 1972–90). Translations are my own, unless otherwise specified.

13. This is the so-called humanitarian passage of *The Overcoat.*

Dostoevsky created several versions of the poor clerk "with a psychology": Devushkin, of course, but also Mr. Prokharchin (in a story of that title, 1846), Mr. Goliadkin (in *The Double*, 1846), and several others. In this series one may discern a critique of Gogol and, in fact, a correction—on principle—of his position. In "The Overcoat" we are struck by the subject's loss of his human self, caused by the deadening bureaucratic routine that transforms a human being into a copying machine. A man is turned into a "scale model," such as appear on drawings of pyramids and other tall buildings,[14] and enters a shadowy world of nonbeing.[15] Akakii Akak'evich, who is routinely replaced by another copying clerk when he dies, acquires "his own place" (*svoe mesto*), becomes a person, and even earns the attention of his superiors only after his death—exactly like his patron saint, the blessed Acacius, in his *Vita*.[16]

The phantasmagoria of "The Overcoat" exposes the nonbeing and phantom reality of a world of petty, shadowy figures. Giving the poor clerk a psychology, Dostoevsky neutralizes Gogol's metaphysical thematics. His response to Gogol's metaphysical grotesque is a tale of real life, psychologically motivated. In *Poor Folk,* all is as sad and funny as in Gogol's story, and the people who populate it are neither worse nor better, but they are live human beings, not "scale models" or puppets, like Gogol's. There is no doubt that Dostoevsky was aware of the difference between Gogol's vision and his own. A passage in his "Petersburg Dreams in Verse and in Prose" (1861) makes this quite clear:

> And suddenly, being now alone, I got to thinking about it. And I began to take a closer look at it and all of a sudden perceived some strange personages. They were all strange, odd figures, wholly prosaic, by no means Don Carloses or Posas, but entirely titular councilors and yet at the same time some kind of fantastic titular councilors. And somebody was making faces at me, hiding behind that whole fantastic crowd, and was pulling some kind of strings and springs, and these puppets were moving, while he was guffawing, guffawing all the time! And then a different story began to haunt me, in some kind of somber roominghouse, some kind of titular heart, honest and pure, decent and devoted to his superiors; and with him, some kind of a girl, wronged and sad, and this whole story was tearing deep into my soul. (*PSS* 19:71)

14. "Masshtabnaia figurka," Shklovsky's witty term.
15. I am following Vladimir Nabokov's reading of Gogol. See his *Gogol* (Norfolk, Conn.: New Directions, 1944), p. 145.
16. See John Schillinger, "Gogol's 'The Overcoat' as a Travesty of Hagiography," *Slavic and East European Journal* 16 (1972): 36–41.

Of course, Dostoevsky created in *Poor Folk* something incomparably more important than a sentimental tale that "was tearing deep into [his] soul." What is most significant in this passage is the "somebody making faces" —Gogol, of course—who is pulling the strings of his puppet theater. In the same "Dreams," explicit mention is also made of "The Overcoat." It develops, then, that Dostoevsky read Gogol's story almost the way Boris Eichenbaum would read it many years later.[17]

One must keep in mind that the early Dostoevsky was, like Gogol, close to the poetics of Romanticism, in which the puppet theater is routinely used as a symbol of the mechanization of life that threatened modern humanity, and of the transformation of man into an automaton.[18] This theme appears particularly often in the tales of Hoffmann, which the young Dostoevsky read avidly. The image of the puppet appears in Dostoevsky's own works with precisely the same ominous meaning. In "Mr. Prokharchin," the poor rebellious clerk is likened to Pulcinella, who after each performance "is put away into his box by a traveling '*artiste*-organ grinder.' " Similarly, Mr. Goliadkin's movements in *The Double* almost from the beginning resemble a puppet's jerky zigzags. Goliadkin no longer has control of his movements but operates "as if somebody had released a spring inside him" (*PSS* 1:133).

Goliadkin and Prokharchin are men who are perishing, or have already perished, as human beings, lost in the deadening atmosphere of bureaucratic Petersburg. They have lost their free will, their human dignity, and their human heart. Dostoevsky's first hero, Devushkin, is different. He was created in response to Gogol's Akakii Akak'evich, whom Dostoevsky judged to be a lifeless puppet. To Gogol's Bashmachkin (from *bashmak,* "shoe") Dostoevsky opposes Makar Alekseevich Devushkin, a name thrice symbolic of his humanity, for *Makar* means "blest," *Aleksei* is the proverbial "man of God," and *Devushkin* means "(son) of the maiden."

Devushkin believes that it ought to have been said about Akakii Akak'evich that he "believed in God and died (if he absolutely wants him to die) mourned by all." This introduces, in Dostoevsky's very first work, the theme of divine justice, for one may choose to read an ominous irony into this passage: God's reward for a virtuous life and faith in Him is death! The young Dostoevsky's answer to the question of theodicy appears to be a negative one, for we hear this from Devushkin:

17. B. M. Eikhenbaum, "Kak sdelana *Shinel'* Gogolia" (1919).
18. Cf. Heinrich von Kleist's celebrated essay "Über das Marionettentheater" (1811).

Of course, everything goes according to God's will; this is the way it is, this must be the way it is, no question about it; and the Providence of the Heavenly Creator is of course beneficent and unfathomable, and likewise Fate, which is the same thing. (*PSS* 1:101–2)

Devushkin's faith depends on his mood of the moment. At moments of well-being, we hear, he "repented, with tears in his eyes, before God the Lord, praying that God might forgive all the sins he was guilty of in those sad days: his murmur, his liberal ideas, his debauchery and recklessness" (*PSS* 1:96).

The world of "The Overcoat" is very much unlike Devushkin's. The question of divine justice may be heard as a remote echo, at best, in Akakii Akak'evich's plaintive exclamation: "Why are you hurting me?" Gogol's world is one in which man may not have forgotten God so much as God has forgotten man. Precisely for this reason, Gogol's world is far more terrible than the world of any work by Dostoevsky. A world that God has forgotten is so alien to Dostoevsky that God will appear in his works, at least by virtue of the denial of His existence, even in moments of doubt and rebellion.

Surely many readers shed tears over Varen'ka's sad future as Mrs. Bykov. Dostoevsky himself explicitly approved such a reading.[19] But some readers will be inclined to give the screw another turn, and the happily married Dunia of "The Stationmaster" is there to give it a push. There is enough between, and even in, the lines of Varen'ka's last few letters to suggest to an unsentimental reader that she will be just fine.

Stylistically, *Poor Folk* presents a marvel of Dostoevskian ambiguity. The author uses the two voices of his correspondents, to create a variety of subtexts that contradict the unwary reader's first, superficial impression. Devushkin, meekly resigned to his lowly status in the world, turns outright patronizing when he meets someone even less fortunate than himself. Devushkin, the budding writer who unwittingly presents a series of paro-

---

19.   See the passage quoted above from "Petersburg Dreams in Verse and in Prose," where Dostoevsky tells of "a girl, wronged and sad," whose "story was tearing deeply into my soul" (*PSS* 19:71). In a letter to A. E. Wrangell, dated March 23, 1856, Dostoevsky observes, having reported that the lady he is courting is considering marriage to a middle-aged well-to-do gentleman: "Poor dear! This will be too much for her to suffer. Should she, with that heart and mind of hers, spend all her life in Kuznetsk? And God knows with whom! She is in a situation like that of my heroine in *Poor Folk* who gets married to Bykov (did I prophesy something for myself there?)" (*PSS* 28/I:218). Dostoevsky was not a very good critic of his own works. When rewriting his early works in the 1860s, he consistently cut passages that made good sense. See n. 12 above for an example.

dies with breathless admiration, suddenly comes up with lines of somber pathos in a vignette of a beggar boy who "is already coughing . . . and death is awaiting him, somewhere in a stinking corner, with no care, no help — and this will be his whole life!" (*PSS* 1:87–88). Devushkin, the timid and chaste lover, will, on occasion, become simply coarse, as when he compares a poor man's shame to Varen'ka's maidenly shame: "Why, you won't take your clothes off before everybody, will you?" (*PSS* 1:69). Devushkin, the naive believer, utters strong arguments against God's world, much as Devushkin the loyal subordinate gleefully tells of embarrassing scenes he has observed at the office.

Altogether, the young Dostoevsky understood a great deal about "The Overcoat," perhaps in part subconsciously. Apparently, Gogol's grotesque disquieted him. He realized that Gogol's basic device was the metamorphosis of a human being into a puppet, and the world of "living life" (*zhivaia zhizn'*) into a hell of nonbeing. He could not fail to protest against such a metamorphosis, and so he transformed Bashmachkin into Devushkin, the overcoat into Varen'ka Dobrosiolova, and Gogol's metaphysical grotesque into "the first Russian social novel" (Belinsky). This change came at the cost of metaphysical depth, which was replaced by social realism, and Gogol's demonic humor, replaced by a rather shallow irony.

However, Dostoevsky's irony may be deeper than suggested by his own pronouncements on the genesis and intent of *Poor Folk*. True, Dostoevsky lets his hero produce "a piercing vision of the contrasted lives of the rich and the poor," as Joseph Frank observes,[20] but he also makes it rather clear that the poor are born losers rather than victims of social injustice. Devushkin's analysis of poverty (*PSS* 1:68 and passim) leaves little doubt about this. True, Dostoevsky lets Devushkin express his respect for the poor man who earns his bread in the sweat of his brow. But he also undercuts the argument by letting Devushkin choose an organ grinder as an example of such an honest toiler — apparently a dig at his friend Dmitry Grigorovich's physiological sketch "The Organ Grinders of St. Petersburg" (1845).

The Double has attracted more critical attention, especially in the West, than seems to be warranted by this work's artistic quality. Dostoevsky himself brought it into question by rewriting it in the 1860s, as well as by admitting

---

20. Joseph Frank, *Dostoevsky: The Seeds of Revolt, 1821–1849* (Princeton: Princeton University Press, 1976), p. 145.

explicitly that he had failed to give a proper form to the idea he had tried to express. He never identified this idea, and many attempts have been made to do it for him.[21]

A. L. Bem saw in *The Double* an echo of Gogol's story "The Nose," and indeed a critique of and an "improvement" on it.[22] If this is correct, *The Double* is an attempt to give the allegory of Gogol's story a psychological basis—that is, to realize Gogol's metaphor. Viktor Shklovsky, in what I believe to be the most convincing interpretation of *The Double*,[23] makes the point that it is in effect a travesty of the romantic *Doppelgänger* theme. The Goliadkins Junior and Senior are equally trivial "nonpersons," as the "evil" in Goliadkin Junior is as petty as the "good" in Goliadkin Senior. What difference does it make which of the two, or if either, occupies a desk at the "department," a flat on Shestilavochnaia Street?

Shklovsky's interpretation squares with Dmitry Chizhevsky's,[24] which sees the reality of human existence as the central theme of *The Double:* as the difference between the opposing poles of human nature approaches zero, human existence becomes nonexistence. Gogol had made an allegory of this theme by letting a nose walk the streets of St. Petersburg in a uniform that identifies it as a person of high rank. Dostoevsky "realizes" the allegory.

The basic tone of the narrative is ironic, which has puzzled some critics, since it is not immediately clear why the narrator should make fun of his sorry hero.[25] If the story is seen as a travesty of the romantic double theme, the irony becomes well motivated. The fear, the anguish, the frantic rushing around of the two Goliadkins revolve around ludicrously trivial matters, in fact, about nothing. The narrator presents Goliadkin's hallucinations as a perfectly normal experience, his disorganized ramblings as logical reasoning, his frenzied dashes into a void as well-planned, sensible activity.

21.   In a letter to his brother Mikhail, dated October 1, 1859, Dostoevsky calls Goliadkin "a very great type in its social significance." And this is what he had to say about *The Double:* "I positively failed with this novel, but its idea was a rather bright one, and I never introduced anything more serious than this idea in literature. But I totally failed in [giving the proper] form to this novel." *A Writer's Diary,* November 1877, chap. 1 (*PSS* 26:65).

22.   A. L. Bem, " 'Nos' i 'Dvoinik'," in Bem, *O Dostoevskom*, 3:139–63.

23.   Viktor Shklovskii, *Za i protiv: Zametki o Dostoevskom* (Moscow: Sovetskii pisatel', 1957), pp. 60–61.

24.   Dmitrii Chizhevskii, "K probleme dvoinika (Iz knigi o formalizme v etike)," in Bem, *O Dostoevskom*, 1:39–64.

25.   The ironic tone in which the narrator reports the misfortunes of his sorry hero is under attack in N. K. Mikhailovsky's famous article "A Cruel Talent" (1882), reprinted in N. K. Mikhailovskii, *Literaturno-kriticheskie stat'i* (Moscow: Gosizdat, 1957), pp. 181–263.

Goliadkin, who stands for Russian man as created by Peter the Great (his patronymic is Petrovich!), believes in the reality of his existence, thinks that he possesses "his own place" (*svoe mesto*),[26] even if temporarily deprived of it by the other Goliadkin, hopes that he will eventually recover it and be again the sole and real Mr. Goliadkin. But the fact is that there is nothing to recover, because the other Goliadkin no more possesses his "own place" than the "original" Goliadkin did. Goliadkin thus stands for the ghostly nonexistence of the philistine, Hoffmann's *gespenstisches Philistertum,* as represented by the imperial bureaucracy of Peter the Great's making.

The nature of *The Double* as a travesty is underscored by a formal trait that was first pointed out by V. V. Vinogradov. Along with the main plot, developed through an account of the hero's stream of consciousness, there runs what might be called a "motor plot," carried on by a veritable orgy of verbs of motion, many of which are inherently grotesque. Here the two Goliadkins appear as twin puppets, jerkily zigzagging through a cinematic sequence of action shots, very much like a silent film starring Charlie Chaplin or Buster Keaton. As a matter of fact, some of these scenes are silent, perfect pantomime, in which neither Goliadkin says a word. The antics of the two Goliadkins may well be viewed as a travesty of the frenzied sciamachies of Hoffmannesque *Doppelgängers.*[27]

Another formal element, also pointed out by Vinogradov, fits in with the ironic narrative and the *grotesquerie* of the motor plot. A liberal dose of expressions comical *per se,* called *slovechki* in Russian, trivial witticisms, including some involuntary ones by the hero, contributes to the atmosphere of comedy, even farce, in what is on the surface a sad story.

Where did Dostoevsky go wrong in realizing his indictment of the "socially significant type" represented by Goliadkin, which may also have been a confession of the "Goliadkin" in Dostoevsky himself?[28] Chizhevsky suggests that Dostoevsky obscured his message by making his hero a trivial stock character in the manner of the Natural School. I suggest rather that

26. The focal role of the expression *svoe mesto* is emphasized in Chizhevskii, "K probleme dvoinika."

27. In Hoffmann's works, *Doppelgängers* may be authentic and fateful, as in his great novel *Die Elixiere des Teufels,* or they may travesty the role, as in "Signor Formica," "Die Brautwahl," and "Die Abenteuer der Sylvesternacht."

28. In a letter to his brother Mikhail (undated, 1845), Dostoevsky calls himself "a veritable Goliadkin" (*nastoiashchii Goliadkin*). In another letter, written in January or February 1847, he says of *Netochka Nezvanova:* "This will be a confession, like Goliadkin, though in a different tone and key" (*PSS* 28/I:139).

the ample psychological and even clinical detail about Goliadkin's condition diverts the reader's attention from the existential core of the story. The reader is apt to gather that Goliadkin's world is meaningless because he is mad. Dostoevsky's message was that Goliadkin's very existence is meaningless, and hence mad. The fault is really the reader's. But it was Dostoevsky's fate to be underinterpreted and underestimated by his critics.

"The Landlady" is perhaps the only outright failure Dostoevsky ever produced. Belinsky was right for once in his negative judgment of this story; he said that Dostoevsky "had tried to reconcile Marlinsky to Hoffmann, adding a bit of humor after the latest fashion, and covering the whole with a thick veneer of Russian *narodnost'*." [29] Indeed, one is amazed to see Dostoevsky use the very same language he had ridiculed in the spirited parodies of *Poor Folk*.

The connection with Hoffmann is even more specific than Belinsky suggested. Important elements of "The Landlady" were lifted from one of Hoffmann's less well known stories, *Erscheinungen,* where the hero, a dreamer like Ordynov, meets a demonic old man, who at one point tries to kill him, and an angelically beautiful, but demented, peasant girl, Dorothea, who fancies herself to be Agafia, a Russian princess. Dorothea-Agafia is expecting the return of her betrothed, Alexei, who seems to have drowned crossing a wide and deep river, while Dorothea and the old man reached the other shore safely. The visions that make up this tale are as dreamlike and disconnected as Ordynov's experiences in "The Landlady," where the heroine's betrothed, Aleksei, was drowned in the Volga River by a demonic old man, Murin. The latter at one point tries to kill Ordynov. There are also many stylistic and figurative details that strongly resemble Hoffmann. [30]

Various efforts have been made to attach an allegorical meaning to "The Landlady." To begin with, it may be viewed as a "realized" version of the romantic theme treated by Gogol in "A Terrible Vengeance." [31] Viacheslav Ivanov observed that Katerina, the heroine, may be an early version of Mar'ia Timofeevna Lebiadkina in *The Possessed:* that is, an allegorical image of the soul of Russia. [32] It has also been noted that Ordynov has some traits

29.   V. G. Belinskii, "Vzgliad na russkuiu literaturu 1847 goda," in *PSS* 10:351.

30.   See Victor Terras, *The Young Dostoevsky (1846-1849)* (The Hague: Mouton, 1969), pp. 90–91 and passim.

31.   See A. L. Bem, "Dramatizatsiia breda (*Khoziaika* Dostoevskogo)," in Bem, *O Dostoevskom,* 1:77–124.

32.   Vyacheslav Ivanov, *Freedom and the Tragic Life: A Study in Dostoevsky,* trans. Norman Cameron (New York: Noonday, 1952), p. 59.

in common with Ivan Karamazov. Both are interested in the history of the Church, and Ordynov, like Ivan Karamazov, has hit upon an important idea in this connection. Katerina, "a faint heart," then stands for the simple soul in the clutches of organized religion, represented by the outwardly devout but evil Murin, who is then a forerunner of the Grand Inquisitor. More recently, Rudolf Neuhäuser has developed an interpretation according to which Ordynov's "idea" is utopian socialism and his planned work "on the history of the Church" something along the lines of *De la célébration du dimanche* or *Das Wesen des Christentums*.[33] Ordynov, symbolic of the Russian progressive educated class, is struggling to save Katerina, symbolic of the Russian people, from the tyranny of her reactionary husband.[34]

Neuhäuser's observations, based on "The Landlady" and other early works, suggest that the young Dostoevsky was skeptical towards Christian ideology and replaced it by faith in a social utopia. This is probably correct, since even the mature Dostoevsky was to face similar charges from conservative churchmen. What is wrong with the story is its stylistic execution.

The story begins in a nervous, precariously balanced style, neither ironic nor stylized, just tense and highstrung. But then, beginning with the second scene at the suburban church, it turns into a steady flow of unabashed romantic *colportage,* crass color effects, and hyperbolically emotional sensuality. Needless accumulations of adjectives, trite metaphors, and hackneyed similes abound. Time and again, one cannot help seeing a rift between statement and drama, or between statement and image, without any indication that we are dealing with stylized or ironic diction. There is an impersonal narrator, so there is nothing to indicate that he moves on a different plane from either author or reader. Apparently Dostoevsky was trying to produce a dramatization of the hero's feverish ravings, as Bem has suggested — but failed.

"White Nights" comes as a pleasant surprise after the failure of "The Landlady." In this story, Dostoevsky has truly captured the spirit of German Romanticism. The story features rich nature and music imagery, gentle irony, usually directed at the first-person narrator himself, and a warm pathos that is always ready to turn into self-parody. It is delightful also in the

---

33.   Pierre Joseph Proudhon's *La célébration du dimanche* was one of two prohibited books found in Dostoevsky's flat at his arrest. Ludwig Feuerbach's *Das Wesen des Christentums* was one of several works seeking to demystify religion by reducing it to a product of human culture and seeing it in a historical context. It was widely read in Russia.

34.   See Rudolf Neuhäuser, *Das Frühwerk Dostoevskijs: Literarische Tradition und gesellschaftlicher Anspruch* (Heidelberg: Winter, 1979), pp. 136–47.

dialogue: the sweet naïveté and ready mother-wit of the coquettishly imp-ish, charmingly selfish, deliciously self-assured heroine, seventeen-year-old Nastenka; the fiery tirades of the young romantic dreamer who, according to Nastenka, "talks as if he were reading from a book," but so well that the Serapion Brotherhood would have welcomed him to their midst. This, by the way, is one of his dreams.

The serious theme at the bottom of it all is the romantic dreamer's losing struggle against his fear of reality. This fear has been looming large for some time, we learn; it recedes briefly in the excitement of enamoration, but comes back in the end, more oppressive than before. The story ends in a passionate invocation to a lost love, culminating in the words, "My God! A whole minute of bliss! Isn't this enough for a whole human life?" But earlier we have heard this:

> or, perhaps, I saw in a flash the whole perspective of my future, uninviting and sad, and I saw myself as I am now, exactly fifteen years later, aging, in that same room, just as lonely, with that same Matriona, who has not grown any smarter over those years. (*PSS* 2:141)

No doubt the dreamer of fifteen years later will be none other than the dis-illusioned romantic of forty in *Notes from Underground*.

Rosenshield has advanced good arguments, specifically the highly sug-gestive epigraph of the story, to prove that the voice of the implied author is dominant in "White Nights," subordinating all other points of view, includ-ing those of the dreamer and the narrator (the two are not identical, since the story is told in retrospect, fifteen years later). Rosenshield contends that the contradiction between the alleged sterility of the hero's dreams and the palpable beauty that they generate is contrived by the implied author to suggest that the clash between a Hoffmannesque escape into a world of cre-ative fantasy and the pragmatic facts of life results in an ambiguity.[35]

Dostoevsky's first full-length novel, *Netochka Nezvanova,* which remained uncompleted because of the author's arrest in April 1849, shows the clear imprint of two contemporary French novelists, George Sand and Eugène Sue. The influence of the former is obvious: *Netochka Nezvanova* has a female narrator who tells the story of her life as a mature woman, appar-ently a singer of some accomplishment, like Sand's Consuelo in the novel

---

35. Gary Rosenshield, "Point of View and the Imagination in Dostoevskij's 'White Nights,'" *Slavic and East European Journal* 21 (1977): 191–203.

of that title. The extent of Dostoevsky's stylistic or psychological borrowing has not been established, although a good deal of literature focuses on Dostoevsky and Sand.[36] The romance of two little girls in the second part of the novel was lifted largely from Sue's novel *Mathilde ou Confessions d'une jeune fille*, as Malcolm Jones has demonstrated.[37]

It appears that *Netochka Nezvanova* was planned as a realist novel of social and psychological conflict. However, the theme of the first of its three parts, which tells the story of Netochka's stepfather, the fiddler Efimov, is the romantic one of a conflict between the artist and his environment, leading to his defeat and tragic end. This theme is treated in a most original way, for Efimov is not really an artist of genius, but rather a moderately talented performer who is, besides, "a profound instinctive critic of art."[38] The conflict is not between Efimov and society, but within Efimov himself. He might have admitted that he is only a second-rate performer, though good enough to make an honest living with his fiddle and make the most of his ability to appreciate great musicianship in others. He refuses to do so, and his life turns into a nightmarish flight from the moment of truth. Rather than play second fiddle, he will not play at all, and lets his family starve. He drives away his faithful friends and prefers to associate with the dregs of society, among whom he can feel and act superior—all to avoid putting his musicianship to a decisive test. The moment of truth comes when Efimov hears the great Z———tz play. He returns from the concert, still with a faint glimmer of hope that he might duplicate the great fiddler's performance. It matters not that he finds his wife dead, a suicide, the frightened child at her bedside; he must play. And play he does. A lesser writer would have let Efimov play as a requiem to his wife, as well as in competition with Z———tz, for it is the last time he will play the fiddle. Not so Dostoevsky: Efimov is oblivious of the presence of the dead body, and he does not play

36. See Terras, *Young Dostoevsky*, pp. 88–90, 101–3; Komarowitsch, *Urgestalt der "Brüder Karamasoff*," pp. 167–235; Sigurd Fasting, "Dostoevsky and George Sand," *Russian Literature*, N.S. 4 (1976): 309–21. Dostoevsky thought highly of Sand, but still felt that she was a "lady writer." In a letter to his brother, dated January 13, 1856, he says: "Even George Sand, undoubtedly a giant of an artist, only too often did herself a lot of harm by her 'ladylike' traits" (*PSS* 28/I:210).

37. Malcolm V. Jones, "An Aspect of Romanticism in Dostoyevsky: *Netochka Nezvanova* and Eugène Sue's *Mathilde*," *Renaissance and Modern Studies* (University of Nottingham) 17 (1973): 38–61.

38. "He felt and understood it [art] so strongly that it was no miracle that he got lost in his own opinion of himself and took himself, instead of for a profound instinctive critic of art, for a priest of art itself, a genius" (*PSS* 2:149).

well. He finally must admit the truth to himself, and he cannot bear it. He abandons his child, flees blindly, collapses, and dies within a few days. The real theme of the story is thus the artist unworthy of his calling: the dream of fame means more to Efimov than music.

Dostoevsky underwent an emotional crisis after the failure of the stories that followed *Poor Folk,* and apparently projected that experience upon this episode of *Netochka Nezvanova.*[39] He could see himself as a "profound in-stinctive critic of art, rather than a great artist," for the one successful work he had produced was in fact a piece of perceptive literary criticism, not an original creation. Dostoevsky knew he was a "reader of genius." Among the great novelists of the nineteenth century, he was by far the most "literary," a writer who wrote his best pages in response to existing works of literature, past and present.

Efimov's unpleasant traits Dostoevsky must in moments of prostration, have seen in himself. Didn't he have a nasty habit of antagonizing people with caustic remarks, though he himself was excessively thin-skinned? Wasn't he, like Efimov, terribly vain and self-conscious? The one feature that makes Efimov a distinct character who *is not* Dostoevsky is the master-ful social stylization of his speech. Efimov is sordid in his servility, pathetic in his hollow self-assurance, repulsive in his callous egoism; all these traits have an air of coarseness, ignorance, and the bad manners of the semiliter-ate; there is much of the lackey about Efimov, albeit a rebellious lackey. This, of course, Dostoevsky was not.

Whether this interpretation of Efimov is correct or not, the first part of *Netochka Nezvanova* is yet another "realization," or "travesty" of a romantic theme. Various details of the episode are also lifted from romantic literature, as Passage has amply demonstrated.

The first part of *Netochka Nezvanova* is written in a terse, matter-of-fact, somewhat colloquial style, which seldom betrays the fact that the narrator is a woman. The second part, a study in child psychology featuring a rather shockingly carnal "romance" between two girls of about eleven or twelve, shows a more subjective and emotional tone, especially in its unconcealed sultry eroticism, the object of which is the pretty little princess Katia. The third part, rather nondescript (perhaps not quite finished, and certainly lacking the final touch, as it was printed after the writer's arrest), is very George-Sandian, in both style and theme. It is the story of the sufferings of

---

39. See n. 28 above.

a beautiful young woman, who is married to a pedantic tyrant but loves—platonically, it seems—a young man of no consequence. It teems with emotionally charged clichés, sentimental moralizing, and carelessly formulated revelations concerning the inner life of a passionate but virtuous young lady (the narrator), all very much in the style of the early Sand. It is impossible to determine whether all this is due to an effort to impersonate a "lady writer" or to a naive imitation of Sand.

A few remarks about the remaining stories will suffice. "A Faint Heart" [40] and "An Honest Thief" are fairly typical of the Natural School. The former, told by an impersonal narrator in a mildly sympathetic but matter-of-fact way, consists for the most part of colloquial dialogue. The latter is told by a semiliterate veteran soldier in what seems to be close to the authentic diction of this type. "A Christmas Party and a Wedding" is a piece of social satire and, in its form, a journal sketch rather than a short story. All of these stories, like those discussed in some detail above, bear out the traits that will remain characteristic even of Dostoevsky's mature work.

What, then, are the distinctive traits of the young Dostoevsky's art? To begin with, his works are remarkably literary in a variety of ways. Explicit or implied allusions to Russian as well as to foreign works of literature play a major role in several of them. Among Russian writers, Pushkin and Gogol are dominant. They will remain so until the very end, as a reading of *The Brothers Karamazov* will show. Several texts appear to have been written in response to either Pushkin or Gogol. Among foreign authors, Hoffmann, Sand, Sue, the French utopian socialists, Rousseau, and perhaps Balzac may be recognized.

Neuhäuser has made a plausible case that the early Dostoevsky developed some of his characters in terms of Fourier's psychology, using his schema of perversion of natural human passions by an unnatural social order. It is a fact that the moral found at the conclusion of "An Honest Thief" (in the earlier, journal version) is closer to Fourier than to the views of the mature Dostoevsky:

---

40. Katharine Strelsky, "Dostoevsky's Early Tale 'A Faint Heart,'" *Russian Review* 30 (1971): 146–53, believes she has found a subtext suggesting a homosexual love story in "A Faint Heart." Renate Lachmann extends this notion by reading a slew of further subliminal signs in and between the lines of the text. She has not convinced me. See Renate Lachmann, *Memory and Literature: Intertextuality in Russian Modernism,* trans. Roy Sellars and Anthony Wall (Minneapolis: University of Minnesota Press, 1997), pp. 262–82.

A man will die of a vice, as of a lethal poison, and therefore vice is an acquired, human thing, and not native to man—it comes and it goes: if this weren't so, Christ wouldn't have come to us, that is, if we were destined to remain sinful for ever and ever from original sin. (*PSS* 2:42)

Frank recognizes Dostoevsky's concern with moral freedom in this passage (p. 328). But we know that the mature Dostoevsky believed that good and evil were equally inherent in human nature.

W. J. Leatherbarrow's interpretation of "Mr. Prokharchin" deserves careful attention. He sees in Ustin'ia Fiodorovna's lodgers a caricature of a Fourierist commune, and in their putdown of Prokharchin's "willful individualism" a parody of socialist rhetoric. Leatherbarrow also draws attention to allusions to Prevost's *Manon Lescaut* in "A Faint Heart," finding the theme of both works identical: the inability of a "faint heart" to master life. Leatherbarrow attaches a symbolic meaning to poor Vasia's visit to Mme Leroux's millinery shop, considering it no accident that she is a namesake of the utopian socialist Pierre Leroux. "Everything great and beautiful" that enthralls him there will prove irrelevant when crisis strikes. Leatherbarrow's interpretation suggests that Dostoevsky was no longer taking Fourierism seriously when he wrote this story.

Dostoevsky belonged to the generation of Russian writers who were brought up on romantic literature and German idealist philosophy. Hoffmann's influence thus acquires an active meaning as a dialogue with both. This dialogue, too, will continue until the end of Dostoevsky's life as a writer.

The young Dostoevsky habitually presents existential problems in socially concrete but psychologically paradoxical form. The middle-aged clerk in love with a teenage girl, the prosaic titular councilor who develops a *Doppelgänger* complex, the dirty miser "with an idea," the "honest thief"—all make a travesty of their roles.[41] Dostoevsky will continue this pattern in his mature works.

The fact that practically every story is written in a different style suggests that Dostoevsky is looking for the proper formula to express his ideas. In most instances he fails to find the right combination of content and form, so that the stories either are outright failures, like "The Landlady," or are

---

41. In much the same way, *Poor Folk* as a whole is a travesty of the sentimental epistolary love story: a middle-aged, semiliterate lover, with holes in his shoes and liquor on his breath; a heroine with a tarnished reputation; a torrid love affair in which a kiss is mentioned only once—in the first letter.

too easily misunderstood, as is the case with "The Double" and "Mr. Prokharchin," where ironic diction and humorous detail obscure the author's
intent. Only in "White Nights" is there a perfect match between content and
form. As for *Poor Folk,* the short epistolary novel that many contemporaries
considered Dostoevsky's best work, its success was mostly due to the fact
that its readers misread it: they saw in it a message of "sentimental humani-
tarianism," as Apollon Grigoriev put it, while it was in fact a parody that put
in question precisely the notions on which a humanitarian view of poverty
is based. Makar Alekseevich Devushkin is poor and will die poor because he
is a born pauper, not only socially, but congenitally.

One thing is clear, though: even the young Dostoevsky works very hard
at giving a quality of markedness to his style. There is always a thirdness
between signifier and signified: stylized diction, parody, irony, travesty,
pathos — whatever. He may not always hit it right, but he is trying. In this,
too, he anticipates the mastery of his mature years.

3

Fact, Fiction, and Psychology in Dostoevsky's Art

AFTER his return from Siberia, Dostoevsky had some difficulty finding himself. "Uncle's Dream" and "The Village of Stepanchikovo and
Its Denizens" were comedies made into short stories. The former is rather
forgettable; the latter has had some success on the stage but is remarkable
mostly for its cruel caricature of Gogol as he appears in his ill-fated *Correspondence with My Friends,* particularly if seen through the eyes of Belinsky's "Letter to Gogol." Foma Opiskin (from *opiska,* "slip of the pen") is one
aspect of Gogol, but only one, and Dostoevsky knew it.[1]

The Insulted and Injured is a Dickensian potboiler (the debt to Dickens is
duly acknowledged by calling the waif heroine Nelly and making her grand-
father an Englishman). Dobroliubov was not so wrong when he said, in an
otherwise sympathetic review, that the novel was below artistic criticism.
But then Dostoevsky did what he did time and again in his life: he pulled
himself up, as it were, by his own bootstraps, and lifted his art to a new
level, while also taking it into uncharted regions. He did so by abandoning
the familiar characters and settings of the Natural School and expanding in
two directions: down, to the lowlife of *The House of the Dead,* and up, to the
world of the modern intellectual, in *Notes from Underground.*

Notes from the House of the Dead belongs to a genre that was in vogue in
the 1840s and lingered on into the 1850s and 1860s, the physiological sketch

---

1. See Iurii Tynianov, "Dostoevskii i Gogol' (K teorii parodii)," in *Arkhaisty i novatory*
(Leningrad: Priboi, 1929), pp. 412–55.

of the Natural School. In this work Dostoevsky joins the other two giants of the Russian novel, the Turgenev of *A Sportsman's Sketches* and the Tolstoi of the Caucasian tales and Sevastopol sketches. Dostoevsky enjoyed success with a work of the literature of fact toward the middle of his career; success with such works had come at the beginning of theirs.

All three authors were pursuing social and psychological as well as moral truth in their works, besides describing facts that they knew through personal observation and experience. In retrospect it was apparent that Turgenev's sketches had not been free of bias. Tolstoi himself later condemned his Sevastopol sketches as basically false. Dostoevsky's work suffered no such adverse verdict. It even withstood the severe judgment of the old Tolstoi.

Notes from the House of the Dead was received as a work of the literature of fact by contemporary readers. The most significant review, Dmitry Pisarev's "Those Who Have Perished and Those Who Are Perishing" (1866), and a whole series of other reviews all reacted to it as to a statement of fact, often voicing, almost in the same breath, their disagreement with the ideological slant of Dostoevsky's journal *Vremia*. When Saltykov indulged in some rather insipid raillery at the expense of *Notes from the House of the Dead*, Varfolomei Zaitsev, otherwise an enemy of Dostoevsky's, wrote in *Russkoe Slovo*:

> It is quite all right to let *Vremia* have it—it is indeed a hideous piece; but to laugh at *The House of the Dead* is to expose oneself to the hazard of having one's attention called to the fact that such works are written in the subject's own blood, rather than in ink from a vice-gubernatorial inkwell. (*PSS* 4:296)

As in earlier reviews (like, say, Dobroliubov's essay "Downtrodden People"), most of the praise for *Notes from the House of the Dead* was inspired by Dostoevsky's sympathy with the "insulted and injured" and his exposure of the arrogance, brutality, and stupidity of their oppressors. Radical and liberal readers saw the convicts at the House of the Dead as victims of a monstrously unjust society—the way Tolstoi still saw things in *Resurrection*. Dostoevsky's facts do not support such a reading. They are complex and if anything suggest that at least many of the prisoners are criminals by choice, and, moreover, that there is such a thing as a criminal mentality. The following passage, by the way, follows the pattern of the physiological sketch:

> The naive ones and the simpletons, as I have already pointed out, were generally looked upon as downright fools and held in utter contempt. Everybody was so ill-tempered and self-centered that he would despise a man of kind and

selfless temper. Aside from those naive and simpleminded gabby people, all the rest, the silent ones, that is, could be sharply divided into *kind* and *mean* ones, or into ill-tempered and mellow ones. There were incomparably more ill-tempered and mean ones. (*PSS* 4:196)

This reminds one of Tolstoi's physiological sketch of the Russian soldier in "A Woodcutting Expedition." But Dostoevsky, who may have had Tolstoi's sketch in mind, does not stop here:

> Here I am, however, trying to categorize our prison (*podvesti pod razriady*), but is this at all possible? Reality is infinitely diverse, as compared with every construction of abstract thought, even the shrewdest, nor does it tolerate any sharp or large-scale divisions. Reality aims at differentiation. We, too, had our peculiar life, whatever it may have been. We certainly did, and not only an official, but also an inner, life of our own. (*PSS* 4:197)

This leads us to an antinomy that dominates all of Dostoevsky's aesthetic thought. On the one side, he is a great believer in facts. Mrs. Dostoevsky reports that whenever her husband was greatly intrigued by something he had heard, he would exclaim: "Let's have the facts, the facts, the facts." And many passages in Dostoevsky's writings suggest a veritable cult of fact. Sven Linnér has collected many of these passages in his *Dostoevskij on Realism*.[2] Dostoevsky himself often declared his opposition to mere theory.[3]

But, on the other side, Dostoevsky believes that not all normally endowed and educated human beings have the same ability to perceive facts:

> One can know a fact, one can see it a hundred times oneself and still fail to get the same impression as when someone else, a man with special gifts, stands beside you and points out that very same fact to you, yet in his own peculiar fashion, explains it to you in his own words and makes you look at it through his eyes. A real talent is recognized by the sort of influence he exerts.[4]

We have in Dostoevsky's aesthetics a hierarchy, where "theory," that is, abstract statements about life, has the lowest truth value, simple facts a

2. Sven Linnér, *Dostoevsky on Realism* (Stockholm: Almqvist and Wiksell, 1967). See also G. M. Fridlender, *Realizm Dostoevskogo* (Leningrad: Nauka, 1964).

3. "No, you haven't got it! You haven't got a sense of reality. Your idealism stupefies, distracts, and deadens you, and you yourself have no clear understanding of that which you are boasting that you understand so well." "Poslednie literaturnye iavleniia; gazeta *Den'*," 1861 (*PSS* 19:63–64).

4. Linnér, *Dostoevsky on Realism*, pp. 143–44.

higher one, and the same facts as perceived by an artist with true intuitive powers the highest.

The position of Notes from the House of the Dead is, in this scheme, different from that of Dostoevsky's other works of fiction. We know that some of the mere "facts" reported in this work were eventually converted into an artist's insight. The prisoner who is serving twenty years for parricide (his name was Il'insky) became Dmitry Karamazov, the prisoner A———v (Aristov) became Svidrigailov, the prisoner Petrov became Fed'ka the convict, and so forth. It is difficult to deny that the products of Dostoevsky's imagination are in a way superior to their prototypes as presented in Notes from the House of the Dead, nor is it absurd to claim that there may be more "truth" in Dmitry Karamazov than in the character described there. Being much more "simple fact" and less "creative fiction" than Dostoevsky's major works, Notes from the House of the Dead as a whole would stand below Crime and Punishment, The Possessed, and The Brothers Karamazov, all of which utilize some material from Dostoevsky's prison experience.

There is one exception: the episode "Akul'ka's Husband," which Dostoevsky himself felt was on the highest level of his art. In "Akul'ka's Husband," however, Dostoevsky clearly leaves the realm of simple fact and enters the realm of fiction. This great story tells of the vagaries of Eros: those in his power follow him unquestioningly, leaving those untouched by him uncomprehending victims.

One may assume that Turgenev was right when he said that truth, alas, is always banal, or one may agree with Belinsky, who said that there are periods in history when telling the simple and unadorned truth is more important than the greatest creation of the imagination could hope to be. Much of the success and impact of Notes from the House of the Dead had to do with the shocking facts reported in it. By any standards, it is a social document of great interest. Dostoevsky's ability to overcome all Victorian squeamishness and his refusal to abandon the solid ground of observed fact are indeed remarkable. For instance, Dostoevsky's handling of the facts of the convicts' sex life is honest, matter-of-fact, and wholly unsanctimonious. He finds a way to introduce the reality of open homosexual practices, mentioning that of the fifteen or so men who, it seemed, granted sexual favors to their fellow convicts, "only two or three had passable looks, while all the rest were lop-eared, ugly slobs, some of them even gray-haired" (PSS 4:40).

Today we are in a better position than were contemporary readers to consider the relative role of fact and fiction in Notes from the House of the Dead. We have Dostoevsky's Siberian notebooks with 484 entries, variants to the printed text, Dostoevsky's letters, memoirs of other prisoners, such as those of Szymon Tokarzewski, one of Dostoevsky's fellow prisoners, and a great deal of background research. Dostoevsky's later works also throw some light on his prison experience: for instance, "The Peasant Marei" (1876).

From today's vantage point it appears that "fact" and "fiction" are both transformed, in *Notes from the House of the Dead* no less than in Dostoevsky's other works, into "figures of fact" and "figures of fiction." In other words, Dostoevsky, who kept a notebook all his life, refused to be a "writer from the notebook" even in this work, but insisted on letting every detail of fact pass through the crucible of his creative imagination.

I suggest that the structure of *Notes from the House of the Dead* resembles Chinese boxes (or a Matriosha doll), where every figure of fiction contains a figure of fact, and every figure of fact contains a figure of fiction. The veracity topos is a recurrent figure; for instance, after a lyrical description of springtime in Siberia, the narrator observes: "I am not poeticizing at this moment and I am convinced of the truthfulness of my observation" (*PSS* 4:173). On the other hand, this introductory passage occurs in "Akul'ka's Husband," a piece of fiction:

> I remember how once, on a long winter night, I overheard a story. At first sight it appeared to me as a feverish dream of some sort, as though I were down with a raging fever and had dreamed all this in my feverish ravings. (*PSS* 4:165)

Or, after the great scene of "death in the hospital," which Tolstoi so admired: "But I have digressed from my subject matter" (*PSS* 4:141). The very title of the work provides another illustration: "Notes" is a figure of fact (the "Notes" are really quasi-notes), while "the House of the Dead" is a figure of fiction (the phrase sounds like Gothic fiction, though it designates something all too real). The introduction starts out as a figure of fact, a feuilletonistic piece on the advantages of life in Siberia, and one is prepared for a work of the journalistic genre. But then, rather unexpectedly, there comes a transition to a figure of fiction, the character of Gorianchikov, clearly a fictitious character. But then, isn't he really a self-portrait of the author?

Then comes the story of the "manuscript," a blatant fiction, it would seem. But as we begin to learn its content, we realize that the figure of fiction contains a figure of fact:

> An entirely new world, wholly unknown up to now, the strangeness of certain facts, some particular observations on those lost people, fascinated me, and

I read some of these things with curiosity. Of course I may be wrong. I have
selected two or three chapters for trial. Let the public be the judge. (*PSS* 4:8)

Note "the strangeness of certain facts," a figure of fact, followed immediately by a figure of fiction: "Let the public be the judge."

Ultimately it may well be that the truth is as elusive in *Notes from the
House of the Dead* as it is in Dostoevsky's other works. Some will see the
ultimate truth in its facts, confirmed as they are by the first letters Dostoevsky wrote to his brother after his release from prison. Others will see the
truth in edifying scenes such as "death in the hospital" and in the mood of
"The Peasant Marei," or in the discourse on freedom in the fifth chapter of
Part One (*PSS* 4:66–67).

While *Notes from the House of the Dead* as a work of the literature of fact is
obviously connected with the physiological sketch, its fictional nature may
be aligned with the many prison episodes in romantic literature, and in the
Gothic novel in particular. The recurring freedom motif and especially the
eagle episode link *Notes from the House of the Dead* with this tradition.

Dostoevsky's search for truth focuses on his exploration of human existence, or as he put it, finding "the man in man" (*cheloveka v cheloveke*).
Much as there is a hierarchy in the understanding of facts, there is also one in
the understanding of human existence. Comparing Dostoevsky's approach
to Tolstoi's may illustrate this point.

Tolstoi's heroes and heroines are ordinary people, engaged in typical relationships, mostly normal ones. The forces that move them are the ones
that most men and women know well—for example, the sex drive, plain and
simple, most nakedly in "Father Sergius," perhaps. The same drive, social-
ized, is the drive to perpetuate one's kind. Of course one hears of various
excesses, specifically illicit, adulterous passion. But they are still typical of
the society in which they occur.

These typical relationships and characters appear only on the fringes of
Dostoevsky's works. Dunia and Razumikhin and their happy union are
marginal to the action focused in Sonia and Raskolnikov. The happy marriage of the Epanchins is marginal to the twisted relationships that form the
plot of *The Idiot*. Dostoevsky justifies this practice by claiming that a deeper
truth is found precisely in exceptional characters and relationships:

For not only is an eccentric "not always" a particularity and a separate element, but, on the contrary, it happens sometimes that such a person, I dare say,

carries within himself the very heart of the whole, and the rest of the men of his epoch have for some reason been temporarily torn from it, as if by a gust of wind. ("From the Author," in *The Brothers Karamazov, PSS* 14:5)

The main characters of Dostoevsky's novels are invariably exceptional types, though they are placed in a world populated by ordinary people. The plots of these novels are built around capital crimes, perpetrated under unusual circumstances. It is Dostoevsky's art that gives credibility to his fantastic plots and eccentric characters, raising a claim for the reality of his fictional world, "realism in a higher sense," in which Dostoevsky believed.

Normal love affairs do not interest Dostoevsky. Even simple adultery is a nontopic. Dostoevsky is fascinated by passions that seem to be a manifestation of a metaphysical yearning for an absolute, for something that defies reason — in a word, the Eros of Plato's *Symposium*. Eros has many forms: the earthy lust of Fiodor Pavlovich Karamazov, who dies lusting for Grushenka, Dmitry's sensual but more exalted "aesthetic" love, Ivan's cold intellectual passion, Aliosha's spiritual *agape*.

One will find expressions of these passions in Tolstoi's works also, but they will tend to be marginal. This is consistent with the marginality of "Dostoevskian" characters, such as Dolokhov or Iashvin, in Tolstoi.

In Dostoevsky, Platonic Eros may take the form of homoerotic passion. Like Princess Katia of *Netochka Nezvanova,* her successors (who may bear her name) are seen spurning their male lovers and developing torrid passions for their female rivals: Nastas'ia Filippovna for Aglaia, Katerina Ivanovna for Grushenka. There is the strange relationship between Trusotsky, the cuckolded husband, and Velchaninov, the Don Juan. There is Piotr Stepanovich Verkhovensky's infatuation with Stavrogin.

Attempts at presenting characters who have the gift of true Christian *agape* are central to Dostoevsky's art. As Rozanov observed, the real test of Christianity is precisely the renunciation of carnal love: only if the afterlife and the rest of Christian metaphysics are accepted as reality do celibacy and chastity make sense. Dostoevsky stakes the success of his major novels on the credibility of Sonia Marmeladov, Prince Myshkin, Mar'ia Timofeevna, and Book Six of *The Brothers Karamazov,* entitled "A Russian Monk." Opinions may differ regarding Dostoevsky's success on this score, but the effort is certainly there.

It might seem that at this point Dostoevsky meets the old Tolstoi, who also celebrated chaste love. However, the keynote of Dostoevsky's feeling is different. Nowhere in Dostoevsky is there a real challenge to, much less a putdown of, that powerful god, Eros. There is nothing resembling the old Tolstoi's squeamish distaste for sex in Aliosha's extreme chastity, or in Myshkin's virginity. Myshkin and Aliosha are both bridegrooms. The Dostoevskian saint is chaste because of too much, not too little, Eros.

Tolstoi's oeuvre is dominated by a negative attitude toward romantic love. It is seen as an unclean, destructive "civilized" perversion of the natural sex drive. Tolstoi's attitude is that of an enlightener (*prosvetitel'*) and rationalist. Dostoevsky's oeuvre is dominated by a positive attitude toward romantic love in all of its forms. Dostoevsky accepts the romantic deification of Eros, which makes love a metaphysical absolute.

Dostoevsky's plot is characteristically a phenomenology of the human spirit, or, better, an Odyssey of the human spirit. It is the romantic plot, close to the Christian *Heilsgeschichte* of a human soul, its fall, and its salvation through suffering. Tolstoian man, on the other hand, is concerned essentially with society, justice and injustice, factual truth and untruth.

Dostoevsky's subject is a self-conscious individual, which leads to a centrifugal psychology. Dostoevskian heroes, like romantic heroes in general, keep surprising us. The romantic hero's self-consciousness may lead to alienation, to doubling, and to disintegration of his personality — all Dostoevskian specialties. Tolstoi's psychology is centripetal: his characters grow and are enriched, but they never transcend themselves.

Romantic intuitivism is opposed to the rationalism of the Enlightenment. The wisdom of the heart triumphs over cold reason. An interest in and respect for the child are romantic — and Dostoevskian. Tolstoi's is an adult world. It is symptomatic that Dostoevsky is disappointed in the hero of Tolstoi's educational trilogy. A passage in the notebooks for *The Possessed* says: "A type wholly contrary to that scion of a noble family of Counts, degenerate (*izmel'chavshiisia*, literally "grown shallow") to the point of swinishness, whom Tolstoi has depicted in his *Childhood* and *Adolescence*" (*PSS* 9:28). In the notebooks for *A Raw Youth* he comments: "*Childhood* and *Adolescence*. A poet of petty vanity" (*PSS* 16:67).

The romantic perception of time is dominated by *kairos* rather than by *chronos*. Time is seen as the creator of values, its flow is goal-directed, it is emotionally and aesthetically charged. Dostoevsky's time perception is romantic all along. Perishability is no concern of his. Fear of getting old and dying is a marginal concern. In Tolstoi's world death and aging are central facts of life. Bad timing is one of the most prominent themes in Tolstoi's plots. In Dostoevsky's plots one is struck by the fantastic number of lucky coincidences. Dostoevsky has a strong historical sense, the ability to perceive the identity of an epoch. Tolstoi has very little of it, as the critics of *War and Peace* have pointed out.

Tolstoi was a realist in the best sense of that term. Dostoevsky's novels do not represent or explain life. Rather, they are attempts at creating a symbolic counterpart (Schelling's *Gegenbild*) of life.[5]

The fantastic and even the supernatural have a place in romantic art, as do psychological extremes. Dostoevsky found ways to combine all these things with an enhanced concreteness of expression. His striving for concreteness — through individualization, carefully chosen detail, an insistence on markedness, and dramatic presentation — is also a romantic trait. It is opposed to the striving for the normal and typical in realist art. The world of Tolstoi's fiction knows no huge and terrifying spiders, nor the little red ones that Dostoevsky uses so effectively as symbols of emotional experience.

This raises the question of the place of psychology in Dostoevsky's art. Granted that his works contain a great many descriptions of the workings of the human psyche, granted that the plots of his novels tend to unfold in a medium of inner life, and granted that the actions of Dostoevsky's characters seem psychologically motivated, what role and value did Dostoevsky himself assign to psychological insight and psychological interpretation? Would it be correct to say that Dostoevsky's main concern is to solve human problems in psychological terms? Is Dostoevsky a psychological novelist in the same sense that another novelist who seeks to clarify social issues and to enhance readers' social awareness is considered a social novelist? Is the point of a Dostoevskian novel psychological?

The critic Valerian Maikov suggested, as early as 1847, that Dostoevsky, a psychological novelist, was interested in society only as a medium stirred by the movements of the human soul, as Gogol, a social novelist,[6] was interested in the individual only insofar as he was affected by society. Maikov, then, saw his friend Dostoevsky as primarily an explorer of the human psyche. Apparently the young Dostoevsky felt so himself. Indeed, the point of some of his better early works seems to be decidedly psychological. Dostoevsky's first work, *Poor Folk* (1846), may well be described as a "psychology of poverty," rather than a sociological approach to the problem. His first

5. " 'You must depict reality as it is,' they say, but meanwhile such reality does not exist at all, nor has there ever been such a thing here on earth, because the essence of things is inaccessible to man and he perceives nature as it is reflected in his idea, after having passed through his senses. Consequently one must give free rein to the idea and not be afraid of the ideal." *A Writer's Diary*, 1873 (*PSS* 21:75). Needless to say, Dostoevsky's "idea" and "ideal" are not theoretical constructs, but living intuitions.

6. See Vladimir Seduro, *Dostoyevski in Russian Literary Criticism 1846–1956* (New York: Columbia University Press, 1957), p. 11.

major novel, *Netochka Nezvanova* (1849), which remained incomplete because the writer was arrested while still working on it, is a psychological *Bildungsroman,* possibly inspired by George Sand's novel *Consuelo.* In the three episodes of the novel that Dostoevsky was able to complete, the author's interest seems to be focused on one or several psychological discoveries. In each instance, his satisfaction with his insights is quite apparent, and there seems to be no point beyond the psychological insight at hand.

In the first episode, the writer discovers that an erotic relationship may exist between a fortyish man, the half-mad and drunken fiddler Efimov, and a little girl of nine or ten, his stepdaughter Netochka, who at this stage believes that he is her natural father. Netochka's first childhood memory is of an argument between her parents. For some reason the child thinks that her father is being wronged and rushes to his side. In the ensuing scene, Netochka's mother inadvertently hurts the child, and Netochka finds herself sitting on her father's lap. This is the beginning of their romance, which bears the features of Dostoevsky's later treatments of the love theme. The lovers are matched unevenly both in the strength and in the quality of their love. Efimov does not deserve the love of the little girl, does everything possible to destroy it, but is loved all the more. His love, if indeed he feels any, is entirely selfish: he needs Netochka, for she alone believes in his childish dreams of fame and fortune. Netochka's love is quite complex. There is an element of pity in it:

> I'd say that this was rather a kind of compassionate, *motherly* feeling, even though such definition may sound slightly ridiculous when used with regard to a mere child. (*PSS* 2:164)

The child, who intuitively sees through the pathetic weakness of the man, seeks to accommodate him, laughs at his sorry jokes, listens to his endless soliloquies, even if she cannot understand a word he says. Father and daughter are united by the bond of a shared dream as well, but there is also a bond of guilt, for their dream contains a wish that Netochka's mother may die. There is an element of possessiveness about it, too:

> Little by little I felt that I was gaining ascendancy over him, that I was gradually assuming the role of mistress, that he no longer could be without me. I was secretly proud of it, as I triumphantly realized how much he actually needed me. So much that I would occasionally play the coquette with him. (*PSS* 2:173)

Certainly Netochka's attachment to her father is an erotic one. The little girl is in love. She will spend hours on the cold staircase waiting for her father, in the hope that he will caress her on his return home. Physical eroticism is a part of her love, but the spiritual element, the desire to do something for the beloved, is more important. In a word, it is a genuine romance (the narrator uses the word *roman*). Most interestingly, Dostoevsky de-emphasizes the daughter–father relationship and lets Efimov and his stepdaughter meet as individuals. Another striking feature is the boldness with which the erotic aspect of the relationship is pointed out and emphasized.

In the second episode of *Netochka Nezvanova* we meet Laria, an orphan boy of about eleven, who was supposed to become the hero of the novel. Laria, the sickly, homely, redheaded son of a poor clerk, has always been a problem child. Abused by his schoolmates, he would seek compensation in a kind of tyranny over his weak parents. He develops a neurotic, sado-masochistic personality. Then, one Christmas Eve, after Laria has distressed his parents by demanding expensive presents, his father dies of a heart attack. His mother, overwhelmed by grief, dies within the week. Netochka's foster father takes the child into his house. Unlike Netochka, Laria does not respond to his guardian's kindness. He sulks in dark corners, cries a lot, refuses to study, and withdraws into a world of torturous daydreams. He has developed a depressive neurosis: he imagines that it was he, and only he, who caused his father's death and derives a morbid satisfaction from a fatalistic belief that he will soon join his parents in death. In fact, he tells Netochka that of late his mother has been seeing him every night. He has firmly decided to run away, go to his mother's grave, and die there. The psychological point of Laria's story is his strange relationship with his parents. It becomes clear from the boy's account that while he loved them dearly, especially his mother, he also tormented them with his capricious and selfish behavior, knowing full well how much he was hurting them. The whole story is an amazingly convincing study of childhood neurosis.

Next we have a torrid homosexual love affair between two young girls, Netochka and Katia, the daughter of Prince Kh—y, who is Netochka's foster father. In this case, Netochka is the weaker, quasi-feminine partner. It is love at first sight on her part, while the vivacious and pretty brunette does not seem to be much interested in her melancholy blond playmate. For a while we see Netochka pining away, without any hope that her adoration might ever be appreciated. Their relationship develops in a series of conflicts of the kind that might occur between heiress and poor orphan. Katia is haughty, brusque, and condescending, generous on occasion; Netochka is submissive, patient, grateful for every bit of attention.

Gradually, Katia begins to care, as she seeks to impress Netochka with her brilliance and courage. Netochka, now completely overwhelmed, can

no longer restrain herself. With much excitement and trepidation, she pur-
loins some articles of Katia's wardrobe to fondle and cover with kisses — a
flagrant exhibition of erotic fetishism. We then witness this display of sultry
eroticism:

> Sometimes I would sit on the edge of her bed, bend over her face and inhale her
> hot breath. Stealthily, trembling with fear, I would then kiss her little hands,
> her shoulders, her hair, her little foot, if it happened to protrude from under
> her blanket. (*PSS* 2:210)

As we learn later, Katia only pretends to be asleep during these visits and
greatly enjoys them. It takes a chance occurrence (Netochka heroically suffers the punishment for some mischief perpetrated by the other girl) to
bring the romance to its consummation. After a coquettish preview in the
presence of the unsuspecting governess, the real love scene finally begins, as
Netochka and Katia are now alone:

> She quickly leaped up from her seat and, all flushed and with tears in her eyes,
> rushed to embrace me. Her cheeks were moist, her lips tumid like little cher-
> ries, her curls all in disarray. She began to kiss me madly, she kissed my face,
> my eyes, my lips, my neck, my hands; she wept as if she were in a fit of hyster-
> ics; I pressed her to myself, and we embraced sweetly, joyfully, like friends, like
> lovers after a long separation. Katia's heart was pounding so violently I could
> hear every heartbeat. (*PSS* 2:217)

That same night the two little girls sleep together and engage in the most
passionate lovemaking. They treat each other to hundreds of kisses "until
their lips are swollen from so much kissing," and exchange other caresses.
"Ah, what shameless hussies we are!" Katia exclaims, which suggests that the
girls, like, of course, the narrator, are aware of the forbidden nature of these
goings-on. The point of the whole episode seems to lie, once again, in the
psychological novelty of the experiences described.

This pattern of psychological discoveries continues after Dostoevsky's return from Siberia. *Notes from the House of the Dead* features several stories
told by the narrator's fellow convicts in which unexpected psychological reactions are reported as a matter of fact, without any theorizing. It is *Notes
from Underground* (1864) that is the turning point. We have in this work, on
the one hand, a perceptive, almost clinical, study of neurotic behavior, with
a wealth of specific, graphically presented symptoms. A Freudian psychoanalysis of the antihero, as Dostoevsky calls him, is clearly indicated. Here,
for example, is a passage that will give a Freudian analyst an excellent start:

How can one, after all, have the slightest respect for a man who tries to find pleasure in the feeling of humiliation *per se?* I'm not saying that out of any mawkish sense of repentance. In general, I couldn't stand saying, "Sorry, Papa, I'll never do it again." And it wasn't at all because I was incapable of saying it. On the contrary, perhaps it was just because I was only too prone to say exactly that." (*PSS* 5:107)

But, for the first time in Dostoevsky, there is also a suggestion that psychological analysis, correct and brilliant though it may be, is not what really defines the human condition. *Notes from Underground* contains passages such as the following:

Don't I know myself, like twice two makes four, that the Underground isn't any good at all, but that there is something else, something entirely different, something for which I thirst, but which I simply cannot find. (*PSS* 5:121)

This "something entirely different" never shows up in the text, but in a letter to his brother Mikhail, Dostoevsky wrote:

It would have been much better not to print that next-to-last chapter (the most important, where my idea is really expressed), than to print it "as is," that is, with phrases plucked out and the resulting contradictions. But what can you do? Those pigs, the censors, let pass the passages where I was ostensibly mocking and at times blaspheming, but where, from all this, I developed the need for Faith and for Christ, they didn't. (*PSS* 28/II:73)

In *Crime and Punishment* (1866), psychological analysis celebrates its greatest triumphs, yet it is in this novel that it is also cut down to size, exposed for what it is, and left, as it were, in the antechamber of a higher level of human understanding. *Crime and Punishment* is a *roman policier* in which the search for the killer is replaced by a search for the killer's motive. Dostoevsky himself wrote in his notebook: "Establish the motive by all means!" The fact is that he never did. The killer himself duly racks his brain after the deed, trying to answer this question, which neither he nor his creator, nor any of the book's many excellent critics, has answered. Pisarev, the positivist, said the motive was, ultimately, money. N. N. Strakhov, a conservative idealist, said it was misguided ideology, a "political" murder, in a way. Others have pointed out the thrill motive, the *Übermensch* motive, the motive of self-inflicted punishment, and even a Freudian Oedipal motive. In the end it turns out that the question is irrelevant. The saintly Sonia does not show any interest in the motive at all: Raskolnikov has killed a human being, he has sinned, and he must be saved. In the Epilogue, Raskolnikov finds the way to salvation when he rids himself of all his subtle thoughts and begins to feel—simply, like Sonia. Raskolnikov the thinker and psychologist is dead; Raskolnikov the believer is born.

Nor is this dénouement unprepared for. Porfiry Petrovich, a master detective who uses psychology with superb skill, is also the first to admit that psychology is inherently double-edged. He does not trust psychology. He knows Raskolnikov well and can "read him." He assumes that he will not kill himself, but he still asks him, just in case, to leave a note saying where he hid the money. Yet this is the same Porfiry Petrovich who easily reads Raskolnikov's brilliantly staged entrance, when the killer walks into the detective's living room in a fit of merry laughter.

What is the reason for this apparent contradiction? The point is that it is one thing to understand another person intuitively, to the point of "slipping under his skin," but another thing to predict what that person will do. Porfiry knows that he who predicts the actions of another human being, as he would predict those of a mechanical contraption, may fare as badly as General von Mack and the Austrian *Hofkriegsrath,* who had figured out how to capture Napoleon with his whole army. It turned out that Napoleon did not act as he "should have," and it was von Mack, not Napoleon, who was led away into captivity. Quite simply, man has free will. Only Raskolnikov can decide whether to kill himself or not. The wise Porfiry accepts this.

Raskolnikov's greatest mistake was trusting psychology. Having studied the psychology of crime and in particular the state of the criminal's mind during and after the commission of a crime, he was confident that he would be able to handle a criminal's "problems." He soon discovered that the psychological problems were the least of what he had to face and that there were entirely new dimensions of existence that his psychology was quite unaware of.

Finally, the most important point about psychology in *Crime and Punishment:* it has often been said that the final scene of the Epilogue is out of character. Psychologically, Raskolnikov's conversion to Sonia's evangelic faith is implausible. But this is precisely what Dostoevsky wanted it to be. He went against psychology in the one point that really delivers the whole meaning of the novel. As Dostoevsky once put it: "If I have to choose between scientific truth and Christ, I choose Christ."[7] In other words, moral values take precedence over any other values. Morally, this is the correct conclusion for *Crime and Punishment,* and hence psychology will have to pass.

7. Letter to N. D. Fonvizina, dated February 20, 1854 (*PSS* 18/I:176), the first evidence that Dostoevsky had experienced a change of heart while in prison.

After *Crime and Punishment* every work of Dostoevsky's involves to some extent psychology's comeuppance. Time and again we meet clever psychologists who discover that people do not behave as predicted by psychology. *The Eternal Husband* (1870) is one of Dostoevsky's lesser works. Yet some critics, K. V. Mochulsky among them, consider it one of his masterpieces as far as structure and composition are concerned.

The plot is simple and symmetrical. Aleksei Ivanovich Velchaninov, a fortyish *bon vivant* and Don Juan, realizes one day that he is being followed by an unknown man with a black crepe band on his hat. Eventually the man comes to Velchaninov's flat, and the latter recognizes Pavel Pavlovich Trusotsky, a government official from the provinces with whose wife he had had a love affair nine years earlier. Trusotsky's wife has died recently, leaving him with their eight-year-old daughter, Liza. Velchaninov realizes that Liza is his daughter. Trusotsky soon tells him that he had discovered, shortly after his wife's death, a stack of letters from her various lovers. Velchaninov recalls, with a sigh of relief, that he had never written her a letter. A strange friendship develops between Velchaninov and Trusotsky. In view of Trusotsky's drinking problem, Velchaninov offers to place Liza with the family of an old friend. Trusotsky has no objections. Formerly the most tender of fathers, he no longer cares for the little girl, believing that she is not his daughter. But Liza falls ill and dies. Meanwhile Trusotsky keeps up his debauch and cannot be induced to see the ill girl, or even to attend her funeral. However, two weeks later, after a visit to Liza's grave, Velchaninov meets Trusotsky near the cemetery. Back in Petersburg, they go to Velchaninov's flat, where Trusotsky, for the first time, appears to be quite at ease and sincere: he has always loved and admired the handsome, brilliant, and witty Velchaninov, and still does. That night he has occasion to prove his devotion. Velchaninov suffers a bad attack of liver colic, and Trusotsky nurses him with eager affection. He stays overnight, even though Velchaninov feels much better and is no longer in pain. In the middle of night, Velchaninov is awakened by a noise, reaches out, and grasps an open razor. In spite of a badly cut hand, he soon overpowers Trusotsky and ties him up. When he releases him at dawn, neither man has said a word. On the next day Velchaninov gets a letter from Trusotsky. It contains only some pages that Mrs. Trusotsky had written to Velchaninov but never mailed. Trusotsky had known all along.

The next-to-last chapter is entitled "Analysis." As Velchaninov thinks back on all that has happened, he stumbles from one ambiguity to another. Trusotsky must have thought of murdering him before (in fact, Velchaninov recalls an earlier situation, similar to that of the previous night), yet his actual attempt must have been made on the spur of the moment, for the razor was the host's. Velchaninov finally decides that Trusotsky "had wanted to kill him, but did not know that he wanted to kill him." Similarly, Trusotsky's "declaration of love" had been sincere, in a way: "He had loved him *from spite* — and that is the strongest love." Whatever Velchaninov tries to tell himself about Trusotsky turns into a paradox, culminating in the insight that Trusotsky is "a moral monster with noble emotions."

The Eternal Husband is, after a fashion, a variation on the theme of Turgenev's comedy "The Provincial Lady." In fact, we are told of an amateur performance of that play in which Mrs. Trusotsky played the title role, a young artillery officer (and one of her lovers) the lover, and Trusotsky himself the husband. The point is that Trusotsky is in the flashback (and again in the epilogue to the novella) the familiar vaudeville cuckold, the "eternal husband" (a mocking echo of the "eternal feminine"), while the middle episode reveals the complexity of this seemingly simple character.

The Eternal Husband, while it is one of Dostoevsky's strongly "psychological" works (note the chapter entitled "Analysis"), is also significant in its evaluation of psychology: the result of Velchaninov's shrewd analysis is exactly zero. In the end he knows Trusotsky as little as before. Velchaninov, through whose consciousness the whole story is seen, remains equally ambiguous — even to himself. It is also intimated that "the provincial lady," whom Velchaninov thought he understood fairly well, was in fact a much more complex character than he had believed.

Unlike most of Dostoevsky's later works, *The Eternal Husband* contains little or no metaphysics. Its message may be read as the negative one that psychology alone is circular, meaningless, and sterile. Thus, *The Eternal Husband* is an "antinovella," an impression enhanced by a certain flippancy in the tone of the narrative.

A final and definitive deflation of psychology takes place in the last book of *The Brothers Karamazov.* At Dmitry's trial we see two fine psychologists in action, the public prosecutor and the counsel for the defense. The prosecutor has an airtight case. He has a motive — in fact, several. He has overwhelming eyewitness and circumstantial evidence. In fact, he has an eyewitness who saw Dmitry run from the scene of the crime with the door of the victim's house wide open. Yet the prosecutor still makes a point of resolving any psychological questions that may arise. Dmitry claims that, having been entrusted with 3,000 rubles by his fiancee, he spent half of that amount on a debauch, then sewed up the remaining 1,500 rubles in a small cloth bag that he carried on a string around his neck until the night of the murder. Dmitry's explanation for this strange behavior is that he is "a scoundrel, but not a thief." He was capable of squandering money entrusted to him on the spur of the moment, but not of embezzling it in cold blood. The prosecutor reasons as follows. If Dmitry's story were true, being the irresponsible spendthrift that he is, he would soon have taken a hundred more rubles from the bag, saying to himself: "If I return 1,400, I'm still not a thief." And then a hundred more, and so on. And when only a hundred was left: "What's the use of returning a hundred? I'll better drink it up, too!" The prosecutor's psychological analysis seems perfectly convincing, but it is false: Dmitry's story was true.

The prosecutor then proceeds to analyze Smerdiakov, the actual killer, and demonstrates to everybody's satisfaction that "to assume Smerdiakov to be guilty of this crime is perfectly absurd." So it is, but Smerdiakov was the killer. The same thing happens as the prosecutor proceeds to account for Ivan Karamazov's abortive confession. Again, his reconstruction of what went on in Ivan's mind is most plausible, but it is not what happened.

By now it is clear that Dostoevsky is engaged in a cat-and-mouse game with psychology and its hapless exponent, the worthy Ippolit Kirillovich. The concluding chapter is entitled "Psychology under Full Steam." The prosecutor overplays his hand. Even the provincial audience finds that "there has been a little too much psychology." The highlight of this chapter is a dazzling, many-layered montage of ambiguities. Ippolit Kirillovich likens the story of the accused to a poorly constructed novel, then exclaims: "And here, then, we shall rout our exultant novelist with the aid of some details, these very details in which reality always so abounds and which are always ignored by these luckless and involuntary novelists." The point is that the "novelist" has told the truth, an implausible truth, but the truth nevertheless.

Next the counsel for the defense, the wily Fetiukovich, takes the stage. The chapter is subtitled "A Stick with Two Ends," which means as much as "double-edged psychology." Fetiukovich takes up the prosecutor's challenge: if the story of the accused is a poorly constructed and poorly motivated novel, is it possible that the prosecutor's version is merely a well-motivated psychological novel? And Fetiukovich proceeds to show that one can give the screw another turn and create a version that is deeper, more subtle, and more credible yet than the prosecutor's, for each and every psychological argument produced by the latter is double-edged.

Dmitry had claimed that, after felling Grigory with the brass pestle, he jumped back down from the fence "simply because he had felt sorry for the old man." He then spent several minutes trying to stop the blood gushing from the victim's head and, when Grigory failed to come to, finally left him there. The prosecutor suggested, most plausibly, that if the accused had indeed stopped, it was only to make sure the witness to his crime was really dead. Now the defender objects that such a course of action would have been unlikely for a man who had just left the most incriminating evidence on the floor next to his father's body and did not even bother to pick up or hide the murder weapon. He could not have been completely reckless one moment and coolly calculating the next. And even if this were the case, the logical thing to do would have been to make sure Grigory was really dead by breaking his skull with a second, well-aimed blow. The defender concludes his demonstration by exclaiming:

> "Gentlemen of the jury, I have used psychology on purpose myself to show how one can prove anything with it. Psychology tempts even the most serious people to start composing novels, and quite against their own intentions. I am talking here of excessive psychology, gentlemen of the jury, I am talking about an abuse of psychology." (*PSS* 15:8)

Shrewd as he is, Fetiukovich is in the end himself a casualty of psychology. Having discredited all of the circumstantial evidence accumulated by his opponent, the defender implicitly admits that his own version is also a psychological "novel," when he concedes the possibility that Dmitry killed his father after all—why else would he hedge and plead extenuating circumstances, "just in case"? In the end, both psychologists achieve the exact contrary of what they would have wished. Fetiukovich, a clever but unscrupulous man, loses his case. Ippolit Kirillovich, a righteous man, convicts an innocent one.

The failures of overconfident psychologists do not, of course, discredit psychology as such. *The Brothers Karamazov* contains some of the deepest psychological analysis in all of Dostoevsky's works. Ivan Karamazov's struggle with his conscience is surely among the finest examples of psychological analysis in fiction. Yet truly deep psychology, presented not as someone's psychological fiction but as psychological truth, is just as inconclusive as the speculations of Fetiukovich and Ippolit Kirillovich. The real solutions are reached in terms of visions, intuitions, and free decisions. No psychological motivation is involved in Father Zosima's decision to become a monk, in Aliosha's mystical vision and its consequences, in Dmitry's decision to accept suffering, or in Grushenka's willingness to follow Dmitry to Siberia.

Altogether, one sees a pattern of deprecation of psychology in Dostoevsky's later works. Psychological motivation, psychological subtlety, and psychological complexity tend to be associated with weakness, lack of faith, and negativism. The more important psychology is in a character, the farther removed he is from Grace. Kolia Krasotkin's psychological problems are manifold, deep, and intriguing—and he will be a very unhappy man some day. No psychology is required to understand the brave and generous Iliusha Snegiriov. Katerina Ivanovna is psychologically complex—and a very unhappy young woman. Grushenka is her opposite: she needs no analyst. Ivan Karamazov is the prime example of psychological complexity—and he is far removed from Grace. His two brothers are simpler, and the saintly Aliosha has no "psychology" at all. It is significant that Father Zosima, a saint, has no "psychology" either: nothing is said, or needs to be said, about his inner life.

What is it about psychology that makes it so negative? The answer can only be that it deals with that aspect of the human condition which excludes the higher faculty of free will and the miracle of divine Grace. Its proper area is therefore limited. Any man whose life can be accounted for in purely psychological terms is lacking free will and is without divine Grace. The Grand Inquisitor is a subtle psychologist, and so are the Devil and his disciple, Ivan Karamazov. Even Smerdiakov is not a bad psychologist. None of them love or respect people, or believe in divine Grace. Father Zosima and Aliosha are lovers of mankind and they love God. They are no psychologists.

Certainly, by going against psychological verisimilitude Dostoevsky compromises the credibility of his plots and the lifelike quality of his central characters. In the following chapters I try to show how he deals with this problem.

4

The Art of *Crime and Punishment*

> A literary creation can appeal to us in all sorts of ways—by its
> theme, subject, structure, characters. But above all it appeals to
> us by the presence in it of art. It is the presence of art in *Crime
> and Punishment* that moves us deeply rather than the story of
> Raskolnikov's crime.
>
> Boris Pasternak, *Doctor Zhivago*

D OSTOEVSKY was a master of montage. He skillfully covers the
seams that join the several distinct themes, genres, and styles of which
the novel is composed. The duel between Raskolnikov's godless Nietzschean
humanism and Sonia's Orthodox faith is high (if you want) religious drama.
The sad story of the Marmeladov family is vintage naturalism.[1] The story of
Svidrigailov is melodrama, with a touch of Gothic horrors. What else could
one call this passage: "Never had he seen her so beautiful. The fire that was
blazing from her eyes at the moment when she raised the revolver virtually
burnt him as his heart winced in pain" (*PSS* 6: 301–2).[2]

Svidrigailov's story is integrated with that of Mrs. Raskolnikov and her
daughter Dunia, though rather carelessly (where are the children Miss Ras-

---

1. We know that Dostoevsky was at one time working on a piece entitled "Dear Drunks"
(*P'ianen'kie*). It became the nucleus of the Marmeladov episode.

2. Dunia is a rarity in Dostoevsky's work: an entirely one-dimensional and stereotypical
character.

kolnikov is supposed to teach?). In that story we recognize the British novel about the virtuous but indigent governess and her rakish and/or mysterious employer. The Pecksniffian solicitor Luzhin, to whom Dunia is engaged as the novel starts, adds a Dickensian flavor to the governess's story. The detective novel enters the plot through the presence of Porfiry Petrovich, a master investigator. The detective is not really needed in the plot, since the perpetrator of the crime is known to begin with and eventually surrenders of his own free will, induced more by Sonia's pleas than by Porfiry's promise of a lighter sentence.

Throughout the novel, scraps of Platonic philosophical dialogues, sophisms, and aphorisms appear, almost always topically related to the ideological struggles of the 1860s. Elements of satire appear throughout the text, some with a point (the socialist Lebeziatnikov is presented as a ridiculous character), some quite gratuitous: the all too familiar "Poles of Dostoevsky," the Jewish fireman, unsavory German (of course!) landladies, madams, and procuresses.

Like most of Dostoevsky's novels, *Crime and Punishment* is a psychological and an ideological novel. The action develops on three levels: that of physical action and spoken discourse, that of the workings of the characters' minds, and that of the philosophical argument, developed in part explicitly, in part as a subtext.

In spite of various spurious insertions, *Crime and Punishment* is a *roman à thèse* of the dramatic type with a dominant central theme.[3] The theme is an age-old one: "What is the greatest good?" The question is asked in terms of a confrontation, on an existential plane, between Sonia Marmeladov's unshakable Christian faith and self-effacing humility and the carnal hedonism of Svidrigailov, the Benthamite utilitarian ethics of Luzhin, the socialist positivism of Lebeziatnikov, and, of course, Raskolnikov's notion that power is the greatest good. At one point the question is reduced simply to Svidrigailov's amoralism versus Sonia's submission to God's law: "Here I must go either her way or his" (p. 354). Inasmuch as the ideological plane is synchronized with the character traits of its bearer, the confrontation is apparently arranged so as to present the Christian answer in an attractive light while discrediting all opposing views. It must be observed that Dostoevsky has managed to introduce at least one significant encounter between Sonia and all four characters whose views oppose hers.

3. A fairly accurate description of the central theme is found in Dostoevsky's notebooks. See *PSS* 7:154–55.

Sonia has all the Christian virtues. Though she has suffered much injustice, she never claims to be a victim but, on the contrary, calls herself "a great sinner," reminding herself of an act of unkindness to her stepmother. Her whole being is penetrated by Christian *agape*. The impression that she is really a saint is supported by the wealth of New Testament symbolism associated with her.[4] It is made explicit in the Epilogue when we learn that the convicts "even went to her to be healed." Sonia, like other characters in the novel, has literary antecedents of which Dostoevsky was well aware, particularly a saintly prostitute called Fleur-de-Marie in Eugène Sue's novel *Les mystères de Paris*. Even her name is symbolic: Sophia is Divine Wisdom, in both the Orthodox and the romantic tradition.

Svidrigailov, a former guardsman, is literate and has the air of a gentleman. He is a more subtle version of Valkovsky in *The Insulted and Injured* and, as it were, a study for Stavrogin of *The Possessed* (down to the theme of an abused child in his past). All these characters are versions of the supercilious dandy (or "libertine") of the English novel, with a hint of Byronic ennui and satanism. Utterly amoral, Svidrigailov follows his appetites and impulses, which lead him to heinous crimes but also to acts of kindness. He can be cynical and overbearing, but also tolerant and understanding, depending on his mood of the moment. Svidrigailov kills himself, apparently because he can no longer stand the nightmares that well up from his subconscious. In a way, he admits defeat by becoming a benefactor and savior of Sonia and the Marmeladov children.

Luzhin, a self-made man of humble origins (his education was paid for "in small change," he admits), prides himself on his hard-earned fortune and middling rank in the civil service. He lacks Svidrigailov's gentlemanly scruples. Where the former guardsman is ruthless, Luzhin is mean in a self-righteous way. Foiled in his clumsy attempt to frame Sonia, he disappears from the novel, a loser.

Lebeziatnikov is a more attractive figure. He naively parrots the socialist line, but in a pinch acts like the silly but harmless little man he is. He betrays his socialist principles ("free love," in this case) when put to the test of applying them in real life (when Sonia is forced into prostitution), but also shows he is an honest man with a kind heart when he foils Luzhin's plot and later tries to help the crazed Katerina Ivanovna.

Raskolnikov, aside from being a murderer, has much going against him.

---

4. See George Gibian, "Traditional Symbolism in *Crime and Punishment*," *PMLA* 70 (1955): 979–96.

He is intolerant of the foibles of others and sounds downright priggish in his encounters with Svidrigailov. He is naively conceited:

> "A thought then occurred to me, for the first time in my life, which no one before me had ever thought of! No one! It became suddenly clear to me, like the sun, that nobody had ever dared, or dares, to walk past all this absurdity, to grab it all simply by the tail and send it to the devil." (P. 321)

After a few condescending gestures, Raskolnikov is, inexplicably and without self-awareness, drawn to Sonia. He is much the weaker party in all of their encounters, right to the end of the novel. His mental imbalance, his uncontrollable swings from momentary bravado to animal fear, from spontaneous generosity to cold heartlessness, cannot stand up to Sonia's moral strength and integrity.

The argument is complicated, however, by deep ambiguities that emerge if one views the novel as a whole. Like Sonia, her father, a drunken derelict, is a believer. He dies in a state of grace, confident that God will forgive him. Meanwhile, his virtuous and hardworking wife dies in a state of acedia, a mortal sin, rejecting the sacraments: "I have no sins to confess! . . . God must forgive me even without [the sacrament of Penance]. He knows how I have suffered! . . . And if He will not forgive me, I have no need of it!" (p. 333).

The crux of the argument appears more clearly and more poignantly in the case of Marmeladov. Sonia's faith is accompanied by every conceivable human virtue. Her father's faith did not prevent him from taking his daughter's last thirty kopecks to keep his binge going. Pleading the case for faith with Sonia is playing with loaded dice. Her father presents the argument on a razor's edge.

Crime and Punishment is a novel with a less than elegant and streamlined plot and a less than clear and convincing argument. What gives it unity and sustains the reader's interest is not to be sought in a linear dimension, but rather in the drama of each successive scene and the variety of particular effects that energize the text.

Dramatic qualities prevail. A series of dramatic scenes follow one another: "duels" (Raskolnikov's duel with Zametov at the "Crystal Palace," his two duels with Porfiry Petrovich, his two duels with Sonia, Dunia's duel with Svidrigailov); mass scenes (the scene at the police station, the wake, Katerina Ivanovna's death); "conclaves"[5] (in Raskolnikov's room, in Porfiry's, at

---

5. L. P. Grossman's term for a scene in which the key characters meet to reach some momentous decision.

the rooming house); a series of dreams (Raskolnikov's and Svidrigailov's); some great silent scenes (the scene where Razumikhin suddenly, without a word's being said, realizes the truth about his friend). Narrative passages are filled with action: the "rehearsal" and the murder, Raskolnikov's aimless but eventful wanderings, Svidrigailov's last hours.

Dialogue is the dominant form of the text, particularly if one considers the inner dialogue Raskolnikov and some of the other characters (Razumikhin, Luzhin) conduct in their own minds. The narrator often engages in a dialogue with the words or actions he reports. His observations on tone of voice, mimicry, and gestures, which accompany dialogue and action with great consistency, often amount to stage directions. The dialogue between Raskolnikov and Sonia that finally states the opposing positions of hero and heroine (pp. 311–14), essentially a dialogue of the deaf, since each speaker ignores the position of the other, comes alive precisely through the narrator's comments on the emotions that animate the speakers.

Time and space are treated dramatically and figure in the action directly and explicitly. The locales of several scenes are symbolic of the action: the sleazy tavern in which Marmeladov meets Raskolnikov, Sonia's monstrously misshapen room (symbolic of the perverseness of her condition), Raskolnikov's room, which resembles a coffin. The circumstance that Svidrigailov rents a room adjoining Sonia's, and is thus able to overhear Raskolnikov's confession to her, is of course a purely theatrical device.

Clock time is crucial to the commission of the murder. We are told that Raskolnikov took exactly 730 steps going from his lodging to the pawnbroker's residence. The plot hinges on a series of coincidences in time, such as the summons delivered to Raskolnikov the morning after the murder.

A pattern of playacting dominates many of the scenes of the novel. Several of the principal characters are presented playing a role other than their natural selves, for various reasons. It is made explicit that Marmeladov is in fact putting on a show at the tavern, and that it is a repeat performance (pp. 9–10). The novel actually begins with Raskolnikov's rehearsal of his planned crime. Subsequently he is forced to put on a show at the police station. He then stages a dramatic scene with Zametov at the Crystal Palace and stages his entry to Porfiry Petrovich's flat. He affects a pose throughout, even with Sonia. His attempt at a public confession in the square turns into grotesque comedy.

Luzhin, as he appears at Raskolnikov's room, tries to present himself as a liberal in step with the times. He puts on a show of righteous indignation when trying to frame Sonia. He is a bad actor throughout.

Katerina Ivanovna tries to play the role of a lady even in the sordid ambience of a slum tenement. She ends up staging a heart-rending street scene with her children and even dies dramatically. Sonia's first scene shows her, too, playing a role: she appears at her father's deathbed dressed up in her streetwalker's finery, carrying a parasol (it is night).

Svidrigailov plays the role of a suitor and bridegroom, knowing full well that it is a farce. Further examples of roleplaying may be readily adduced. They all add dramatic tension to the action.

Individualization of his characters, even minor ones, is characteristic of Dostoevsky's art. The concreteness that it gives them is one of his main assets. A *dramatis persona* has a specific function in the plot and, in most instances, also a function in the development of the ideological argument. In any case, a Dostoevskian character has a personality and a story of his or her own. Another tendency of Dostoevsky's art is to give his characters more idiosyncratic traits, more eloquence, wit, and imagination, than might be expected of average individuals. A favorite device is marking a character by polarized contradictory traits.

Porfiry Petrovich, the detective, is a case in point. To begin with, he does not look like a master detective: he is a rolypoly little man with a round face, a snub nose, and an unhealthy dark-yellow complexion. His face

> might have even appeared goodnatured, but for the expression of his eyes, which had a kind of watery luster and were covered by almost white eyelashes, continually blinking, as if winking at somebody. The gaze of these eyes clashed strangely with his whole figure, which actually had something womanish about it, and made him look much more serious than might have been expected at first glance. (P. 192).

The contradictions in this description are typical of Dostoevsky's manner of characterization.

Porfiry Petrovich's speech and mannerisms are highly idiosyncratic and, again, hardly typical of a successful detective. Who ever thought of a garrulous detective? Porfiry is in perpetual motion and appears nervous and self-conscious, yet is in full control of the situation. He suspects from the very first moment of their first meeting that Raskolnikov is his man. Raskolnikov has staged his entry to Porfiry's flat so as to appear casual and carefree, needling his friend Razumikhin about the latter's incipient infatuation with the beautiful Dunia. The embarrassed Razumikhin looks very funny, and Raskolnikov joins the rest of the company in a good laugh. This is the first instance of what Porfiry calls "double-edged psychology." No guilty man would enter a detective's place laughing—unless he is a truly formidable fighter, reasons Porfiry, realizing that it will take patience to get his man. So he enters into the spirit of goodnatured camaraderie and light banter, then springs his first surprise on Raskolnikov: the latter's article "On Crime." He soon steers the discussion to the question of those extraordinary individuals who have a right to break established laws. In the ensuing discussion (a Platonic dialogue, really), Raskolnikov parries Porfiry's probing questions well enough. They are slyly aimed, as it were by a narrow-minded philistine, at the practical consequences of Raskolnikov's subtle (Hegelian!) theory. The discussion ends when Zametov overplays his hand by blurting out: "Wasn't it perhaps some future Napoleon who last week did in our Aliona Ivanovna?" Porfiry tactfully changes the subject, only to spring another surprise. He asks Raskolnikov a question that he could have answered only if he was at the pawnbroker's the day of the murder. Double-edged psychology enters the picture once more: Raskolnikov sees the trap and answers "correctly," in the negative. But the fact is that an innocent but flustered man might have given an incriminating answer, and Raskolnikov's correct answer merely proves that he is on his guard. Porfiry profusely apologizes for his "mistake."

Eye to eye with Raskolnikov at their next meeting, Porfiry welcomes him warmly, and with the greatest solicitude, calling him "sir" and even "my dear sir" (*batiushka,* literally "little father"). Raskolnikov observes, however, that Porfiry stretches out both hands to greet him, yet does not shake hands. Porfiry agrees with everything Raskolnikov has to say (not much) and even with what he has not said: "Just as you, my dear sir, deigned to observe justly and wittily" (p. 258). The detective assumes a self-deprecating stance, complains about his health (he ought to quit smoking, his doctor told him), ruefully admits his weakness for military history (though himself a civilian, he might have made it to major, though not to Napoleon). This follows a long tirade on the fiasco of the Austrian *Hofkriegsrath,* who planned the capture of Napoleon in minute detail, only to see its own General von Mack surrender to him instead.

There are moments when Porfiry seems to be in a dither, mouthing strings of empty phrases, developing his ideas on investigative and interrogation strategy. Of course he is playacting, trying to provoke Raskolnikov into an angry outburst that would be tantamount to an admission of his guilt. He comes close, but Raskolnikov is saved when the interview is interrupted by the young painter's sudden confession to a crime he did not commit. At this point both antagonists quit playacting for a moment, as Porfiry observes: "Why, my dear, you didn't expect it either. Look how your hands [*ruchki,* "little hands"—Porfiry is very fond of diminutives!] are shaking!

He-he!" Raskolnikov responds: "Why, you are shaking, too, Porfiry Petrovich!" And Porfiry: "Yes, I am shaking, sir, I did not expect it, sir!" (p. 272)

When they meet for the last time, Porfiry puts his cards on the table. He quits playacting and coolly assesses the situation. He is convinced that Raskolnikov is guilty, but admits that he has no hard evidence (he had his room searched, but *umsonst!*—the German word emphasizes his frustration). He offers Raskolnikov a few more days of freedom to confess his crime, which would mean a reduced sentence, but warns him that he will have to arrest him if he does not take advantage of the offer. Here, finally, Porfiry abandons his self-deprecating bantering manner. He speaks with precision and authority, though not without a note of sympathy for the young man. He is aware of his duty as a magistrate and asks Raskolnikov to leave a brief note in case he chose "to resolve the matter in a different, fantastic manner, to raise your hands [*ruchki*, again!] against yourself." After all, Nikolai the painter, a wholly innocent man, is still in prison.

Altogether, Porfiry Petrovich remains psychologically ambiguous. We learn little about his personal life, except that he is thirty-five, a bachelor, and very sociable. We know also that he likes to play pranks on his friends: at one time he made them believe that he planned to become a monk, and recently, inspired by the acquisition of a new suit of clothes, he had intimated that he was about to get married—all in jest. Is Porfiry Petrovich a believer? He asks Raskolnikov if he believes in God, in a new Jerusalem, and in the raising of Lazarus. Raskolnikov, an unbeliever, answers in the affirmative. Porfiry gives no indication of his own position. His argument in favor of a confession is purely utilitarian: no mention is made of moral or religious reasons. One may suspect that behind Porfiry's cheerful and playful façade is hidden a rather sad character, a "finished man," as he says at one point. But perhaps he is only joking.

A pattern of inner contradictions prevails in other characters of the novel. Marmeladov is in some ways close to Porfiry. Like the latter, he is a middle-aged civil servant of some education. But he is older, and he is from the provinces, so his literate Russian sounds old-fashioned and smacks of the seminary. Like Porfiry, he is playing a role. Like Porfiry, he keeps qualifying, retracting, and conceding points. For example, as he talks about his efforts to impart to his growing daughter some knowledge of history and geography, he concedes that they did not get very far, for "whatever books we had . . . well, we no longer have those books [note the "doubletake," a favorite mannerism of his!] . . . so that was the end of it. We got as far as Cyrus of Persia" (p. 16). That is, they stopped after the second lesson.

Marmeladov's performance at the tavern is deeply ambiguous. It is, of course, a *cri de coeur*, but it is also, after all, a repeat performance before drunken strangers in a lowly tavern. The following passage may serve as an example:

> Marmeladov knocked himself on the forehead with his fist, clenched his teeth, closed his eyes, and firmly dug his elbow into the table. But in a moment his face suddenly changed, and he looked at Raskolnikov with a feigned show of roguishness and simulated insolence, laughed and said: "And today I went to Sonia and asked her for some money for a drink to cure me of my hangover!" (P. 6)

Thus, Marmeladov's version of the Last Judgment may be understood as an expression of true faith, but also as a carnivalesque — and, to some, blasphemous — travesty of scripture.

Marmeladov's performance, like Porfiry's, is clearly far too brilliant and imaginative to be taken for honest realism. Besides the spirited, metaphysical Judgment Day passage, he comes up with several other memorable aphorisms — about the difference between poverty and beggarliness; about the condition of no longer having a place to go; about begging without the faintest hope of being heard — each more poignant than the other. There are some marvellous clashes of pathos and bathos, as when a pompous Slavonic word clashes with a sordid vulgarism: "When my firstborn and only daughter [the adjective is *edinorodnaia,* usually applied to Jesus Christ in relation to God the Father] was certified a prostitute" (*po zheltomu biletu poshla,* "got her yellow ticket," which she would have to renew by submitting to medical examination). Marmeladov's monologue also establishes a list of *realia* that will keep returning in the course of the novel and acquire symbolic status, such as the "family" shawl and Katerina Ivanovna's finishing school diploma. All around, a sense of the marked detail prevails: Marmeladov actually sold his wife's stockings for drink — "not her shoes, for that would have been still in the order of things, but her stockings" (p. 16).

The whole story is marked by contradictions. Marmeladov lost his first job through no fault of his own but lost his second for drunkenness; he was given a second chance and blew it. He knows that his long-suffering wife will pull his hair and beat him when he comes home drunk, but "such beating, sir, causes me not only pain, but enjoyment" (p. 22). Katerina Ivanovna has cruelly forced her stepdaughter into prostitution, yet when Sonia comes home after surrendering her virginity for thirty silver rubles, she "knelt down before Sonia's bed and kissed her feet" (p. 17).

Katerina Ivanovna's character is as full of contradictions as her husband's. "She was by nature of cheerful and peaceloving disposition, and much inclined to laugh easily" (p. 296). But the misfortunes of her life have made her shrewish and quarrelsome. She beats her children when they cry because they are hungry. She is in the last stages of consumption and is beginning to lose her mind. Her fantasies invade reality. She introduces Raskolnikov to her guests as a young scholar who "is getting ready to take over a professor's chair at the local university" (pp. 293–94). Katerina Ivanovna's fantasizing and roleplaying lack the imagination and wit of her husband's, being confined within the narrow experience of the daughter of a minor provincial official. The highlight of her life was the graduation ceremony of her finishing school, at which she "danced a *pas de châle*" before the Governor and other personages of high rank.

Pulkheria Aleksandrovna Raskolnikov is another figure associated with deep ambiguities. Her long letter to her son is heavily stylized to create the effect of a painful and at times comical contrast between the scandalous and sinister happenings at the Svidrigailov estate and the writer's naive efforts to downplay their impact and her own reaction to them. This contrast grows even sharper when Mrs. Raskolnikov faces Luzhin's sordid actions and, finally, the perplexing predicament of her only son, which she cannot fathom. Dostoevsky mercifully avoids the climax of a mother learning that her son is a murderer by letting Mrs. Raskolnikov fall ill and die without being told the terrible truth. But he cannot resist adding yet another ambiguity by suggesting that in the final stages of her illness, "in her feverish ravings, some words escaped her from which it could be gathered that she suspected much more about her son's terrible fate than had been assumed" (p. 415).

Svidrigailov is of all the characters in the novel the most literary. Dostoevsky in a way apologizes for this by letting Svidrigailov say: "What the devil? I see that I may in fact appear to some people like a person from a novel" (*litsom romanicheskim*, p. 315).[6] Svidrigailov, too, is a deeply contradictory figure:

> This was a strange face, rather resembling a mask: white, red-cheeked, with bright red lips, a light-blond beard, and still rather thick blond hair. His eyes were somehow too blue; their gaze was somehow too heavy and too immobile.

6.   In the notebooks, Svidrigailov emerges more clearly as a murderer, sadist, and child-abuser, a Gothic character. In the definitive text, his nature is covered by a veil of ambiguity. For some excellent observations on Svidrigailov, see Joseph Frank, *Dostoevsky: The Miraculous Years, 1865–1871* (Princeton: Princeton University Press, 1995), pp. 94–95.

There was something terribly unpleasant about this handsome and extraordinarily youthful face, considering his age. (P. 357)

The demonic and evil is lurking behind Svidrigailov's gentlemanly façade: "Svidrigailov took an attentive look at Raskolnikov, and it appeared to the latter that in this glance there flashed momentarily, like a bolt of lightning, a malevolent sneer." Svidrigailov is very literate and, his mind is sharp. He can be civil, tolerant, and capable of self-criticism, but he can also be cynical and overbearing:

"Considering that Avdot'ia Romanovna is essentially a pauper (oh, excuse me, I did not want to be . . . but isn't it all the same, if the same concept is expressed?), in a word, she lives by the labor of her hands and has to support her mother and you (oh, the devil, you are frowning again . . .)." (P. 367)

Svidrigailov, like Porfiry and Marmeladov, delivers himself of occasional aphorisms and words of wit. An expert at seduction, he declares that flattery is the surest way to even a virtuous woman's heart: "If a straight approach contain even a hundredth part of a tiny note of falsehood, the result is an immediate dissonance, and thereafter a scandal. But if flattery is utterly false to the last tiny note, it still pleases" (p. 366).

The ultimate function of Svidrigailov in the novel's argument may be sealed by the good deeds that he does before killing himself. He undoes the evil done to Sonia and Katerina Ivanovna's children. Paradoxically, Marmeladov dies in a state of grace, while Svidrigailov is damned. The point of this can only be that the subject's salvation depends solely on his emotional state, not on his deeds. This notion will be pursued further, and more explicitly, in *The Idiot.*

Razumikhin, to whom Svidrigailov superciliously refers as "a seminarian, most likely," is also marked by contradictions, but in a wholly different way: "This was an extraordinarily cheerful and sociable lad, goodnatured to the point of being considered a simpleton by some. However, beneath this simplicity there were hidden both depth and dignity" (p. 43). Razumikhin is the very last to realize that his friend Raskolnikov is a murderer. But he sticks with him all the way and is rewarded by winning the hand of Raskolnikov's beautiful sister. Razumikhin is always his own honest self. But he is never dull. His views are in accord with his character. Speaking of his socialist friends, he observes:

"They demand complete loss of individuality and find it very much to their taste! How not to be themselves, how to resemble yourself as little as possible!

This they consider the highest progress. If they would at least talk rubbish in
their own way . . ." (P. 155)

Razumikhin's speech is laced with students' jargon: "Let us now proceed
to the United States of America, as they used to be called at our school,"
he says as he presents a pair of trousers to Raskolnikov. But he can argue a
point with logic and eloquence, though without subtlety. Razumikhin, too,
has his moments: the wonderfully carnivalesque paean to talking rubbish
(*vran'e*, a word that means "telling lies, fibbing, talking nonsense, make-
believe"), delivered in a state of advanced intoxication on a sidewalk in the
middle of the night before two mildly frightened ladies, and followed by a
spontaneous declaration of love uttered while kneeling on the sidewalk.

The hero and heroine of the novel are less challenging, Raskolnikov because we are allowed to follow the workings of his mind all along, and Sonia
because her character and mind lack psychological complexity. In contrast
to the characters already discussed, the speech of neither has any idiosyncratic traits.

Raskolnikov is a bundle of contradictions. Razumikhin says of him:
"Really, it is as though two contradictory characters were taking turns in
him" (p. 165). The contradictions in Raskolnikov's mind prior to the crime
may be reduced to a conflict between the normal emotions of an intellectually alert but emotionally immature young man (his normal, healthy self
is released by the dream that returns him to his childhood) and a paranoid
obsession with an idea that leads to a compulsive crime. After he commits
the crime, the struggle is between the criminal's natural desire to evade detection and the growing sense of isolation and alienation that results in a
subconscious desire to rejoin the human race by accepting the punishment
for his crime. Raskolnikov's efforts to escape detection are subverted, time
and again, by compulsive actions that put him in jeopardy: virtually admitting his guilt to Zametov, returning to the scene of his crime, challenging
Porfiry needlessly. All along he puts himself into a position that forces him
to playact, something that is in crass conflict with his proud and self-assured
nature. At Porfiry's, he is tricked into declaring not only that he believes in
God, a new Jerusalem, and the raising of Lazarus, but also, implicitly, that
he is a failed pseudo-Napoleon who ought to and will rightly suffer the full
severity of the law.

With Sonia, Raskolnikov can be himself. He develops his gloomy view of
life, his denial of God's existence, and his idea that power is the only good
worth pursuing — not as well as he had developed his idea of the exceptional
individual and his right to transgress at Porfiry's, but in a rambling, staccato
monologue. He believes that he can overpower Sonia with the force of the

"facts of life" that are destroying her and will similarly destroy Polechka, her ten-year-old stepsister. He is foundering in a sea of bitterness, self-pity, and hurt pride. When he confesses his crime to Sonia in their second meeting, he shows no remorse, only self-hatred and despair.

Sonia is, of course, the winner all the way, even if Raskolnikov refuses to admit defeat until the last page of the Epilogue. Her second dialogue with Raskolnikov is a masterful composition of dissonant tonalities. Raskolnikov is trying to analyze the motive of his crime and passes judgment on himself in terms of a Darwinist anthropology and anticipated Nietzschean ethics. Sonia responds, point after point, in terms of New Testament ethics and the movements of her heart:

> "But I only killed a louse, Sonia, a useless, repulsive, noxious louse!" — "So a human being is a louse?" (P. 320)

> "I had to find out, find out precisely, if I am a louse, like all, or a man? Find out if I can cross the boundary or not? Find out if I dare reach for it and take it, or not? Find out if I am a trembling creature or have the right . . ." — "To kill? You have the right to kill?" (P. 322)

The point is that neither can convince the other, because Raskolnikov's heart is not ready to accept Sonia's truth, and because she loves him and will not give up on him until he is saved.

Sonia, too, has her great moment:

> "What to do?" — she exclaimed, suddenly leaping up from her seat, and her eyes, filled with tears up to this moment, flashed: "Get up" (she grabbed his shoulder; he arose, looking at her almost in amazement). "Go right away, this very minute, stop at the crossroads, bow down, first kiss the earth, whom you have desecrated, and then bow down to the whole world, in all four heavenly directions, and say to all, aloud: 'I have killed!' Then God will return you to life. Will you go? Will you go?" she asked him, all trembling, as in a seizure, clasping him firmly by both hands and fixing a fiery gaze at him. (P. 322)

The narrator of *Crime and Punishment* is different from Dostoevsky's other narrators, in part because some of the initial first-person narrative mode was left in the text. The narrator's frequent remarks pointing to a future when Raskolnikov will look back at the events related are one trace of this circumstance.[7] As is, *Crime and Punishment* has a narrator without a distinct

---

7. "He later remembered that he was actually very attentive, cautious" (p. 63). Other examples: pp. 92, 270, 316, 422. For an excellent analysis of the narrator in *Crime and Punishment,*

voice. The narrative mode of this novel is uneven and takes different forms. Basically, we have a selectively omniscient narrator who follows action and dialogue rather as a careful director would follow the performance of his ensemble. But the narrator enters the text in other ways as well.

Occasionally, the narrator's observations stand apart from the drama; for example:

> There are some encounters, even with people entirely unknown to us, in whom we begin to take an interest at first sight, suddenly, without a word having been said. (P. 12)

The passage introducing Raskolnikov's first dream (pp. 45–46) provides another example:

> In a diseased condition, dreams are distinguished by an unusual plasticity, expressiveness, and extraordinary resemblance to reality. Sometimes a monstrous image develops, but the setting and the entire process of the representation are so plausible nevertheless, and have details so subtle, unexpected, yet artistically perfect, that no person awake, including the dreamer himself, even if he were an artist like Pushkin or Turgenev, could imagine them.

In a few instances the narrator makes his presence felt by referring to the text itself: "We shall omit the whole process by way of which he reached his final decision" (p. 59); or: "I shall not describe what took place at Pulkheria Aleksandrovna's that night" (p. 240). But these instances are hardly characteristic of the whole text.

Sometimes the narrator will let his own emotions come to the fore: "And this unfortunate Elizaveta was so simpleminded, downtrodden, and frightened that she did not even raise her hand to defend herself" (p. 65). Here, "unfortunate" belongs to the narrator, for the murderer cannot have had this reaction as he was striking her with his axe. (He may have said this later, when recalling the scene in a confession.)

When we read: "Sonia understood that this somber catechism had become his creed and his law" (p. 328), these are clearly the narrator's words, not Sonia's. Then there is this famous passage: "The candle was barely flickering in the crooked candlestick, dimly illuminating in this beggarly room the murderer and the harlot, who had so strangely come together reading

---

see Gary Rosenshield, *Crime and Punishment: The Techniques of the Omniscient Narrator* (Lisse: Peter de Ridder, 1978).

the eternal book" (pp. 251–52). Here "harlot" is *bludnitsa*, a biblical word not used in ordinary speech. The pathos is the narrator's. By the way, this solemn scene has a counterpoint. We learn, a page or so later, that the whole scene was witnessed by Svidrigailov, whose reaction was not at all like the narrator's.

Throughout the text, in narrative as well as dialogue, many comments that amount to inner hermeneutic or semiotic analysis occur with some regularity. Raskolnikov interprets his mother's letter (p. 35); Raskolnikov's analysis of a criminal's state of mind (pp. 58–59) fully applies to him, as he will soon learn; Zosimov's observations on mental disease describe Raskolnikov's condition (p. 174); Porfiry and Raskolnikov discuss interrogation techniques (pp. 256–62); Porfiry reviews Raskolnikov's article (pp. 345–46). Other examples are readily found.

The narrator sometimes assumes the role of a chorus responding to the hero's condition at that moment:

> If only he could have grasped all the difficulties of his situation, its whole desperation, its hideousness and absurdity, and understood how many obstacles and, perhaps, crimes he might have to overcome and commit in order to get out of there and get back home, it is quite possible that he would have left it all and turned himself in, and this not even out of fear for himself, but solely out of horror and revulsion for what he had done. (P. 65)

In fact, none of these thoughts occurred to Raskolnikov, for the drama has only just started. An important choral passage introduces the leitmotif[8] of the murderer's profound sense of alienation and isolation from the whole human race:

> A somber sense of excruciating, infinite isolation and alienation suddenly took hold of his soul. It was not the baseness of his heartfelt effusion before Il'ia Petrovich, not the baseness of the lieutenant's triumph over him that was suddenly turning his heart. Oh, what did he care about his own baseness, all those egos, lieutenants, German women, liens, offices, and so on and so forth? If he had been condemned to be burnt at the stake this very moment, he would not have made a move, in fact, he would hardly have listened to the verdict. (P. 82)

Obviously, Raskolnikov was not thinking of being burnt at the stake at this moment. So the image belongs to the narrator, as does the whole tirade, a

---

8.   Other instances in which this leitmotif appears: pp. 90, 150, 176, 201, 324. Another leitmotif involves the raising of Lazarus and the New Jerusalem, about which Porfiry asks Raskolnikov: see pp. 201, 250, 405, 422.

response to an as yet dim and indistinct feeling that is taking hold of Raskolnikov's soul. There is a similar passage in response to the experience that sends Sonia on her way to her part in the drama:

> She was awfully glad that she could finally leave. She walked along, hunched and hurried [. . .] to be at last alone and thus, walking along hurriedly and looking at no one, taking note of nothing, to think, to remember, to take in every word that had been said, every detail. Never, never had she experienced anything like this. A whole new world had entered her soul, dimly and unawares. (P. 187)

The narrator's comments differ in their mode and intensity, depending upon the character in question. When Luzhin first comes to Raskolnikov's room, his appearance and behavior are described in detail and commented upon (pp. 113–14). The narrator proceeds to follow this character's every move and explains his motives as if he were reading his mind. His dislike of Luzhin is obvious. On the other hand, the workings of Porfiry Petrovich's mind are never revealed, while his appearance and behavior are described in meticulous detail. Svidrigailov's treatment is somewhere in the middle between these: up to a point, he is viewed from the outside, though very carefully. But then we are allowed to follow his every thought and emotion, to a degree, we are never given access to the innermost recesses of his psyche. Glimpses of it are provided by Svidrigailov himself (the ghosts he sees and his vision of Hell as a place with spiders) and by a description of his last nightmare.

The narrator comments on the characters' language, behavior, mimicry and gestures, and, occasionally, their motives. For example, the narrator explains why Marmeladov would open his heart to a bunch of drunks in a lowly tavern:

> Obviously, Marmeladov had been known here for a long time. Also, his penchant for flowery language he had probably acquired as a result of a habit of engaging in bar-room conversations with assorted strangers. This habit turns into a need for some drunkards, particularly those who are dealt with sternly at home and hear frequent reproaches. This is why, in the company of other drunks, they try to obtain, after a fashion, some justification and if possible even some respect for themselves. (Pp. 13–14)

This remark also draws attention to a stylistic trait: the flowery language of Marmeladov's monologue. Observations on the style or tone of the *dramatis personae* occur throughout the text; for example: "When Andrei Semionovich concluded his prolix disquisition with such a logical conclusion [. . .]

Alas, he could not even express himself in decent Russian" (p. 307). Or this: "She was saying this as if she were reciting from memory" (p. 319). The characters of the novel occasionally engage in similar observations. Razumikhin and Raskolnikov discuss the style of Luzhin's letter (p. 180). Raskolnikov gives Razumikhin credit for a good synopsis of the scene at the police station (pp. 206–7). At one point Raskolnikov congratulates himself on having found the right word: "I became *angered* (this is a good word!)" (p. 320). The Russian text: *ozlilsia (eto slovo khoroshee!)*.

Sonia's inner life is hardly shown or her words and actions analyzed, while every movement of Raskolnikov's mind and soul is reported and commented upon in a sympathetic manner. Throughout the text, we find hundreds of passages such as the following:

> Let us note one particular trait regarding all these definitive decisions which he had made earlier in this matter. They had one strange quality: the more definitive they became, the more hideous, absurd, they also became immediately in his eyes. In spite of all the torturous inner struggle, he could never for a moment believe in a realization of his plans. (P. 57)

At times, the narrator will illustrate his description with a simile of his own: "It was as if he had gotten a strip of his clothes caught in the wheel of a machine, and it was beginning to pull him inside" (p. 58).

The whole murder scene is observed in minute detail by a narrator studiously producing specifics and avoiding commonplaces. Who would expect a narrator describing a murderer on his way to his victim's place to say: "Fortunately, everything went well at the gate," as Raskolnikov slips by unseen? And what narrator would have thought of a murderer being overcome by "a kind of absentmindedness, or a pensive mood, as it were"? Or this: when Raskolnikov finds a piece of red cloth in the victim's chest, looking for her money, he wipes his bloody hands, thinking, "It is red, and on red the blood will be less noticeable," then immediately: "My God, am I going out of my mind?" (p. 65)

After the murder, the narrator's observations deal mostly with Raskolnikov's enforced roleplaying and his growing sense of isolation. Mood swings from apathy to fierce determination are noted repeatedly:

> He stood there, as it were lost in thought, and a strange, suppressed, half-senseless smile was playing on his lips. He finally took his hat and quietly left the room. His thoughts were getting confused. (P. 208)

But also this, after the threat of a surprise witness has evaporated:

"Now we shall yet put up a fight," he said with an angry smirk, as he walked down the stairs. His anger was directed at himself. He remembered his "faint-heartedness" with contempt and shame. (P. 276)

The key scene of Raskolnikov's second meeting with Sonia begins with this introspective passage. As so often, Raskolnikov's feelings are polarized:

He stopped at her door with a strange question: "Must I tell her who killed Lizaveta?" It was a strange question because suddenly, at the same time, he felt that it was quite impossible not only not to tell her, but even to postpone it, even for a short time. He did not know as yet why this was impossible, he only *felt* it, and this excruciating awareness of his own powerlessness before the in-evitable almost crushed him. (P. 312)

It is almost a foregone conclusion that the passage that first introduces Raskolnikov's love for Sonia would start as it does: "And suddenly a strange, unexpected sensation of a burning hatred for Sonia passed through his mind" (p. 314).

The principle *les extrêmes se touchent* appears here in its crassest form.

The principal qualities of Dostoevsky's art in *Crime and Punishment* are a wealth of factual, psychological, and intellectual detail, an insistence on markedness in every aspect of the text, dialogue or narrative, at almost any cost, and an equally uncompromising ambiguity of every position taken.

Markedness is achieved in various ways. The most pervasive is the steady flow of concrete and meaningful facts, such as the "Zimmermann hat" on the second page of the novel (it will recur a few pages before the end), or this specific detail as we see the hero leave his room on page one: "as if he were trying to make up his mind" (*kak by v nereshimosti*). Such concreteness is often enhanced by presenting extreme facts and conditions. The novel starts with the words: "Early in July, on an extraordinarily hot day a young man was leaving his room"—not "on a warm summer day"! We are immedi-ately told that the young man is dressed in "rags" (*lokhmot'ia*), objectively an overstatement, for we will soon learn that he has not been *that* destitute very long.

The emotions that move the young man are also extreme: "A feeling of the deepest revulsion flashed momentarily in the fine features of the young man." (We already know that he is "remarkably handsome.")

The extremes in the text are often polarized, which marks them even more effectively. After we have heard that "the young man, who was deeply in debt to his landlady, was afraid to meet her," we are immediately told:

"Not that he was fearful and downtrodden, quite the contrary: but for some time now he was in an irritable and tense condition, resembling hypochondria." As early as page three, we find this example of psychological polarization:

> At the time he did not himself believe in his daydreams and merely titillated himself with their hideous but alluring audacity. But now, a month later, he was already beginning to take a different view and, in spite of all his mocking monologues about his own weakness and indecision, had willy-nilly gotten used to considering the "hideous" daydream an undertaking, though still not believing it himself. In fact, he was on his way to make a *test* of his undertaking, and his excitement was growing stronger and stronger with every step. (P. 7)

This example is also typical in that it presents, as it were, an inner dialogue after the fashion of a pendulum swinging wide to both sides — in this case, from disbelief in the possibility of a hideous idea awareness of its actual happening. Many such inner dialogues appear throughout the text. Some have been mentioned earlier. A similar polarization appears in other characters as well. One more example from the Marmeladov episode:

> But there was one very strange thing about him: in his gaze there was a glimmer of, as it were, yes, rapture — perhaps, there was sense and intelligence in it, too — but at the same time, also a flicker of madness. (P. 12)

Extremes and their polarization may assume the form of paradox, such as when Katerina Ivanovna is said to pull her husband's hair "from compassion" (*ot zhalosti serdtsa*); outright overstatement (when Raskolnikov's room is called a "closet," though a group of people meet there); or pathos and bathos (when the story of Dunia's proven innocence becomes the talk of the town).

Suspense, such as when we are not immediately told what Raskolnikov's "undertaking" (*delo, predpriiatie*) might be; surprise, such as when Svidrigailov keeps showing up unexpectedly or even without Raskolnikov and Sonia's being aware of his presence; and symbolic repetition of leitmotifs[9] or "situation rhyme," such as when Katerina Ivanovna's last words ("They have ridden the nag to her death") remind one of Raskolnikov's dream, are some other ways to achieve markedness.

A constant source of markedness is the Sophoclean irony that permeates almost the entire text. Time and again, we observe Raskolnikov listening to

9. See n. 8 above.

conversations about the murder he has committed. At times he almost gives himself away by appearing to know too much. The whole action that unrolls independently of Raskolnikov's crime is marked by its presence. Raskolnikov's strange behavior mystifies his mother and sister, who do not know what the reader knows. This irony becomes particularly cruel toward the end, when everybody except Raskolnikov's mother knows the truth.

Dostoevsky does not spurn any device to achieve markedness. Name symbolism,[10] catachresis,[11] and occasional literary allusions[12] are employed.

Like markedness, ambiguity, itself a form of markedness, assumes various forms. The theme of double-edged psychology extends far beyond its relevance to detection of the perpetrator of a crime. In Dostoevsky's world, any attempt at understanding human nature elicits a dialectic, rather than an unequivocal answer. The "real" motive of Raskolnikov's crime remains unresolved. There is overwhelming evidence that it was an intentional, deliberate "thought crime." In fact, we learn that he had paid little attention to "the material difficulties of the matter" (p. 89). But there is also ample evidence that the crime was committed under irresistible compulsion. Was the murderer in a condition to tell right from wrong? Yes, of course, for Raskolnikov has a conscience (he often blames himself for his base and cowardly behavior, has noble impulses); but, also, no: he considers his undertaking "no crime" (p. 59), suffers no pangs of conscience after the double murder, and says, "I only killed a louse," forgetting that he also killed Lizaveta.

Sonia, a saint, humbly calls herself "a great sinner." Paradoxically, Raskolnikov agrees, showing the gulf between their respective worldviews: to him she is a sinner because she thinks only of others, never of herself; to herself she is a sinner because she once, only once, thought of herself.

Katerina Ivanovna, certainly not blameless, feels she has nothing to con-

---

10.   Raskolnikov, Luzhin, Svidrigailov, Zametov, and Razumikhin have symbolic names: *raskol'nik*, "schismatic"; *luzha*, "puddle"; Svidrigailov has a foreign ring (a Lithuanian prince of that name figured in medieval Russian history); Razumikhin, *razum*, "(good) sense"; Zametov, *zametit'*, "to notice." Further observations may be readily added.

11.   For example, when Marmeladov relates that Lebeziatnikov beat up Katerina Ivanovna "with his very own hands" (*sobstvennoruchno izbil*), using a pompous literary word for a minor domestic squabble.

12.   It has been noted that Raskolnikov uses the very same examples as Hegel when he develops his theory of "extraordinary men" (Hegel's "world-historical personages, who trample on many an innocent flower"). But there are also minor details worth noticing. The State Councilor who refuses to pay Sonia for her sewing because the shirt collars were crooked, and stamps his feet at her, is called Klopstock—a German, of course, but also the namesake of a famous German poet with a ludicrous name derived from *kloppen*, "to give a beating," and *Stock*, "stick."

fess. Her husband, a serious sinner, is eager to confess. She does not want forgiveness; he hopes for it. The slimy Luzhin feels good about himself. The evil Svidrigailov seems secure in his amoral ways but is shown, after all, to have a "deep" conscience, which destroys him. The conclusion to be drawn from all this appears to be that guilt and innocence, and hence right and wrong, are existentially ambiguous.

A peculiar form of ambiguity is due to the presentation of themes and characters, particularly those that are central to the drama, in travesty. By "travesty" I mean an action, sentiment, or thought whose performance or expression falls drastically short of its intended or normal effect, or distorts it so badly that it is in danger of turning into its opposite. Marmeladov's travesty of Judgment Day on the first pages of the novel sets the tone for much of the rest of the text.

The whole story of the Marmeladov family is an exercise in travesty. Theirs is a marriage in travesty, for Katerina Ivanovna married a man twice her age only because she had "no place to go" with her three small children. The St. Petersburg of the slums, where they land, is a travesty of "that magnificent capital city, decorated by numerous monuments" (p. 16). Marmeladov's wake is an ill-conceived affair and ends in a scandal. Katerina Ivanovna's death in the streets of St. Petersburg is an ugly tragedy, a tragedy in travesty.

Raskolnikov's quest for the status of an extraordinary man (a Hegelian "world-historical personage"), who has the right to break the law and seize power, turns into a ludicrous travesty: a future Napoleon climbing under an old woman's bed to steal her few rubles. Worse yet: Raskolnikov is not even a passable common criminal. He must hear Razumikhin say: "He didn't even know how to rob, the only thing he knew how to do was kill! His first step, I'm telling you, his first step; he lost his nerve!" (p. 117). Later, in prison, Raskolnikov must hear from his fellow convicts that killing with an axe was none of his, a gentleman's, business. Only luck keeps him from being caught in the act. He has every chance to escape justice, but manages to compromise himself enough to attract suspicion. The travesty he makes of a clever criminal is compounded by the fact that he actually evokes Porfiry Petrovich's pity.

When Raskolnikov finally yields to Sonia's urging and stages a public confession, as she demands, even this act turns into a travesty. As he kneels down in the square and kisses the ground, he hears this:

> "Look at him, isn't he plastered!" And there was laughter. "He is headed for Jerusalem, my dear brothers, he's saying good-bye to his children, to his native

land, and bows down to the whole world, kisses the capital city of St. Petersburg and its ground," some drunken tradesman commented. (P. 405)

Many other instances of travesty are found throughout the text. Luzhin and Svidrigailov (and even Porfiry, after a fashion) are bridegrooms in travesty. Lebeziatnikov makes a travesty of a socialist believer. Svidrigailov joins the long line of Byronic characters in travesty who have populated Russian literature since *Eugene Onegin.* In fact, Svidrigailov's hell is a travesty.

Even Sonia is, after all, a saint in travesty. She is a "rather pretty blonde" when first presented in her streetwalker's finery at her father's deathbed, but we later learn that she has a "pale, thin face, with irregular and angular features" (p. 248), hardly the image of a traditional Mary Magdalene. She is a very ordinary, very cheap streetwalker, decidedly unglamorous. The Slavonic *bludnitsa,* applied to her in the scene described above, rings false. The point is that she is saintly and firm in her faith even while she walks the streets. In fact, Raskolnikov asks her if she had gone to work the night of the reading of the Gospel, and her answer is yes.

Where, then, is the art of *Crime and Punishment?* First of all, it rises from the vigor of Dostoevsky's imagination, which produces an abundance of wonderfully alive scenes, images, characters, and ideas. Second, it comes from the extraordinary power of his language, activated by a great variety of devices. Among these, the most important are a dramatic technique of scenic presentation, the presence of dialogic form even in narrative passages, the use of polarized extremes in every aspect of the text, and a playing down of the melodramatic effects of the action by travesty. The result is a virtual (or "poetic") reality that makes all but the most critical readers disregard the conventional literary quality of some of the characters and the rather makeshift plot. In *Crime and Punishment* Dostoevsky has not quite reached the consummate dramatic structure of *The Possessed,* nor the superb dialectic skill of *The Brothers Karamazov.* The devil's case is not presented nearly as well, but it is to Dostoevsky's credit that he lets his hero hold out, bloodied but unbowed, almost to the end, and that Sonia is, amazingly enough, almost a credible character.

5

The Hierarchy of Meanings in
The Idiot

T H E nineteenth-century novel is a form of verbal art characterized by inherent contradictions. Its dependence on plot and storyline is in conflict with its purported realism. "Poetic truth" may clash with empirical truth. The nineteenth-century novel tends to advance an ideological, moral, or religious thesis, allegedly of general validity, yet it finds expression in terms of specific individualized characters and particular events. The real thus may clash with the ideal, the universal with the particular. The nineteenth-century novel pretends to the status of a work of art, yet it almost always pursues certain utilitarian ends, such as advocating a political program or catering to the ephemeral tastes of a fickle reading public. The concerns of real life thus make frequent intrusions into a world created by the imagination.

We know that the public, as well as most critics, tended to judge Dostoevsky's novels on their topical and ideological content, paying scant attention to their artistic merit. Yet we also know that Dostoevsky was a highly conscious artist who was much concerned with giving his ideas the proper artistic expression. We know that Dostoevsky believed in certain religious and moral truths, and that he held to fairly narrow political opinions, but also that he was greatly concerned with getting his facts straight.

Dostoevsky's novels are "ideological" in that their author felt that he was fulfilling a Christian and a national commission. He was also a realist who honestly tried to present the facts of life, and Russian life in particular, as he saw them, and even as they were perceived by his ideological opponents. He was inclined to give his opponents a voice in the concert of his polyphonic compositions. Readers have often chosen to embrace a voice or a viewpoint as the message of a Dostoevskian novel, when extrinsic evidence suggests that Dostoevsky had something different in mind, but was playing devil's advocate exceedingly well.

Some readers have interpreted *The Brothers Karamazov,* and "The Grand Inquisitor" chapter in particular, as bearing an anti-Christian, or at least a heretical, message, although we know that Dostoevsky wanted the message to be in full accord with Russian Orthodox doctrine. Other readers have seen an irresoluble conflict between Dostoevsky's psychological realism and his religious message, finding, for instance, the Epilogue of *Crime and Punishment* false and out of character.

The way to account for some of these difficulties is to distinguish, throughout Dostoevsky's novels, a hierarchy of epistemologically distinct meanings: empirical, moral, allegorical, and anagogic.[1]

There is, to begin with, a realistic narrative that develops a plot after the common fashion of a nineteenth-century novel. On this level we also meet digressions of an essayistic nature, as well as various subtexts: journalistic, in the form of allusions to topical events; literary, in the form of allusions or polemical responses to readily identified works of Russian or foreign literature; and personal, in the form of references to Dostoevsky's personal life or an earlier work of his own.

Then there is the moral level. Throughout Dostoevsky's oeuvre, many structured arguments regarding various moral topics are unfolded. Such is, for example, the argument about "ordinary" and "extraordinary" people, conducted in *Crime and Punishment* and in "The Grand Inquisitor" chapter of *The Brothers Karamazov.* Such are also the question regarding the relation between faith and miracle in *The Brothers Karamazov,* and the question of the relative value of good deeds versus emotional attitude, as developed explicitly in *The Idiot* and implicitly in the story of the Marmeladov family in *Crime and Punishment.*

Furthermore, there is an allegorical level. *Crime and Punishment* may be, *The Possessed* must be, read as an allegory of the Russian revolution. *The Brothers Karamazov* is an allegory of fatherhood and sonhood, and of sensual, intellectual, and spiritual man — among other things.

---

1.   Konstantin Mochulsky distinguishes only two levels, the empirical and the metaphysical. See his *Dostoevsky: His Life and Works,* trans. Michael A. Minihan (Princeton: Princeton University Press, 1967), pp. 376–77.

In all of Dostoevsky's novels we observe intrusions of the mystical. While the plot unfolds in a world of ordinary affairs and characters, diabolical and heavenly elements appear from time to time. I am thinking of the massive Christian symbolism introduced in connection with Sonia Marmeladov, or of the various shapes in which the diabolical appears throughout *The Brothers Karamazov*. While the moral and allegorical level are structured and may be "closed" or "open" much as the plot is, the mystical element seems unstructured: we have, as it were, intrusions from other worlds, whose entirety remains unknown and whose logic escapes us. But Dostoevsky's characters are gifted with an intuitive sense that allows them to recognize these intrusions. Of course, much of what may be said to belong to the mystical level may be subjected to a psychoanalytical interpretation — that is, seen as a projection of neuroses peculiar either to Dostoevsky's characters or to Dostoevsky himself. Dostoevsky certainly leaves the door open to such reading.

It is the task of the novelist to harmonize these different levels of meaning. Some critics — Nabokov, for example — have said that Dostoevsky has failed in this task. Not only Soviet critics have found the Christian message, moral as well as mystical, merely a tedious nuisance. I believe that such a view has the corollary that Dostoevsky was not a very good novelist. Nabokov is therefore right — on his terms. I shall not try to show that Dostoevsky is a great novelist in spite of these objections. But I shall try to show that the different levels of meaning are all strong and important, so that to ignore one or more of them is tantamount to misreading and misinterpreting the work in question.

Each of these four levels of meaning is associated with certain featured themes, though some themes and motifs may appear in different versions on different levels of meaning. For example, in *The Idiot* the theme of a condemned man — that is, a man who knows that he will die within a very brief span of time — appears on all four levels of meaning. Several executions are described or mentioned, and one of the main characters, Ippolit Terent'ev, suffers from what was then called "galloping consumption," and dies as expected. His condition has intriguing moral implications. Ippolit points out that he could very well commit a heinous crime with total impunity, since his case would never come to trial, even if the law actually tried to prolong his life.

The whole text of the novel makes it clear that the theme of a condemned man is also presented as an allegory of the human condition. Finally, the same theme stands in the very center of the metaphysical dilemma developed on the anagogic level of meaning. The realization that Christ Himself was a condemned man who was executed and died is introduced with great poignancy.

I shall now try to present some other themes as I introduce the four levels of meaning that I believe I discern in *The Idiot*. In the process, I hope to demonstrate that a satisfactory interpretation of this novel as a *successful* Christian novel is possible and that there is no contradiction between Dostoevsky's Christian faith and his vision of the world as presented here.

The empirical level of *The Idiot* is realized in terms of nineteenth-century novelistic technique. The novel has an intricate and suspenseful plot, a large number of characters, some truly dramatic scenes, and a great deal of social and psychological commentary, some of it quite digressive (for example, the discussion, à propos Gania Ivolgin, of the psychology of an ordinary person who refuses to admit that he is an ordinary person). Topical and polemical detail is abundant. In the Burdovsky episode, for example, Dostoevsky settles scores with the Petersburg scandal sheets and with M. E. Saltykov-Shchedrin, and Myshkin's anti-Catholic harangue at the Epanchins' party certainly reflected Dostoevsky's own views. On this, the simple empirical level, we have a psychologically motivated account of the passions and intrigues surrounding a beautiful woman desired by many men. Her own irrational and self-destructive reactions are made psychologically plausible. Prince Myshkin is, on this plane, a very unusual type, but Dostoevsky has made every effort to make his presentation of a "Christ figure" conform with the standards of a realist novel. *The Idiot* may be read entirely as a socio-psychological study of emergent urban capitalist society in Russia. Many characters and developments in *The Idiot* belong exclusively to that sphere. The Kellers, Ptitsyns, and Doktorenkos are irrelevant to the other levels of the novel's meaning. They may divert the reader's attention from the allegorical or metaphysical meaning of the novel.

Let us proceed to the moral level. A great deal may be found here even without any Christian doctrine. At her nameday party, Nastas'ia Filippovna organizes a game in which each participant must relate the basest action of his life. Her lover, the *bon vivant* Totsky, tells a charmingly innocuous little story that makes him look quite good — not the story of how he used a fifteen-year-old girl's defenselessness and innocence to make her his mistress (that girl was Nastas'ia Filippovna, who was, moreover, Totsky's ward at the time). General Epanchin tells another little story, which also makes him appear as quite a gentleman, but not the story of how he arranged for his secretary and protégé, Gania Ivolgin, to marry Totsky's mistress, in the hope that Gania would return the favor and let the General have an affair with his wife. The theme of love as a commodity, to be bought at a price that depends on the subject's appearance (Nastas'ia Filippovna is a rare beauty), develops into one of the leitmotifs of the novel. Clearly, this theme is quite independent of Dostoevsky's Christian message.

Other moral themes are relevant to it. Marie, the Swiss peasant girl in the story Myshkin tells the Epanchin women, is introduced to contrast with Nastas'ia Filippovna: the humble penitent who suffers society's cruel injustice without complaint, contrasted with the proud woman who lashes out at the men who have wronged her. This contrast may be seen as a simple lesson in Christian morality. Altogether, moral themes permeate the novel. The theme of justice, human and divine, appears in many variations. In this respect *The Idiot* really deals with a world quite similar to that of the almost contemporaneous *Anna Karenina*.

An allegorical meaning suggests itself in *The Idiot* rather naturally, though not as directly as in *The Possessed*. The plot of *The Idiot* may well be perceived as allegory of heavenly love and earthly passion vying for the soul of Beauty. This tragic plot is embedded in a much broader and more complex novelistic plot. From a viewpoint of high tragedy, the novelist's mundane digressions and psychologizing appear banal, as Julius Meier-Graefe observed as early as 1926.[2] In an allegorical reading Nastas'ia Filippovna is the central character, Prince Myshkin a Dionysian figure, and Rogozhin an earthborn Titan who lusts for the heavenly beauty of a goddess.[3]

Another allegorical reading suggests itself more directly. Prince Myshkin is a "Christ figure." As Dostoevsky said so eloquently in a notebook passage ("Masha is laid out"),[4] there is a gulf between the ideal of Christ and human nature. It is this gulf that provides the conflict in *The Idiot*. Like his *Doppelgänger* Don Quixote, Prince Myshkin enters a prosaic world of ordinary people with selfish concerns and worldly passions, the world of a nineteenth-century novel. It would be a perversion of Dostoevsky's thought to consider Prince Myshkin a Christ figure in any supernatural sense. We know from notebook entries that Dostoevsky saw nothing supernatural in the process by which a human being "becomes (a) Christ," a process of self-perfection whose goal is an attitude of total forgiveness, compassion, love, and shared responsibility for all of God's creatures. Prince Myshkin is singularly gifted in this respect. He has a talent for saintliness. The allegory

2. Julius Meier-Graefe, *Dostojewski der Dichter* (Berlin: Rowohlt, 1926), p. 265.

3. See Roger B. Anderson, "*The Idiot,* Duality, Paradox, and Dionysus," in *Dostoevsky: Myths of Duality* (Gainesville: University of Florida Press, 1986), pp. 66–94.

4. See n. 24 to Chapter 1.

of a "Christ figure" cannot possibly end in worldly success (hence Murray Krieger's "curse of saintliness").[5] The Swiss theologian Walter Nigg has said most aptly: "Der Christ muss scheitern."[6] If Dostoevsky had let Prince Myshkin succeed, he would have created a saint's vita, not a novel, much less a tragic allegory. When Dostoevsky took up the idea of a saintly person in the modern world in *The Brothers Karamazov*, he kept the *Vita* of Father Zosima separate from the text of the novel. Father Zosima is a saint. Prince Myshkin is no saint. His tragic flaw is that of acedia, the despair of those who have lost the strength to face this world. Acedia is one of the seven mortal sins. But we are sure that Prince Myshkin will be forgiven. We leave the tragedy in the hope that the Prince has planted the seeds of spiritual resurrection in Rogozhin's soul and left a mark in the souls of others who crossed his path.

Nastas'ia Filippovna is another singularly gifted human being. Her gift is that of great, unforgettable, and irresistible beauty. On a mundane level, Nastas'ia Filippovna is a woman who, having been wronged by a man who has deprived her of the normal life for a woman of her standing, seeks to find an identity with which she can live, but fails. On the allegorical—and metaphysical—level, she is the Beauty of the Eternal Feminine, complementary to the Goodness of Prince Myshkin. Nastas'ia Filippovna's beauty meets the same fate as Prince Myshkin's goodness. It is misunderstood and abused by men who will possess rather than love her beauty. In Rogozhin, the desire to possess this beauty reaches an intensity of passion that carries passion into the regions of the metaphysical.

Nastas'ia Filippovna and Rogozhin face their tragic trials without God, a fact that is brought into focus by the introduction of the negative mirror image of Marie, for Nastas'ia Filippovna, and for Rogozhin by a similar contrast with Prince Myshkin, his chosen brother. But Nastas'ia Filippovna has atoned for her willfulness by her sacrificial death, foreshadowed by her symbolic surname (Barashkova, from *barashek*, "lamb"), and will be resurrected, as intimated by her Christian name, Anastasia (from *anastasis*, "resurrection"). As for Rogozhin, his experience during the vigil over Nastas'ia Filippovna's body must belong to those regions of human feeling which

5.   Murray Krieger, "Dostoevsky's *Idiot:* The Curse of Saintliness," in *The Tragic Vision: The Confrontation of Extremity* (Baltimore: Johns Hopkins University Press, 1960), pp. 209–27.

6.   Walter Nigg, *Der christliche Narr* (Stuttgart and Zurich: Artemis, 1956), pp. 394–95. Translation: "A Christian must fail."

are the desert beyond which revelation and regeneration shine. There is no word for what Rogozhin must have felt.

Prince Myshkin has returned to the darkness from which he had been awakened by the braying of an ass in the market square of Basel — to be awakened again to another, better life. So much for the allegorical meaning.

The anagogic meaning, as always in Dostoevsky, emerges in concrete episodes of spiritual epiphany, in passages in which a human consciousness breaks through the darkness into light:

> "I remember I was insufferably sad; I wanted to cry. I was all the while lost in wonder and uneasiness. What affected me most was that everything was *strange;* I realized that. I was crushed by the strangeness of it. I was finally roused from this gloomy state, I remember, one evening on reaching Switzerland at Basel, and I was roused by the bray of an ass in the marketplace. I was immediately struck with the ass, and for some reason extraordinarily pleased with it, and suddenly everything seemed to clear up in my head." (*PSS* 8: 48)

Nigg comments:

> The braying of an ass in the market place in Basel could become such an important event in his life precisely because he was himself just such a tormented creature, almost a mute creature of God. The suffering of an animal in some mysterious fashion elicited a response in his suffering soul.[7]

The illumination that suffuses an epileptic's soul at the moment when his fit starts almost coincides with a horrible animal shriek that erupts from his chest. Lev Shestov has this to say:

> Now in Russia, the people venerate and even love (one does not know why) their mental cripples. One might say that they somehow feel that the howlings of the possessed are not completely devoid of meaning and that the miserable existence of the simpletons also is not as absurd and repugnant as appears at first sight. And indeed, an hour will come when each of us will cry, as did the most perfect of men: "My God, my God, why hast Thou forsaken me?" And then we shall leave the riches we have accumulated and set out on the road like miserable vagabonds, or like Abraham, who, according to the word of the Apostle, departed without knowing where he was going.[8]

7.   Ibid.
8.   Lev Shestov, *Afiny i Ierusalim* (Paris: YMCA, 1951), p. 254.

A basic theme of *The Idiot* is precisely the one that is expressed in Fiodor Tiutchev's lines:

> Whence, how, did this dissonance arise,
> And why is it that in the common chorus
> The soul sings not what the sea does
> And the thinking reed murmurs![9]

The Idiot deals with man's failure to be in step with the rhythms of Nature, with man's perception of Nature's time, *chronos,* as an enemy, yet also with man's striving to find *kairos,* the right time, a good and auspicious time for his enterprises. The way to a condition that finds man once more in accord with Nature is difficult and must be charted by intuition. There is no return to the unconscious harmony of Nature for human reason. Ippolit's revolt in *The Idiot,* much like Kirillov's in *The Possessed,* seeks to attain this breakthrough in rational terms. This is the wrong way.

The right way is shown by Prince Myshkin, but by some other characters also, men and women who live a "living life" (*zhivaia zhizn'*), which is always an *imitatio Christi.* Myshkin tells Rogozhin about a young mother who crossed herself when her baby smiled for the first time.[10] When he asked her why, she answered: "God has just such gladness every time He sees from heaven that a sinner is praying to Him with all his heart as a mother has when she sees the first smile on her baby's face." Myshkin observes that "the whole essence of Christianity finds expression in this thought." He goes on to say that "the essence of religious feeling does not fall under any sort of reasoning or atheism, and has nothing to do with crimes or misdemeanors." The point is that at the moment the young mother crosses herself, she has no doubt as to life's meaning, has no doubt about the existence of God, and is living life to the fullest. She has made that decisive breakthrough into the light of God's truth.

Of all the characters in the novel, Myshkin has incomparably the largest number of these moments. When he says to Gania, "Oh, how ashamed you will be of what you have just done!" after Gania slapped his face, when he exchanges crosses with Rogozhin, when he offers his friendship to young Burdovsky, and on many other occasions, Myshkin acts as a Christian —

---

9.   The poem is "There's Melody in the Waves of the Sea" (1865). "The thinking reed" is Blaise Pascal's *roseau pensant* — that is, man.

10.   This episode (p. 184) produces several examples to the effect that God is a living presence, often descending on man unexpectedly.

and implicitly believes in God, knows the meaning of life, and lives life to the fullest. In these moments he is perfectly free, and Nature is not the cruel monster of Ippolit's dream, nor an inexorable mathematical formula, but a living harmony of which one is a part. What is the secret of this blessed state? Myshkin defines it *per negationem* as he pictures a man without God:

> "Every blade of grass grows and is happy! Everything has its path, and every-thing knows its path, and goes forth with a song, and returns with a song. Only he knows nothing, neither men nor sounds: he is outside of it all, an outcast."
> (P. 352)

The secret lies in overcoming isolation and alienation. Myshkin, once he has recovered from his illness, gives everybody object lessons in communion. The simple secret of his apparent clairvoyance is that he takes a genuine and personal interest in people. He is free because he is utterly selfless. He loves God because he loves life. He is Christlike also in the negative sense: he can be despondent, and he knows despair. The secret of Dostoevsky's way of introducing the mystical level of his thought is very simple as well: it amounts to presenting it in concrete terms by creating a credible human character who is extraordinary enough to live the mystical life of an *imitatio Christi.*

The Idiot is not a *roman à thèse.* There is no structured metaphysical argu-ment to prove the Gospel of Christ right. The novel presents Dostoevsky's understanding of life, not a structured philosophy. It shows that the road to God, to faith, and to freedom is very difficult, strewn with failures. But Christ has shown the way (obviously, the figure of Christ must be perceived in the subtext of *The Idiot*), and Prince Myshkin has been a good disciple. The world at large is not any better for it, but neither was it after Christ Himself walked the earth.

A quotation from Alexander Solzhenitsyn may explain what Dostoevsky was trying to do in *The Idiot:* "We all lived beside her, and never understood that she was that righteous one without whom, according to the proverb, no village can stand. Nor any city. Nor our whole land" ("Matrionin Dvor," 1963). Solzhenitsyn's Matriona is a fictional character, like Prince Myshkin. His message must therefore be modified to say: "Or so long as a writer or poet can create such a character."

Such, then, is the Christian—or anagogic—meaning of *The Idiot.* Dosto-evsky created a saintly, Christlike character who moves, excites, fascinates, and exasperates the reader. Some readers will embrace him; others will re-ject him or try to give him a Freudian or Lacanian psychoanalytic interpretation.[11] By placing this Christlike character in a thoroughly modern, secular, and urban world, Dostoevsky challenged his reader to decide whether the Gospel of Christ was alive. If meeting Prince Myshkin caused the reader to experience an ever so slight "contact with other worlds," Dostoevsky succeeded in fusing the ideal with the real.

11.   See, for example, Elizabeth Dalton, *Unconscious Structure in* The Idiot: *A Study in Literature and Psychoanalysis* (Princeton: Princeton University Press, 1978).

6

Dostoevsky and the Drama
The Possessed

D OSTOEVSKY'S novels have often been converted into stage or screen versions. This is not in itself proof of their affinity to tragic drama, but the dramatic quality of Dostoevsky's novels was observed even by his contemporaries. Curiously, the first to see a connection between Dostoevsky and Greek drama was Ivan Turgenev, who observed that he had been "made fun of in the manner of Aristophanes" in *The Possessed*. It was Viacheslav Ivanov who forcefully advanced the thesis that Dostoevsky's art was akin to Greek tragedy in spirit as well as in structure.[1] It was also Ivanov who first called Dostoevsky "the Russian Shakespeare."[2]

Ivanov believed that Dostoevsky, guided by a tragic view of life, expressed certain tragic antinomies in antinomic action.[3] A tragic view of life is Dionysian, embracing passion, exaltation, violence, suffering, and death. Dostoevsky's novels present man as self-willed and free to make a choice between life in a godless world with no absolutes or a world of good and evil ruled by God's law. This is analogous to the worldview of the Greeks, as expressed most poignantly in Aeschylus' *Prometheus*.

Much like Greek drama, Dostoevsky's novels focus on the centrifugal

6

1. I am referring to Vyacheslav Ivanov, *Freedom and the Tragic Life: A Study in Dostoevsky,* trans. Norman Cameron (New York: Noonday, 1952), and its Russian version, *Dostoevskii i roman-tragediia,* in vol. 4 of Ivanov's *Collected Works* (Brussels: Foyer Chrétien, 1987), pp. 399–444.
2. *Dostoevskii i roman-tragediia,* p. 415. All translations are my own.
3. Ibid., pp. 412–13.

6

workings of the individual soul as it meets the world. Hence, the inherently dialogic nature of Dostoevsky's world: "Thou art — this means not merely 'thou art perceived by me as existing,' but 'thine existence is experienced by me as my own,' or 'through thine existence I know that I am.' *Es ergo sum.*"[4]

The "limiting situations" (*Grenzsituationen*) of utter despair, desolation, and guilt, but also fateful passion, lofty hubris, and noble self-sacrifice, in which the heroes and heroines of Greek drama appear are also found in Dostoevsky's novels and, like their Greek counterparts, may be reduced to *Urmythen*.[5] The action of a Dostoevskian novel, like that of Greek tragedy, proceeds on three levels: external action, its complex and often ambiguous psychological motivation, and the symbolism of the metaphysical antinomy that is its mover.

As to structure, Ivanov observes the musical ("symphonic") quality of Dostoevsky's composition, its contrapuntal thematic development, which also aligns it with tragedy. He also stresses the "liberating energy" of Dostoevsky's language, which transcends the conventions of the realist novel. Hence he labels Dostoevsky's style "mystical realism."[6] Ivanov also notes the direct application of stage technique in Dostoevsky's novels, such as "dialogues that might be impressive behind the footlights, but are not true to life."[7] He does not go into details, or give examples, but clearly perceives this trait as an artistic flaw.

Ivanov's views need to be confronted with Mikhail Bakhtin's assertion that Dostoevsky is no more and no less than the quintessential novelist. His style incorporates a variety of novelistic styles, from the classical adventure novel to the romantic novel, the Gothic novel, and the *roman-feuilleton.* Bakhtin also emphasizes the dialogic quality of the Dostoevskian novel, seeing it not as a device, but as an end in itself.[8] It must be stressed that Bakhtin sees no connection between the drama as a genre and dialogic composition — even in Shakespeare.

Bakhtin defines the novel as "an artistically organized social medley of speech [*raznorechie*] — at times a medley of languages [*raznoiazychie*] — and an individual discord of voices [*raznogolositsa*]."[9] He concedes that an author will try to organize the various discordant voices into a symphony,

---

4. Ibid., p. 419.
5. Ibid., p. 518.
6. Ibid., p. 514.
7. *Freedom and the Tragic Life*, p. 14.
8. M. M. Bakhtin, *Problemy poetiki Dostoevskogo* (Moscow: Sovetskii pisatel', 1963), p. 339.
9. Ibid., p. 71.

creating from these his personal style. Bakhtin stresses the social diversity of voices in a novel and suggests that a novelistic character is inherently an "ideologue," and his words "ideologuemes" (*idiologemy*). In his ground-breaking study of 1929, Bakhtin called Dostoevsky's novels "polyphonic," in that they present a concert of many voices, one of which is that of the narrator. Eventually he got around to admitting that such polyphony is, at least to some extent, present in many novels by other authors as well, that polyphony is in fact characteristic of the modern novel in general.

It is obvious that the modern novel both continues the epic tradition and departs from it in some ways. It tends to have a subjective personal narrator, who may be a participant in the action. It may have lyrical interludes. It may usurp aspects of the drama. It may also incorporate a variety of sub-genres, such as the Platonic dialogue, the biography, the essay, and satire. In short, it is an open form, ready to respond to social and literary stimuli.

In examining the novel's relationship to other forms of verbal art, it may be useful to recognize some elementary characteristics of lyrical, epic, and dramatic imagination. The lyric genre is associated with the first person, demanding the listener's merging with the poet's consciousness, which is facilitated by the many iconic traits of lyric poetry. The epic is associated with the third person, since it is told by an anonymous narrator who is not himself involved in the action. Drama is dialogic in more ways than one. Its *personae* address not only other *personae*, but also an audience — and themselves, in monologues and asides.

An epic relates to the past, a lyric poem to the present, while drama combines past and present, working forward to the future. A lyric poem may be perceived as a single utterance. An epic is a series of coordinate clauses; a drama, a maze of subordinate clauses: "if," "because," "in spite of" dominate.

The drama's action is finite and goal-directed, while the epic is potentially endless, its structure open: there may always be a "Twenty Years Later." The drama tends to be focused on a central theme, like *Dike* (Justice) in Aeschylus' *Oresteia*. An epic is less focused and may develop several themes. The presence of a *telos* in the drama causes foreshadowing of the eventual catastrophe, a common trait in Greek drama.

The scenic quality of drama may not be a decisive distinction, since an epic may also be broken down into diverse scenes. Yet the tendency is against it. Plato's Socrates, in the *Lesser Hippias,* points out the inconsistencies in the character of Achilles, depending on what scene he appears in, while his opponent believes he sees a single, consistent character. Most readers of the *Iliad* will agree with Hippias, however.

The more intensely dialogic nature of drama causes sharper individualization and a more intensely marked quality of speech and circumstantial detail. Dramatic characters are subject to Sophoclean irony and tend to become involved in inner contradictions and multiple motivation. Does Clytemnestra plan the murder of Agamemnon merely to avenge the death of her daughter, as she says, or does she resent his paramours, the last of whom, Cassandra, he brazenly commits to her care? And hasn't she also taken a lover in his absence? Besides, Agamemnon, while a mighty warrior, is a man of limited mind and spirit, unworthy of the high-minded Clytemnestra.

A dramatic character's speech tends to have a subtext, psychological, ethical, or metaphysical. Note, for instance, the undercurrent of resentment in Hephaestos' words as he forges the chains that bind Prometheus to the rock in the Caucasus, with *Cratos* (Brute Force) supervising the procedure. In *Choephoroe*, l. 243, the chorus asserts that there are only three powers: *Cratos, Dike,* and Zeus, the most potent of the three, creating a subtext that asks whether Zeus is with *Dike* or with *Cratos*.

The dramatic chorus introduces what may be in fact the key element of dramatic art: it comments on the action, takes sides, and judges the characters. It represents the moral, political, and ethical aspect of drama. When the chorus is abandoned, it functions are taken over by the *dramatis personae*. In a dramatic novel, the narrator, usually an interested or partial observer or even a participant, assumes the role of the chorus.

The scenic quality of dramatic composition fosters improvisation in the form of casual digressions from the main line of action, such as inserted aphorisms, words of wit and wisdom, puns, and other word play. A good deal of this is to be found in Greek tragedy, starting with Aeschylus. Like a personalized narrator in a novel, the chorus will dispense aphorisms of worldly wisdom and experience not necessarily relevant to the plot, as when the chorus of *Agamemnon* comments on the infirmities of old age.

The ritual origins of Greek drama are still apparent in Aeschylus. The religious essence of the emergence of a new *Dike* is made quite explicit in the *Oresteia*. The language of Aeschylus is accordingly exalted, even extravagant. In Sophocles, a descent from the mythically heroic to the nobly human takes place. In Euripides, there is a further descent to the merely human. Aristophanes' parody of Aeschylus and Euripides in *The Frogs* shows that the audience was well aware of this development. Aristophanes has Euripides charge Aeschylus with using a pompous, ornate style: "When you talk, you give us [blocks] the size of Lycabettus and Parnassus. Is this the proper way to teach one how to speak in human fashion?" (*Frogs*, ll. 1055–56).

Euripides, in turn, is charged with having debased the noble and sublime tragedy of Aeschylus by introducing into the mythic world of Homer various trivial details of everyday life, such as "Achilles threw a two and a four at dice" (l. 1400), alluding to a scene in Euripides' *Telephus,* where the Achaeans are shown playing at dice. Aristophanes' comedies persistently make fun of *Telephus* for having the hero, a king, appear on stage in a beggar's rags. Aristophanes also chides Euripides for what he sees as his moral relativism and sophistry, as opposed to the heroic worldview of Aeschylus. When Euripides bitterly complains about the shameful injustice of being left behind in Hades in spite of Dionysus' initial promise to return him to life, the answer is a quotation from Euripides' *Aeolus,* where the crime in question is incest: "Shameful is what so appears to those who see it." And, besides, quoting another drama by Euripides: "Who knows, perhaps life is really death"—so what's the difference?

Clearly, one may see in Euripides' drama a "novelization" of tragedy: a descent to the mundane concerns of the audience, from myth to "real life," and from religion to psychology.

In Shakespeare's tragedies, further steps in this direction are taken, while some dramatic traits are intensified. The heroes are less heroic; their characters are more complex and more contradictory. There are more characters, and the action is more involved. Some lowly personages are introduced, causing comedy and satire to enter tragedy. While the action is set in a—more or less—contemporary and realistically seen world, a great deal of license is taken to arrange for the extravagant *peripeteiai* of the plot. A great deal of graphic violence is presented on stage. Digressions from the main plot at times obscure the *telos* of the play.

The mythical hypostases of human passions that we find in Greek drama are now replaced by complex and contradictory individuals. The moral message is not always clear. Villains, like Edmund in *King Lear,* are apt to fascinate the audience more than the righteous.

But the characters are still extraordinary, larger than life, whether good or evil. Their language is highly marked, and marked in a great variety of ways, including iconic effects and lyric interludes. Scenic effects are pursued more strongly than in Greek drama. The action is broken down into many more scenes. Vastly more detail is aimed at immediate scenic effect.

Tolstoi's essay "On Shakespeare and the Drama" will provide us with a vehicle to organize our comparison of Dostoevsky's novels with the drama, and with Shakespeare's plays in particular. Tolstoi challenges Shakespeare on three issues: the language is "unnatural," that is, exaggeratedly marked; the characters are not credible, unless one assumes they are mad, like Lear; the plots are absurd, arranged to produce immediate scenic effects. Tolstoi's challenge is based on two heterogeneous considerations: his own mimetic aesthetic, in whose terms the characters, plot, and language of Shakespeare are "unnatural," and his idea that a work of art ought to be properly structured: it ought to have a beginning, a middle, and an end, and it ought to have a definite meaning, and hence a recognizable *telos*.

To Tolstoi's charges, there are answers. A Shakespearean drama is a poetic text, subject to a different contract with the audience than a realist novel, while the characters are extreme versions of real people, men and women driven to extreme actions by fate or strong passions. The plot enjoys the privileges of dramatic license, and, besides, the audience is so fascinated by the action that it hardly notices the absurdities of chance coincidences, compression of time and space, and *deus ex machina* that occur in the drama.

We shall now take a look at Dostoevsky's novel *The Possessed* and try to determine to what extent Tolstoi's critique of Shakespeare applies to Dostoevsky. At the same time, we shall measure Dostoevsky's novel in terms of Greek tragedy.

A point Tolstoi chose to overlook is that the drama was from its very beginnings a part of literature at large. Aeschylus said that his works were only crumbs from the table of Homer. Allusions to one myth or another are common in the dialogue of Greek drama, such as when Clytemnestra likens her husband to the three-headed monster Geryon, who had to be killed three times (she has at least twice previously received news of Agamemnon's death). In Shakespeare, whose plays are derived from literary or historical sources no less than the Greeks', literary quotations and allusions appear quite routinely. Vergil and Ovid appear in *Hamlet,* for example, and a Greek Hecate shows up in *Macbeth.*

Dostoevsky's novels are exceptionally rich in literary connections, so much so that some of them were in fact conceived in antiphon to a particular work of literature, as *Poor Folk* responds to Gogol's *The Overcoat. The Possessed* has ample literary connections. It features a reckoning with Dostoevsky's one-time friend and now enemy Ivan Turgenev, who appears as Karmazinov, "a great writer." Several of his works are presented in travesty, and his liberal westernizing is branded as a betrayal of Russia. Several other characters have more or less recognizable literary prototypes. The Bible, Shakespeare, Goethe, and a host of Russian writers (Pushkin, of course, but also N. G. Chernyshevsky's *What Is To Be Done?*) are introduced, and various literary questions are brought up. There is a great deal of direct reference to literary life, in the 1850s as well as in the 1870s.

Furthermore, Dostoevsky clearly is pursuing effects that are extrinsic to purely artistic or objectively mimetic ends throughout the text. The caricature of Turgenev, a masterpiece of satirical invective and parody, also delivers a political message equivalent to Aristophanes' lampooning of Euripides and Socrates. The novel as a whole was perceived by contemporaries as a political pamphlet, which is how it was initially conceived by Dostoevsky. Analogous concerns are by no means alien to Greek drama. Aeschylus' *Oresteia* was aimed at asserting the authority of the institutions of the Athenian state and glorifying Athens' patroness, Pallas Athene. Similarly, bows in the direction of the recently enthroned Stuarts may be seen in *Macbeth*. The very nature of drama invites political and ideological partisanship.

The ideological quality of *The Possessed* is enhanced by ample symbolic detail, including even name symbolism. Stavrogin's name is a contamination of Greek *stavros*, "cross," and Russian *rog*, "horn," hence a fusion of Christ and the Devil. Kirillov and Shatov live in Epiphany Street. Shatov's name is derived from the verb *shatat'*, "to waver, to vacillate," which describes his position. Aleksei Nilych Kirillov carries in his name the memory of Alexis, Man of God, Nilus Sorsky, and Cyril, apostle of the Slavs, three venerated saints. The lame madwoman's family name, Lebiadkin, is derived from *lebed'*, "swan," which squares with her folkloric fantasies. The Governor's family name, Lembke (he became von Lembke only when promoted to a decent rank), means "little lamb" in German and fits his role in the novel. Other names in the novel, like Karmazinov, Virginsky, Liputin, and Liamshin, have also been recognized as having symbolic power.

The Possessed is a *roman à thèse* with an explicitly stated dominant idea: a revolt against God, religion, and the existing social order leads to death and destruction. The revolt is fomented by diabolic agents. Diverse forms of possession appear. This may be seen as a modern version of the revolt of the Titans against the Olympic gods and similar myths, not excluding the Apocalypse and the myth of the Antichrist. Traces of ancient myths may be observed in details of the novel. Ivanov has drawn particular attention to the figure of Mar'ia Timofeevna. This lame madwoman perceives herself as the bride of a fair prince whose place has been usurped by a murderous pretender who threatens her life. Prince and usurper are one and the same person, Nikolai Vsevolodovich Stavrogin, the nihilist hero of the novel. The madwoman's fantasies are prophetic. In one scene of the novel, Piotr Verkhovensky reveals his mad plan to fashion Stavrogin as "Prince Ivan," who is to lead the uprising against the existing order. Ivanov suggests, not implausibly, that Mar'ia Timofeevna is symbolic of the soul of Russia and of Mother Earth herself, raped by the nihilism of the westernized upper class.

Piotr Verkhovensky is a version of the mythical trickster, or clever demon, who has an uncanny ability to create confusion and disorder. Other characters are also given demonic traits. The mad theorist of the revolution, Shigaliov, has monstrously large ears, reminding the reader of a vampire. Liputin and Liamshin, two other members of Piotr Verkhovensky's quintet, are fashioned as nasty imps. Nevertheless, much as in Shakespeare's *Macbeth*, the demons and the possessed live in a world in which ordinary people pursue their ordinary affairs.[10]

The novel has a *telos,* announced in the epigraph that then enters the text at the novel's conclusion. At that point Stepan Trofimovich Verkhovensky, remembering the passage in Luke 8:32–34, has it read to him and says that it applies to the current situation in Russia. But unlike most Greek tragedies, whose *telos* leads to a cathartic conclusion, *The Possessed* leaves the world no different than it was at the outset. (This is also true of Shakespeare's tragedies, where the carnage at the end of *King Lear* or *Hamlet* hits good and evil characters alike, as it does in *The Possessed*.) The main villain escapes justice, and the theorist of the revolution, surely unrepentant, will not be prosecuted. The stage is set for another round of madness.

The idea of a return to the religion of the Russian people gets lost in all the violent action. It dies with Shatov and, again, after a brief flicker of recovery, with Stepan Trofimovich. *The Possessed* lacks the promise of faith and hope seen in the conclusion of *The Brothers Karamazov*. The religious message is there, but perversely it comes through the voices of unreliable witnesses: the madwoman Mar'ia Timofeevna; the dying gasp of a vain, weak-willed, and frightened Deist, Stepan Trofimovich; Shatov, who, by his own admission, is still struggling for his faith. The brigand and murderer Fed'ka, who has recently robbed a church and killed its warden, also defends the faith in a conversation with Piotr Verkhovensky. Thus, the message of the novel is reduced to an ambiguity that is in fact predicted even by the presence of a second epigraph, two stanzas from Pushkin's poem "Demons" that contain no message of hope.

The ambiguity of the novel's message extends to its negative elements. Some of the socialist revolutionaries are honest idealists, whose social protest is, moreover, justified. The greatest threat to a world ruled by God's law comes from Aleksei Nilych Kirillov, a madman, certainly, but a pure and noble soul.[11] Kirillov believes that, with God dead, it is up to man to take His place and strive to become godlike. The main obstacle to this being fear of death, Kirillov will kill himself gratuitously to show that man can conquer

---

10. As observed by Thomas de Quincey, "The Knocking at the Gate in *Macbeth*" (1823).

11. A similar position, with a somewhat different, less heroic slant, is presented by Versilov in *A Raw Youth.*

that fear and, godlike, choose his own hour of death. Kirillov's symbolic name and the fact that he lives on Epiphany Street suggest that he is the prophet of a new religion. Of course, he may be a false prophet—it is really the reader's choice.

The worldview that emerges from *The Possessed* is tragic. Death is the only certainty; all the rest is clouded in doubt and ambiguity. There is no human justice, as good people perish senselessly while evil people thrive, and divine justice on earth remains a mystery. The conclusion one draws from *The Possessed* is no different from that which seems to be unavoidable in Shakespeare's tragedies. The innocent Mar'ia Timofeevna and Liza perish, as do Cordelia and Ophelia.

A feature of drama is an exaggerated markedness of the principal characters, meaning that they have qualities that almost immediately establish them as unique individuals. This is in conflict with mimetic realism, for one rarely meets such characters in real life. Tolstoi charges that Shakespeare's characters are overstated as well as inconsistent: they act and talk not like normal people but like, well, stage characters or madmen. In part, this is explained by the fact that Shakespeare yields to the temptation to let his characters "make speeches," say something striking, witty, or otherwise effective to keep the audience interested, instead of being concerned with creating credible characters. Lear, for example, is not only a raving madman but also produces veritable fireworks of provocative wit and profound wisdom.

This is also true of some of the great characters of Greek drama. Clytemnestra makes long and brilliant speeches at which both the chorus and Agamemnon marvel. The chilling stichomachia of Orestes and Clytemnestra in *Choephoroe* (ll. 907–29), shows mother and son trading spirited aphorisms in the very face of death. Aeschylus' superb skill allows him to present the deceptive game played by the Queen with convincing psychological verity; yet it is still obvious that Clytemnestra, as a character and as a speaker, is raised to a higher power: the truth of her character is symbolic and poetic, not empirical.

The main characters of *The Possessed* are all "marked," overstated, and travestied. By "travesty" I mean giving content a downgraded, inferior, or inappropriate form without actually changing its substance. (In parody, it is the substance that is downgraded, while the form remains intact.) A common example of travesty is failure to live up to a role: Stepan Trofimovich makes a travesty of his scholarship, Governor von Lembke of his role as administrator, Karmazinov of his position as a recognized "great writer."

Stavrogin is the one character who has a claim to heroic stature, albeit a negative one, perhaps best described as that of a Byronic hero in travesty. His role may be readily compared to that of Hamlet—again in travesty. Paradoxically, the center of gravity Stavrogin presents is inert, not unlike Hamlet's role in Shakespeare's play. Stavrogin is nihilism, the denial, driven to an extreme, of all values. A terrifying figure from the outset, he is gradually revealed as a man without a conscience, or a soul, a man reduced to appetites and impulses, incapable of emotion. Stavrogin is strikingly handsome, but his face is "like a mask." It has been observed that Stavrogin leaves a void in the novel.[12] He probably says less than any of the main characters. His speech is not perceptibly marked, being laconic, careless, at times abrupt and cutting. The narrator comments that Stavrogin's letter to Dasha showed "the style of a Russian gentleman who had never quite mastered Russian letters, in spite of all his European education" (*PSS* 10:513).[13] If Stavrogin leaves a void, it is a void that sucks in all around him. He does not do all that much in the course of the novel (there is more in the *Vorgeschichte*, though, even if one ignores "Stavrogin's Confession"), yet the whole action gravitates toward him. Stavrogin is indifferent to good and evil.[14] He inspires Shatov's Christian ideal, but also Kirillov's atheism. He makes a mockery of the sacrament of marriage, but leaves Mar'ia Timofeevna a virgin (Fiodor Pavlovich Karamazov does not spare the *iurodivaia*, one may recall). Stavrogin spares Gaganov's life, but we know he has killed in cold blood before. He did not, in fact, order Mar'ia Timofeevna's murder, but readily admits that he is guilty of it, which is true.

With all these ambiguities, Dostoevsky still makes sure to mark Stavrogin as a diabolical figure, even explicitly. Lebiadkin is reported to have called Stavrogin a "wise serpent" (p. 83), and the following section of the novel is entitled "A Wise Serpent." In it, Stavrogin is twice referred to as a reptile (*gad* and *udav*, pp. 147, 155).[15] Liza, who loves him, finally admits: "I always felt that you would take me to a place where a huge spider the size of a man

12.   See R. M. Davidson, "*The Devils:* The Role of Stavrogin," in *New Essays on Dostoyevsky,* ed. Malcolm V. Jones and Garth M. Terry (Cambridge: Cambridge University Press, 1983), pp. 95–114.

13.   See Leonid Grossman, "Stilistika Stavrogina: K izucheniiu novoi glavy "Besov," in *Poetika Dostoevskogo* (Moscow: Gosudarstvennaia Akademiia khudozhestvennykh nauk, 1925), pp. 144–62.

14.   Dostoevsky's frequent notebook references to the Laodiceans, who are neither hot nor cold (Rev. 3:14–16), seems to refer to Stavrogin. In the text, Stepan Trofimovich brings up this passage (p. 497).

15.   See N. M. Chirkov, *O stile Dostoevskogo* (Moscow: AN SSSR, 1963), pp. 38–39. Chirkov observes Dostoevsky's tendency to attach grotesque elements to lofty feelings, as well as details of physical ugliness to spiritual beauty (pp. 177–80).

lives, and we will look at him all our lives and be afraid of him" (p. 402). Even without "Stavrogin's Confession," Stavrogin is an unforgettable figure, particularly if perceived in terms of a stage presentation.

While Stavrogin's character is open to question, like that of Hamlet or Prince Harry, to whom he is likened in the text, Piotr Verkhovensky is marked for evil from the beginning. His character, too, seems ambiguous, but only at first sight. The narrator introduces him in detail at his first appearance (pp. 143–44), describing him as a bundle of contradictions between what he appears to be and what he really is. Piotr Verkhovensky is not as deep or complex as Stavrogin, but he is far from simple. He is a fanatic, but in the pursuit of power, without any ideal. He is a tireless worker for the revolution, but not averse to pursuing personal ends. He seems sociable and a "nice fellow," but despises people. He is a master at manipulating people by appealing to their weaknesses, yet he also underestimates them. Piotr Verkhovensky is a lesser demon than Stavrogin — hardly realistic, but unforgettable.

Kirillov is marked by his idea and the fervor with which he preaches it, but also by his lusterless black eyes and his barely grammatical speech. He likes to stay up all night drinking strong tea. He also likes to bounce a red rubber ball to amuse his landlady's baby. He is almost immediately identified as a madman and is quite out of his mind in his last hours.

Captain Lebiadkin, who fancies himself Falstaff to Stavrogin's Prince Harry, is a bear of a man (his physical presence, like that of the other characters, is well described),[16] marked by his drunken buffoonery and, in particular, by his efforts at writing verse, "so bad it is good." Lebiadkin vacillates between aspiration to a gentleman's status and brutish pursuit of gain by any means, including criminal. Semiliterate, he makes a travesty of every line or image he touches.

Stepan Trofimovich Verkhovensky is a caricature of an idealist of the 1840s. He is also a bundle of contradictions. A learned, talented, witty, and eloquent man, he is also silly, vain, and incredibly naive. A keen judge of art and literature, he is like a child in practical affairs. A handsome man, he always finds a woman to lean on. He is marked by many details, such as a weakness for cards (he is a good loser), attacks of cholerine, compulsive let-

---

16. It is remarkable how the scenic quality of *The Possessed* is enhanced by detailed descriptions of the appearance of all the major — and some minor — characters. There is, of course, no description of the narrator's appearance. As the "chorus" of the drama, he needs only a general identification.

ter writing, a love of champagne, and many others. Stepan Trofimovich is an example of an incredible character who is wonderfully alive.

The "great writer" Karmazinov is a transparent caricature of Turgenev, though not in his physical presence. Dostoevsky accomplishes the rare feat of fully integrating a satire (in fact, more of an invective) and literary parody into the plot of his novel.

The story of Andrei Antonovich von Lembke, the provincial Governor, is yet another satirical sortie, well integrated with the plot. Andrei Antonovich is a man of limited intelligence and energy who has made his way to high rank, well, "by belonging to a certain tribe" (never named!) and by marrying a forty-year-old princess (he is also a handsome man). He is marked by his hobby of constructing elaborate scenery (a theater, a railway station) from cardboard and paper. When his wife discovers his pastime, she forbids him to continue, so he turns to writing a novel instead. Andrei Antonovich cannot stand the strain of events that overtake his province and suffers a nervous breakdown. His story, like those of several other characters, might serve as a good short story in its own right.

Even minor characters are given a striking and unforgettable identity by their distinctive language and extraordinary character traits, or the peculiar events in which they are involved. Fed'ka, the escaped convict, is marked by a criminal's self-righteous cockiness. He gets the better of Piotr Verkhovensky, physically and mentally, but respects Kirillov and fears Stavrogin. His speech is a marvel of "jive talk."

Liamshin, one of Piotr Verkhovensky's quintet, has a touch of "Jewishness" about him. He plays the buffoon, and the piano. He has composed an amusing piece called "The Franco-Prussian War" (the narrator intimates that Liamshin has stolen it). Liamshin can walk on his hands, which he does in the "literary quadrille" at the Governor's fete. The Governor orders him to be turned right-side-up. Liamshin suffers a nervous breakdown after Shatov's murder, shaking and breaking into a loud, uncontrollable squeal. He will soon go to the police and confess to the crime. Liamshin's story deserves to be made into a play like *Rosencrantz and Guildenstern Are Dead*. The same is true of Liputin, another member of the quintet. Liputin, a middle-aged low-ranking government official, is a penny-pinching domestic tyrant, a gossip, and a spinner of intrigues. But he is also a Fourierist. Nobody's fool, he is still caught in the web spun by Piotr Verkhovensky. After the murder, he makes his escape to Petersburg, but is arrested in a brothel after a drunken debauch, though in possession of a valid passport. Liputin also has a run-in with Stavrogin, who, at a party, shamelessly kisses Liputin's young and pretty wife.

The women in the novel, fewer in number, are equally well marked. Mme Stavrogin, a homely, horse-faced woman, imperious and self-righteous, has one weakness: Stepan Trofimovich. Their twenty-year love affair never advances beyond his abortive attempt to declare his love, to which Varvara Petrovna reacts by hissing: "I will never forgive you this!"

Iuliia Mikhailovna von Lembke is Mme Stavrogin's rival for leadership of the province's society. A well-meaning but foolish woman, she trusts Piotr Verkhovensky, of all people. She fancies herself a liberal and believes herself to have charmed everybody by her generosity.

Mar'ia Timofeevna, the lame madwoman, is thirtyish, emaciated, with a long neck, stringy black hair, and a heavily powdered and rouged face. But she has tender, loving gray eyes. Her behavior is gentle and girlish — until she erupts in denoucing Stavrogin as "the false prince." She lives in a fantasy world in which dreams are indistinguishable from reality. She believes herself to have borne a child and drowned it, though she is a virgin. She calls her brother her lackey, though he beats her regularly. Her speech is a mixture of folklore, literary romance, and lower-middle-class colloquial diction. She definitely has a touch of Ophelia about her — in travesty, of course.

The narrator dwells on the appearance of Liza Tushin, the novel's tragic heroine. He comes to this conclusion: "Now, remembering the past, I will no longer say that she was a beauty, as she then appeared to me. Perhaps she was in fact homely. Tall, thin, but supple and strong, she actually had quite irregular features" (p. 88). Liza is marked by being the only woman in town who rides horseback, a detail that leads to a grotesque episode. In one of her frequent fits of hysterics, she vividly imagines what would happen if she were thrown by her horse and left a cripple — like her rival, the lame woman. Lebiadkin, in love with Liza, like every man in town, assures her in a poem that "if she were to hurt a limb," he would love her so much more.

Altogether, then, we have a large number of extraordinary characters in extraordinary circumstances, all drawn into the whirlpool of the novel's action, like the characters in Shakespeare's *Hamlet* or *King Lear*. As in Shakespeare's tragedies, we have a most vivid picture of real life, but raised to a higher power through drama's license to condense and concentrate life in time and in space, as well as to present people at the crossroads of their lives, when a moment of truth reveals their deepest nature. Quite extraordinary strings of chance coincidences, encounters, clashes, and crimes thus acquire poetic credibility. The necessary suspension of disbelief by the reader or viewer is achieved through the power of highly marked characters and highly marked dialogue.

A peculiar trait of Dostoevsky's characters in *The Possessed* is that virtually all of them have traits exaggerated in both directions: pathos and bathos, sublime and grotesque, beauty and ugliness. This is particularly true of Stavrogin, Liza, and Mar'ia Timofeevna. The same trait may be observed in Shakespeare, with Lear a case in point.

Dostoevsky was criticized by many, including Tolstoi, for letting all his characters speak alike—like the author-narrator, in fact. Tolstoi leveled the same charge against Shakespeare. The charge is not altogether valid, since both Dostoevsky and Shakespeare differentiate between social levels of speech. Fed'ka the convict is a case in point. But it is true that Dostoevsky's characters tend to be more eloquent and more inventive than might be expected from a like character in real life and that many characters are marked by speaking either too well or too badly—that is, in a way that turns attention to their speech. The same is true of Shakespeare. For example, even the murderers in *Macbeth* seem to be lettered. And, to bring in Greek drama, even messengers are eloquent quite beyond their social status.

Attention to the characters' speech is supported by Dostoevsky's extraordinarily careful attention to intonation, volume, emotional nuances, and accompanying gestures and mimicry, stage directions, as it were, in lieu of what the actor adds to dramatic dialogue.[17]

In *The Possessed,* the marking of the characters' speech is predominantly negative. (In *The Brothers Karamazov,* in contrast, several characters are extraordinarily eloquent in a positive sense.) Stavrogin says little, but it is clear that his speech is a front, concealing a chaotic and hideous inner life. His laconic suicide note is symbolic of the terrible void of emotion in his soul. Kirillov's skewed speech does call attention to his obsessive idea: if it had been expressed in the language of, say, Stepan Trofimovich, it might have slipped by unnoticed. But his speech also tells the reader that Kirillov's mind is in disorder. Stepan Trofimovich is a genuine man of letters, but whatever he says is usually turned into bathos by the context or by the narrator's ironic comments. His speech is laced, often grotesquely, with French phrases, such as when he explains himself to Sof'ia Matveevna, a simple woman of the people. The many other voices also tend to have certain negative markings. There is a general tendency to add a note of bathos or grotesquerie to the personality and speech of every character in the novel. Even so sterling a character as Mavriky Nikolaevich is put down by a casual remark to the effect that "he was not considered to be too bright."

The narrator,[18] who calls himself a chronicler, in fact acts as a chorus. He is

17.   S. M. Solov'ev, *Izobrazitel'nye sredstva v tvorchestve F. M. Dostoevskogo: Ocherki* (Moscow: Sovetskii pisatel', 1979), devotes a whole chapter to this trait (pp. 339–50).

18.   For an excellent treatment of the narrator in *The Possessed,* see V. A. Tunimanov, "The

an eyewitness of most of the action and refers to reliable witnesses for much of the rest. We know his first name and patronymic, Anton Lavrent'evich, but his family name is discreetly left as G———v. He is a middle-echelon government official, a veteran member of Stepan Trofimovich's circle, a member of the Club, meaning that he belongs to the best society in town. He is still a young man, well educated and amazingly well read. Both of these qualities are patently exaggerated, for Mr. G———v has in fact the mind of Fiodor Mikhailovich Dostoevsky, a man of letters and "a reader of genius." Some instances of personal experience remind the reader that Mr. G———v is a real person: he is embarrassed by his awkward behavior the time he ran into the great writer Karmazinov in the street. It is intimated that he, too, had a crush on Liza Tushin. He is an usher at the Governor's fete.

Mr. G———v is a gossip and a busybody, a moderate liberal but loyal to the existing order. Ostensibly a modest and well-meaning person, he actually has a condescending and ironic attitude toward most of his subjects, particularly those who have real-life prototypes: Karmazinov, Stepan Trofimovich, Shigaliov, and others. He seems to share everybody else's awe before Stavrogin but in the end sends him off with a sarcastic: "The citizen of the Canton of Uri hung there, right behind the door" (p. 516). But he can also show sympathy, solidarity, pity, scorn, and outrage. His irony, too, has a wide range of nuances: wry, bitter, sarcastic, good-natured, worldly-wise, amused, self-deprecating, and more.

Mr. G———v engages everybody in the novel in a dialogue, often enough directly. When he is personally present but not participating in the conversation, he will accompany the conversation with a running commentary expressing his reaction to it. Even in those scenes for which the narrator must use his imagination, he still acts as though he were present. For example, in the scene between Stavrogin and Fed'ka, which he did not witness and could not possibly have heard about, he observes: "On his knees, pressed to the ground, his elbows turned to his back, the wily tramp calmly awaited the resolution of the situation, apparently not in the least believing in any danger to himself" (p. 220).

The trick here is to insert an emotional reaction, giving the description a subjective quality. Another example: before describing the terrible beating Piotr Stepanovich suffers at the hands of Fed'ka the convict, the narrator

Narrator in *The Devils*," in *Dostoevsky: New Perspectives,* ed. Robert Louis Jackson (Englewood Cliffs, N.J.: Prentice-Hall, 1984), pp. 145–75.

says: "Here a rapid and revolting scene ensued" (p. 429). By calling the scene "revolting," the narrator projects himself into the picture, as though he were present.

Frequently the narrator carries on a veritable dialogue with a scene he did not witness by inserting observations on its progress. For example, the lengthy conversation between Stavrogin and Lebiadkin (pp. 206–14) is interrupted time and again by observations like the following: "The Captain was speaking with enthusiasm and, of course, believed in the beauty of the American's testament, but he was still a fraud and was trying very hard to amuse Nikolai Vsevolodovich, with whom he had in the past long held the position of a jester."

It must be noted that the narrator assumes not merely the power of an omniscient observer, which is a prerogative of the epic poet, but actually makes himself a participant in the action, precisely as the chorus of a Greek drama does.

The plot of *The Possessed* is dramatically focused, in spite of a very large number of *dramatis personae* and the presence of several side plots. The action takes place within a very short period of time in a provincial capital, gravitating toward Skvoreshniki, the suburban manor of Varvara Petrovna Stavrogin, the widow of an important General. Almost every person or event in the novel has a connection to Stavrogin. Some scenes are set at the Governor's mansion, at a house on Epiphany Street, where Shatov and Kirillov live, and at a house "on the other side of the river," where Captain Lebiadkin lives with his sister. The ballroom of the local Club is the site of the Governor's fete. Time and space are decidedly compressed for dramatic effect, most strikingly in the chapter "A Wise Serpent," which develops a "conclave" (L. P. Grossman's term), staged to introduce the central characters of the novel and tie the knot of the action. The lame woman, her brother, Piotr Stepanovich, and finally Stavrogin himself appear before a gathering that includes most of the other characters. The conflicts that will lead to the eventual catastrophe are set up.

The entire action is presented scenically, with dialogue and outright action dominant all along. There are tense one-on-one encounters, verbal duels (as well as one with pistols), scenes of physical violence graphically described, and some mass scenes (the protest march of the Shpigulin factory workers, Liza's death at the hands of an angry mob) — the whole gamut of a Shakespearean tragedy.

The writing of *The Possessed* is more compact than that of Dostoevsky's other novels. There are relatively few digressions of the kind one finds in

The Idiot or *The Brothers Karamazov*. Still, the narrator engages in essayistic, satirical, and anecdotal digressions on such topics as the literary ambience of the 1850s (pp. 21–24), the peculiar role played by the German community in the imperial bureaucracy (pp. 241–43), and the reaction of Russian conservatives to the emancipation of the serfs (p. 224). He cannot refrain from telling a good story even if it is irrelevant to the progress of the plot — for example, the sad story of a youth who shot himself after gambling away his sister's dowry (p. 255), the story about a pious lady who was reported to have been flogged by the police for no good reason, and then turned out to be nonexistent (pp. 342–43), or the story of how Mme Virginsky, a midwife and nihilist, brought about a successful delivery by frightening the woman in labor with a rude blasphemy (p. 301). There are many other such minor digressions, invariably amusing.

Dostoevsky's characters tend to deliver themselves of long ideological or philosophical tirades. This trait is reduced to a minimum in *The Possessed*. The only character to "make a speech" of any length is Shatov (pp. 198–200), as he expounds to a rather bored Stavrogin the idea of Russia, a "God-bearing" nation, abandoned by Russia's westernized upper class. Stepan Trofimovich's harangues are invariably interrupted. Kirillov does not need much time to express, with inarticulate poignancy, the idea that torments him. Altogether, then, the dramatic quality of *The Possessed* is hardly diluted by extraneous elements.

The Possessed has far more dramatic than epic traits. It has an ideological focus that is announced in the work's title. It has a *telos* toward which the action rushes inexorably. There are several plots, but they run parallel to each other and in the end dovetail into a common catastrophe. I disagree with Joseph Frank, who believes that *The Possessed* "peters out rather inconsistently for reasons very largely outside Dostoevsky's power to remedy by the time he reached the final pages." [19] Dostoevsky may not have delivered the ideological or the Christian message he had in mind, but as far as the tragic drama is concerned, the conclusion is no less fitting than in any of the world's great tragedies. Once again, as in *The Idiot,* Dostoevsky's tragic impulse prevailed over a desire to assert a belief in the existence of divine justice and order on this earth. Once again, Christ is not of this world.

A strongly personalized narrative voice acts as a chorus, maintaining a steady connection between the tragic and irrational action and the more

---

19. Joseph Frank, *Dostoevsky: The Miraculous Years, 1865–1871* (Princeton: Princeton University Press, 1995), p. 497.

ordinary and rational sensibility of the audience. That the narrative voice is deeply ironic is well in line with the ethos of tragedy.[20]

The characters of *The Possessed* are out of the ordinary, highly idiosyncratic, sharply defined, and deeply contradictory. They are motivated by powerful ideas and strong passions, but also by the most mundane considerations in a world of prosaic concerns. As a result, *The Possessed* becomes a tragedy in travesty, meaning that it *is* a tragedy, whose characters, while suffering a truly tragic fate, do not in effect measure up to the lofty standards of Greek tragedy, as pathos is reduced to bathos and a tragic worldview is brought down from the heights of poetry to the valley of prose. The strong presence of satire and parody moves *The Possessed* closer to Shakespeare, and in fact to Aristophanes, while moving it away from Greek tragedy.

The structure of *The Possessed* is scenic rather than narrative, in spite of pretending to be a chronicle. Dialogue and outright action dominate. Space and time are treated dramatically, as scenes are staged in symbolic space and time is arbitrarily adapted to the contingencies of dramatic action.

The novelistic traits of *The Possessed* are the contemporary prosaic setting, the introduction of contemporary social concerns, such as the plight of the Shpigulin factory workers, various digressions of anecdotal, essayistic, and aphoristic nature, and the fact that some portions of the text are narrated by an omniscient narrator. The latter quality may well be shared with a dramatic chorus.

20. The *Oresteia* features many instances of deep irony, as when Clytemnestra presents herself as a faithful wife and guardian of her absent husband's estate, or when Agamemnon, moments before his terrible death, says: "Count him among the blest / Whose life has ended in felicity." In *Prometheus,* Hermes and Prometheus trade ironic barbs. Sophocles' dramas, such as *Oedipus Rex, Ajax,* and *Philoctetes,* rely on "Sophoclean irony" for their main scenic effects.

7

On the Style of A *Raw Youth*

Paced between two *chefs d'oeuvre, The Possessed* and *The Brothers Karamazov, A Raw Youth* may appear second rate. Not a great novel, it is nevertheless quintessential Dostoevsky. In fact, it may offer a more revealing paradigm of Dostoevsky's style than the great novels in which art has smoothed out the rough edges of Dostoevsky's idiosyncratic mannerisms.

In *A Raw Youth*, tendencies that appear in all of Dostoevsky's works show up in an extreme and therefore readily recognized form, allowing one to project observations made here onto Dostoevsky's other works. The plot of *A Raw Youth* is melodramatic, whereas that of the great novels is dramatic. The plot is embedded in an outspokenly subjective and excessively diffuse narrative, whereas a modicum of objectivity is at least pretended and some narrative discipline observed in Dostoevsky's great novels, such as *The Possessed* and *The Brothers Karamazov*. The personalities of the main characters are marked by glaring contradictions, without the effort to resolve them dialectically that tends to be made in the great novels. *A Raw Youth* is a *roman-feuilleton* whose narrative is richly interspersed with philosophical musings, insights into human nature, social commentary, observations on current affairs, literary discussions, aphorisms, poetic conceits, and inserted stories and anecdotes. The same elements appear in the great novels, but less patently, and they are better integrated with the narrative.

Nevertheless, *A Raw Youth* is an immensely entertaining, challenging, and, yes, convincingly credible novel. How is this to be explained? My thesis is that the effect of *A Raw Youth* is due to the intense and unflagging energy of its language, where the striking though momentary effect of each and every detail of the text amply compensates for the sacrifice in long-range consistency and teleology caused precisely by the writer's successful pursuit of immediate scenic, emotional, intellectual, or verbal effects. I believe that this is also true of the great novels, though less obviously. In a way, *A Raw Youth* is a purer novel in the Bakhtinian sense than the great "novel-tragedies," where some of the freedom and openness of the novel is yielded to the stricter formal requirements of classical drama. Yet observations made with regard to *A Raw Youth* may point to flaws even in the structure of the great novels. As the following description of the basic stylistic traits of *A Raw Youth* shows, every trait recognized here also appears in the great novels, being part and parcel of Dostoevsky's style.

While a personalized narrator and an individualized style are characteristic of Dostoevsky, *A Raw Youth* is the only major work of his in which a consistent effort is made to maintain a genuine, rather than merely formal, first-person narrative voice. This objective is realized at the cost of a badly skewed plot, as awkward chance encounters, *ad hoc* messengers, and strained eavesdropping scenes are used to allow the narrator to witness most of the action. These artifices permit the narrator to use dialogue much of the time. When he must resort to indirect speech, he will use *erlebte Rede* laced with frequent quotations (often within quotation marks).[1] The narrator also likes to quote himself.[2] He uses italics for emphasis quite often.[3]

A few letters are quoted verbatim.[4] The voices of several characters, some of them minor, emerge from the text, along with some facial descriptions,[5] but they are well embedded in the narrative, which is dominated by the narrator's own voice. There are a few *intermezzi*: Nastas'ia Egorovna's story (*PSS* 13: 142–47), Versilov's confession (pp. 374–80), Makar Ivanovich's edifying *conte moral* (pp. 313–22), each in the character's own voice.

Dostoevsky's narrators are by no means uniform, but they have one thing in common: they are intensely and in a partisan way interested in the action; they may or they may not try to conceal their bias, but they will always find ways, direct or indirect, to express their sympathies and antipathies. A per-

---

1.   For example, Versilov's account of his love affair with the hero's mother (*PSS* 13: 9–13).

2.   For example, p. 15, ll. 40–45.

3.   For example, p. 9, l. 45, p. 11, ll. 15, 17, 35, p. 19, l. 29, p. 36, ll. 32–33.

4.   Versilov's to Katerina Nikolaevna (p. 258), young Prince Sokol'skii's to the hero (pp. 279–80), Nikolai Semionovich's letter to the hero (pp. 452–55). Olia's brief suicide note is also quoted verbatim (p. 149).

5.   Some descriptions of voices: the hero's, p. 196, ll. 23–27; Alphonsine's, p. 278, ll. 8–10, 35; Anna Andreevna's, p. 194, ll. 13–15; Katerina Nikolaevna's, p. 126, ll. 44–46; Makar Ivanovich's, p. 244, ll. 1–3; Versilov's, p. 219, ll. 41–44, p. 260, l. 11.

sonalized narrator who is himself involved in the action is the ideal vehicle for such an attitude. *A Raw Youth* presents the most drastic example of this type of narrator. Arkadii Dolgorukii is, like the narrators of *The Gambler, The Possessed,* or *The Brothers Karamazov,* ostensibly an inexperienced amateur writer, who also happens to be immensely talented, eminently literate, and intensely conscious of his language.

In *A Raw Youth,* the narrator's point of view is affirmed time and again by stylistic and psychological self-analysis,[6] punctuated by frequent apostrophes to the reader.[7] The narrative's personal quality is enhanced by dream passages (pp. 305–7) and occasional episodes of stream-of-consciousness (pp. 297, 326–27, 361–62). The novel begins and ends with observations on the literary quality of the text and contains frequent comments regarding questions of style and difficulties in expressing emotions and ideas. The crux of these observations is that the author is trying to avoid yielding to the temptation to bring forth "literary beauties" (*literaturnye krasoty,* p. 5) instead of expressing himself. However, he admits that he often lapses into literature, and the literary quality of the text is marked by numerous literary quotations and allusions.[8] The very "idea" on which he intends to build his life is taken from, or at least supported by, Pushkin's tragedy "The Covetous Knight" (p. 75). Ultimately his mentor and only reader, Nikolai Semionovich, whose postface concludes the novel, suggests that life itself will have to become more structured to allow the writing of a more artful novel, for which the present text may serve as a preparatory draft. This raises the corollary that life is at present as formless as the author's narrative. Thus, the relation between life and art becomes an expressly raised issue, as it is in some other Dostoevskian novels, starting with *Poor Folk* and ending with *The Brothers Karamazov.*

6.   For example: "Oh, didn't I anticipate how trivial all rejoinders would be and how trivial I would be myself expounding my 'idea': well, what have I expressed? I haven't expressed a hundredth part of it; I feel that it came out petty, crude, superficial, and in fact younger than my years" (p. 71). Other examples: p. 6, ll. 3–20, p. 263, ll. 18–20, p. 322, ll. 13–24, p. 437, l. 8.

7.   For example: "My idea is to become a Rothschild. I ask for the reader's calm and seriousness" (p. 66). Other examples: pp. 5–6, 32, ll. 25–27, p. 67, ll. 24–28, pp. 76, l. 30–77, l. 14, p. 439, l. 14.

8.   Pushkin is quoted or alluded to repeatedly: pp. 76, 152, 192, 192, 382. So is Shakespeare: pp. 129, 209, 224, 382. Versilov at one time played the role of Chatskii in an amateur performance of Alexander Griboedov's *Woe from Wit* (p. 94) and mentions Nikolai Nekrasov (p. 109) and Alexander Druzhinin (p. 10). The hero declaims Ivan Krylov, Mikhail Lermontov, and Goethe (p. 352). Heine (p. 379), Dickens (p. 353), Lev Tolstoi (p. 454), and others are also alluded to.

The self-conscious nature of the narrative is signaled by occasional slang,[9] *slovechki*,[10] verbal tics,[11] intentional catachresis,[12] and hypostatization of words[13] and names. The hero's surname, Dolgorukii, which he shares with a great aristocratic family, occasions a series of embarrassing, revealing, and funny scenes throughout the novel. The narrator consistently violates every rule of conventional good style. The most characteristic traits are those which are also found in Dostoevsky's other works: hedging and concession,[14] sublation and deconstruction.[15] The text is rich in negative figures of speech: false notes,[16] paradox,[17] bathos,[18] and doubletake.[19] Digressive essays and aphorisms on a variety of topics are frequently introduced—a trait that *A Raw Youth* shares with other Dostoevskian novels, and many other nineteenth-century works.[20]

9.   For example: *fintifliushek* (p. 15), *fru-fru* (p. 25), *podushka* (p. 33), and *fater* (p. 66).

10.   *Slovechki* (literally, "little words") are cute or apt expressions of colloquial discourse, such as "conscience for hire" (a lawyer), which the hero hears from Makar Ivanovich (p. 310).

11.   For example, *slishkom*, "too (much)," which the hero uses excessively.

12.   For example: "I . . . decided to eliminate people" (*reshilsia sokratit' liudei*, p. 69), where the verb *sokratit'* is used in the meaning it has in *sokratit' shtaty*, "reduce the staff." What the hero is trying to say is that he will be less concerned with people.

13.   For example, the hero's "idea," throughout the novel.

14.   Hedging: "There was something in his face that I would not have liked to have in mine, something all too confident, in a moral sense, something like a kind of secret pride, unaware of itself. However, probably I could not have passed judgment so literally then; it does appear to me so now, that I was judging him then in this fashion, that is, already after the fact" (p. 44). Other examples: p. 358, ll. 10–18, p. 421, ll. 15–21, p. 438, ll. 3–11.

15.   Sublation: "To this day I am inclined to perceive this encounter with Lambert as something, well, prophetic . . . at least judging by the circumstances and consequences of this encounter. However, all of it happened, at least from one viewpoint, as naturally as can be" (p. 275). Other examples: p. 15, ll. 12–14, p. 63, ll. 24–26, p. 179, ll. 7–10.

16.   Olia's suicide note provides an example, as does the exchange between young Sokol'skii and Versilov (pp. 155–56).

17.   For example: "So then, as far as my feelings for and relations with Liza were concerned, all that was apparent on the surface was merely a strained, jealous lie on both sides, yet never did the two of us love each other more than then" (p. 293).

18.   Such as when the hero, in expounding his "idea," goes into meticulous detail regarding proper care for his clothes and footwear, including how one must put the whole sole to the ground to reduce wear at the heels and tips (p. 69). By the way, this corrects the practice of Akakii Akak'evich in Gogol's "The Overcoat."

19.   For example: "I don't guarantee that he loved her, but that he dragged her around with him all his life—that is true" (p. 12). Other examples: p. 15, ll. 15–16, p. 42, ll. 30–34, p. 44, ll. 18–20, p. 72, ll. 24–26, p. 159, l. 4, p. 204, ll. 32–33.

20.   An essay on laughter (pp. 285, l. 7–286, l. 8), an essay on the breadth of the Russian national character (p. 307, ll. 19–27), an essay on photography (p. 370, ll. 15–30), Versilov's discourse on the Russian European (p. 377, ll. 8–44), a remark on the bourgeois mentality of the French (p. 418, ll. 21–25), Makar Ivanovich on atheists (p. 302, ll. 38–46), among many others.

The writing is uneven. There is some fine writing, as in the episode describing the visit of the hero's mother to Touchard's boarding school (pp. 270–73), introduced in the form of a dream, from which he is awakened by his boyhood chum Lambert.[21] But all in all the writing can be eloquent or awkward,[22] verbose or elliptical,[23] solemn or breezy,[24] poetic or prosaic,[25] profound or naive.[26] It may affect scientific objectivity or appear heartfelt, even sentimental.[27] Its tone may be assertive and categorical or vague and diffident.[28] Its ethos is rarely neutral. Any given phrase tends to be marked by some form of connotation through allusion, a figure of speech, stylistic peculiarities, ambiguity, solecism, and other traits that make the *signifier : signified* relation complicated and symbolic, rather than simple and indexic. The phrasing tends to be marked rather than unmarked, regardless of the quality of markedness. The first few sentences of the novel may serve as an illustration:

21.   This artifice reminds one of Oblomov's dream in Goncharov's novel. This episode was immediately singled out by critics as a piece of masterful writing. See *PSS* 17:354.

22.   The hero is eloquent at the meeting of the Dergachev group (pp. 48–49). He is awkward when he tries to explain his "idea" (pp. 66–71) and actually notices it himself (p. 71, ll. 45–48).

23.   He is verbose most of the time. But on occasion he will come up with surprising examples of extreme concision — for example: "My idea is the corner" (*Moia ideia — ugol,* p. 48), meaning that he plans to isolate himself from people.

24.   Solemn diction: "She truly respected all her life, in fear, in trembling, and in reverence, her lawful husband and wanderer Makar Ivanovich, who had magnanimously and forever forgiven her" (p. 292). And breezy: introducing Versilov, his natural father, the hero says: "I shall briefly present his *curriculum vitae*" (p. 64), where *formuliarnyi spisok* in the original smacks of "officialese" even more than my translation. Or this: "This is what my 'idea' amounts to; I repeat, all the rest is trivia." At this point the chapter ends and the new chapter begins: "But let us look at the trivia, too" (p. 68).

25.   For a poetic passage, see p. 113, ll. 7–21, where Dostoevsky introduces one of his favorite conceits, St. Petersburg as a mirage that will disappear when the fog enshrouding it lifts. But much of the text is written in a graceless journalese, laced with numerous, often quite unnecessary foreign words, such as *kompetentnyi* (p. 309), *essentsiia* (p. 338), *ekspansivnost'* (p. 308), *radikal'no* (p. 281), *gigienicheski* (p. 307), and *formulirovat'* (p. 281).

26.   The hero's analysis of his mother's fall is mature beyond his years, as is his gradually emerging understanding of his father's character. But when he expounds his "idea," he is very naive.

27.   For example: "One-and-a-half cubic *sazhens* are needed to provide a human being with fresh air for twelve hours, and perhaps these rooms had this much, though probably no more" (p. 126). For sentimental diction, see, for example, the hero's report of the sad fate of his sister Liza (pp. 450–51).

28.   This is particularly true of the hero's judgment of people. He never hesitates to pass judgment on Baron Björing and the latter's friend Baron R. But there is a great deal of hedging and concession in his opinions of the main characters. Cf. nn. 14 and 15 above.

Не утерпев, я сел записывать эту историю моих первых шагов на жизненном поприще, тогда как мог бы обойтись и без того. Одно знаю наверно: никогда уже более не сяду писать мою автобиографию, даже если проживу до ста лет. Надо быть слишком подло влюбленным в себя, чтобы писать без стыда о самом себе. Тем только себя извиняю, что не для того пишу, для чего все пишут, то есть не для похвал читателя.

> Unable to restrain myself, I have sat down to record this history of my first steps in life's arena, while I might have done without it just as well. One thing I know for sure: never again will I sit down to write my autobiography, even if I live to be a hundred. One must be too basely in love with oneself in order to write about oneself without shame. The only excuse I can come up with is that I am not writing with the purpose everybody does, that is, in order to be praised by my readers. (P. 5)

Beginning any discourse with a negative phrase (*ne uterpev,* literally "not having restrained myself") immediately signals the writer's unorthodox style. The concession in the first sentence ("while I might have done without it just as well") does not square with the categorical tone of its first part and conveys diffidence. The second sentence reestablishes the categorical tone, but then wavers by overstating its point ("even if I live to be a hundred"). "To be in love with oneself" is in itself a marked phrase, but the markedness is stressed by "basely," not ordinarily an adverb associated with "being in love," and then, for good measure, by "too." The concluding sentence is marked by the overstatement of its negation.

Similar observations may be made regarding every page of the novel. The author shows a pervasive tendency to produce various kinds of stylistic irregularities and ambiguities, rather than to remove them. What is Dostoevsky's purpose in so consistently introducing a qualifying subtext or, in semiotic terms, making the reader aware of an "interpretant" that affects the relation between signifier and signified? Is this merely to signal an unskilled writer, or does it relate to the content of the novel and hence to Dostoevsky's, rather than merely the hero's, vision? A glance at Dostoevsky's great novels shows that all these traits appear there as well, albeit on a smaller scale. Dostoevsky tends to energize his text by keeping it marked in any conceivable way, from high pathos and flowery oratory to jargon, slang, and stammer. Some of his favorite ideas are put into the mouths of clowns like Lebedev in *The Idiot, iurodivye* like Mar'ia Lebiadkin in *The Possessed,* or scoundrels like the old Karamazov, whom he lets reverse Pascal's famous bet. In *The Possessed,* Dostoevsky lets Kirillov express his breathtakingly bold and novel philosophy in a barely grammatical, fractured stammer. And could there be a more memorable profession of faith than Marmeladov's drunken babble? These examples are readily multiplied. Although a specific strategy is pursued in some instances of marking, they all engage the reader's attention and maintain interest in the text.

The dominant pattern in the novel's psychology is an unresolved tension between opposing character traits. The hero's analysis of his mother's illicit liaison may serve as an example. It is also typical of his hedging and sublation of assertions made only a moment ago. He admits that he has never talked to her on the subject and then proceeds:

Вопрос следующий: как она-то могла, она сама, уже бывшая полгода в браке, да еще придавленная всеми понятиями о законности брака, придавленная, как бессильная муха, она, уважавшая своего Макара Ивановича не меньше чем какого-то бога, как она-то могла, в какие-нибудь две недели, дойти до такого греха? Ведь не развратная же женщина была моя мать? Напротив, скажу теперь вперед, что быть более чистой душой, и так потом во всю жизнь, даже трудно себе и представить. Объяснить разве можно тем, что сделала она не помня себя, то есть не в том смысле, как уверяют теперь адвокаты про своих убийц и воров, а под тем сильным впечатлением, которое, при известном простодушии жертвы, овладевает фатально и трагически. Почем знать, может быть, она полюбила до смерти. . . . фасон его платья, парижский пробор волос, его французский выговор, именно французский, в котором она не поиимала ни звука, тот романс, котрый он спел за фортепьяно, полюбила нечто никогда не виданное и не слыханное (а он был очень красив собою), и уж заодно полюбила, прямо до изнеможения, всего его, с фасонами и романсами.

The question is as follows: how could she, she herself, already married for half a year, and moreover, stifled like a helpless fly by all the notions of the legality of marriage, she, who respected her Makar Ivanovich no less than some god, how could she in the course of a mere two weeks arrive at such a sin? For surely my mother was not a lewd woman? On the contrary, let me say this up front, it is difficult even to imagine a soul purer than hers, then and for the rest of her life. It could be explained, perhaps, by assuming that she did it oblivious of herself, that is, not in the sense lawyers these days assert about their murderers and thieves, but under a powerful impression that, given a certain simplemindedness on the part of the victim, takes possession fatefully and tragically. Who knows, perhaps she came to love fatally the cut of his suit, his Parisian coiffure, his French accent, his French itself, of which she could not understand a sound, the romance he sang accompanying himself on the piano—came to love something she had never seen or heard before (and he was very handsome), and with all that came to love, simply to the point of exhaustion, all of him, with his fashions and romances. (P. 12)

Many details of this passage are marked stylistically, mostly by skewed writing. "The legality of marriage" (*zakonnost' braka*) seems wrong—one expects "the sanctity of marriage." "Stifled like a helpless fly" (*pridavlen-naia, kak bessil'naia mukha*) is, in the given context, hardly an appropriate simile. Loving someone "to the point of exhaustion" (*do iznemozheniia*) is a strange way to describe a great love. Along with this, the psychological analysis presented here is paradoxical. The severity of his mother's sin is overstated, but so is the purity of her character. Her "fateful and tragic" passion was kindled by "the cut of his suit, his Parisian coiffure"—a sudden leap from pathos to bathos. Yet the narrator concludes his analysis with a feeling that he may have come close to the truth, and the reader will tend to agree. Throughout the novel, the relationship between Versilov and Sof'ia Andreevna is a strange mixture of the fated and the banal.

A similar pattern may be observed in the psychology of several other characters, including even the glamorous Katerina Nikolaevna Akhmakova (see especially p. 340, ll. 17–33). The following passage establishes that the narrator is well aware of the contradiction:

Жажда благообразия была в высшей мере, и уж конечно так, но каким образом она могла сочетаться с другими, уж бог знает какими, жаждами —зто для меня тайна. Да и всегда было тайною, и я тысячу раз дивился на зту способность человека (и, кажется, русского человека по преиму-ществу) лелеять в душе своей высочайший идеал рядом с величайшею подлостью, и всё совершенно искренно.

A thirst for godliness was there in the highest degree, and of course it was so, but in what way could it be wedded to other thirsts for God-knows-what—that is a mystery to me. To be sure, it has always been a mystery and I have mar-veled a thousand times at the ability of man (and, it appears, Russian man in particular) to cherish in his soul the highest ideal side by side with the greatest baseness, all of it with complete sincerity. (P. 307)

The most obvious form of this trait appears in some paradoxical situations, such as when the hero bares his soul to his father and to Katerina Niko-laevna, yet in the same breath lies to them about his possession of the fateful document they both covet. In the hero's case, these psychological contra-dictions are revealed in many instances of inner dialogue and self-analysis.[29] In Versilov's case they are explicitly hypostatized as "the double" (*dvoinik*):

---

29. For example: "This pleased me and at the same time displeased me; I shall not ex-plain this contradiction" (p. 281). Other examples: p. 23, ll. 17–20, p. 163, ll. 34–40, pp. 222–24, p. 307, ll. 33–42, p. 358, ll. 12–18, p. 421, ll. 15–20, p. 429, ll. 1–2.

Меня ничем не разрушишь, ничем не истребишь и ничем не удивишь. Я живуч, как дворовая собака. Я могу чувствовать преудобнейшим образом два противоположные чувства в одно и то же время — и уж конечно не по моей воле. Но тем не менее знаю, что это бесчестно, главное потому, что уж слишком благоразумно. Я дожил почти до пятидесяти лет и до сих пор не ведаю: хорошо это, я дожил, или дурно. Конечно, я люблю жить, и это прямо выходит из дела; но любить жизнь такому, как я, — подло.

Nothing can break me, nothing can destroy me, nothing can surprise me. I am as tough as a yard dog. I can conveniently experience two contrary feelings simultaneously — and of course involuntarily so. But I know nevertheless that this is dishonorable, mainly because it is really too reasonable. I have lived almost to the age of fifty and I do not know to this day: is it good that I have lived to this point, or is it bad? Of course, I love to be alive, and this follows directly from the facts; yet it is base for a man like myself to love life. (P. 171)

Elsewhere, the hero explains Versilov's having joined the villainous Lambert by "the double" syndrome (p. 442, l. 33). Versilov's outrageous act of splitting Makar's holy icon in two is explained the same way (p. 410, ll. 18–32).

The entire action of the novel is marked by a glaring contradiction between intense desire and dismal failure. Intent upon becoming a Rothschild by persistent effort and iron self-discipline, the hero drifts into an idle life of self-indulgence. Versilov, whose lofty ideas inspire those around him, is mired in a meaningless and parasitic existence. Young Prince Sokol'skii cherishes his ancient nobility and dreams of returning to the land as an honest plowman. He dies in prison, having been involved in a fraudulent stock scheme. Liza, the hero's sister, who refuses to abandon Sokol'skii and insists on bearing his child, suffers a miscarriage. A whole row of minor characters follow a similar pattern. At one point the hero summarizes his experience in these terms: "Alas, all was done in the name of love, generosity, honor, and later turned out to be ugly, impertinent, dishonorable" (p. 164).

Another unresolved contradiction that permeates the novel is the opposition between a moral and an aesthetic principle. Versilov's life illustrates this contradiction most spectacularly. In the end, his attempt at starting a religious life comes to naught when his aesthetic sense is hurt by some trivial external detail of religious observance (p. 447, ll. 8–12). Even the most positive characters are affected by this contradiction. The saintly Makar Ivanovich has a weakness for the aesthetic: he is rather proud of his aristocratic name, and the quality he cherishes in the edifying stories he tells is *umilenie*, the quality of moving the listener to tears, an aesthetic rather than a moral quality.

It may or may not be intentional on Dostoevsky's part to leave all these contradictions unresolved, but they are certainly effective in creating tension and suspense. At any rate, inner contradictions are also characteristic of many of the main characters of the great novels.

The treatment of ideas in *A Raw Youth* is in line with the pattern observed in its psychology. Ideas are presented with passion, yet remain unrealized. This is true of the hero's idea to become a Rothschild—that is, to acquire freedom through isolation (*uedinenie*) and power (*mogushchestvo*). His idea is never realized; he does not even begin to take the first step to put it into action.

The socialist humanist ideal of Dergachev and his group of conspirators is utterly discredited. Vasin, the best of them, and a superbly reasonable and well-intentioned man, when arrested by the police provides the authorities with "the most precise explanations and most interesting information" (p. 451); he is released. His "notorious" manuscript turns out to be only a translation from the French. Dostoevsky lets his narrator discredit Vasin and the Dergachev group in a rather meanspirited way, it appears. Kraft, another member of the group, has become "mathematically" convinced that the Russian nation is inherently second-rate and, in desperation, commits suicide. Dostoevsky has given him a marked (German) name, though he lets him say that he is Russian.

Versilov's humanist philosophy is discredited by life itself. His belief that a humanity deprived of faith in God will get to love and cherish its neighbors to compensate for its loss is an idle fantasy. Like other rational constructs of humanist philosophy, it is subject to the second law of thermodynamics:[30]

Да зачем я непременно должен любить моего ближнего или ваше там будущее человечество, которое я никогда не увижу, которое обо мне знать не будет и которое в свою очередь истлеет без всякого следа и воспоминания (время тут ничего не значит), когда земля обратится в свою очередь в ледяной камень и будет летать в безвоздушном пространстве с бесконечным множеством таких же ледяных камней, то есть бессмысленнее чего нельзя себе и представить!

Why should I absolutely love my neighbor or your humanity of the future, which I will never see, which will not know of me, and which, in turn, will rot away without leaving a trace or memory (time means nothing here), when our Earth will, in its own turn, become an icy rock flying through airless space

30. For Dostoevsky's concern with the philosophical implications of the second law of thermodynamics, see *PSS* 17:367.

along with an infinite multitude of such icy rocks, that is, something more meaningless than anything one might imagine. (P. 49)

Here, the second law of thermodynamics is used as a metaphor for Nature's inexorable indifference to the affairs of men.

While the case for the irredeemably contradictory nature of human life is made massively and directly, the Absolute enters the text marginally and obliquely. No details of the righteous Makar Ivanovich's inner life are reported, nor are we told how he became the admirable man he is. Makar Ivanovich's tale about the reformed sinner Maksim Ivanovich Skotoboini-kov dwells extensively on his sinful life, but reports his change of heart and eventual decision to become a pious wanderer like Makar Ivanovich simply as a "miracle" (*chudo*, p. 313, l. 45). The hero's mother, a woman of the people, is a saintly character, but, like her husband, Makar Ivanovich, she is shown only from the outside. The language of these saintly characters offers no clue to their inner life.

The conflict between Dostoevsky's quest for form and his quest for expression, between his pursuit of the Absolute and his pursuit of the concreteness of real life, between psychological verity and provocation, a conflict that dominates his entire oeuvre, appears nowhere as clearly as in *A Raw Youth*.[31] More clearly than in his other major works, poignancy of expression and the concreteness of real life prevail over the ideal. The inconsistent and multifaceted, heavily marked style of *A Raw Youth* projects a world, a society, and a human psyche that are chaotic, contradictory, and indeterminate. It challenges the reader to read the text critically, to take sides, inviting approval or disapproval, sympathy or antipathy. It also makes for ambiguity and a wide latitude of interpretation, including misinterpretation of the author's intent. The constant deconstruction of the text may annoy the reader and may irritate his sense of aesthetic form.

The positive message of the novel is introduced mainly through a negation of the negative: the narrator and his characters are trying to escape the chaotic, disorderly life of which they are a part. However, the godly appears only in the background, and there seems to be no avenue to it, save a miracle. The hero himself declares that he will not be able to follow Makar Ivanovich (p. 291, ll. 23–25). Much of this is also true of Dostoevsky's great novels. Many find Raskolnikov's conversion unconvincing. The conclusion

---

31.   I am following a conception first developed by Robert Louis Jackson in his seminal study *Dostoevsky's Quest for Form: A Study of His Philosophy of Art* (New Haven: Yale University Press, 1966).

of *The Idiot* is hardly edifying, nor does that of *The Possessed* offer much reason for optimism. The future of the Karamazov brothers is a matter of conjecture.

A Raw Youth is quintessential Dostoevsky in that its style and psychology feature a consistently high level of markedness. Markedness is obtained by a rich variety of devices, among which a Bakhtinian "other voice" (*chuzhoi golos*), composed of inner dialogue and various subtexts, quotations, and literary allusions, is a major factor. More clearly than in Dostoevsky's other novels, yet typically of all of them, ambience and characters are generated by a generous, free, and often quite random accumulation of factual, psychological, and stylistic detail, rather than by a consistent development of specific traits or observance of a narrative teleology. This makes for an ever-expanding textual ambience and for tantalizingly complex characters. It invites the reader's active intellectual and emotional involvement in interpreting the text.

8

Subtext, Intertext, and Ambiguity in *The Brothers Karamazov*

A S T H E hero of Dostoevsky's first novel, *Poor Folk* (1846), walks through the streets of St. Petersburg on a cold and rainy day in September, he meets a half-naked, shivering, coughing beggar of about ten, whose mother has sent him out into the streets with a note imploring the charity of passers-by. The little beggar seems to be having little success, as most people brush him aside with harsh and cruel words. Devushkin concludes his little vignette with this observation: "Look there, he is coughing already; before long, disease, like a slimy reptile, will creep into his chest, and then, before you know it, death is going to take him, somewhere in a foul-smelling hole, with no care, no help—and there it is, his whole life! That's what life is like sometimes."[1]

We see here Dostoevsky's first hero in open rebellion against God. When Dostoevsky's last rebel, Ivan Karamazov, makes his stand, his principal charge against God's world is still that in it innocent children are allowed to suffer senselessly. In *Poor Folk,* Dostoevsky's own position is equivocal, to say the least, and the conclusion of the novel finds Devushkin once again in deep despair, facing a world that he cannot understand.[2] In *The Brothers Karamazov,* there can be no doubt as to whose side Dostoevsky is on, God's or the Devil's. Ivan Karamazov's negative argument "from design" is met

---

1.   The initial pages of this chapter coincide with my article "Turgenev and the Devil in *The Brothers Karamazov*," *Canadian-American Slavic Studies* 6 (1972): 265–71.

2.   See Chapter 2 above.

by a formidable array of counterarguments. There is the bold counterthrust in little Iliusha's meaningful and inspiring death. There is the more indirect message of the general atmosphere of the novel and of its edifying episodes, such as "Cana of Galilee." They do not cancel the fact of senseless suffering, but provide a strong counterbalance.

Perhaps strongest of all are the *argumenta ad hominem* by which the rebel himself is discredited, morally as well as intellectually. In the "Legend of the Grand Inquisitor," Ivan, who has earlier "returned his ticket" to God's world, proposes an alternative to it: a group of wise and noble men, having discovered the secret of God's nonexistence, will secure the bliss of the ignorant and believing masses by concealing the secret from them, by taking care of their earthly needs, by giving them a show of power and authority on earth as well as a false promise of eternal life in Heaven. Christ, as he appears in the "Legend," is a noble idealist who has sadly overestimated the spiritual capacity of most men. He has offered them beatitude through freedom, which most men do not even want, or which they grossly abuse.

The Grand Inquisitor, Ivan's creation, is a projection of his own innermost thoughts, and so in a sense his "double." But the Grand Inquisitor is only one aspect of his mind, his superego, one might say. After the Grand Inquisitor episode, Ivan is subjected to a devastating and unrelenting assault from many sides, until both he and his philosophy have been totally destroyed. Much of this destructive work is done through the introduction of two further "doubles," Smerdiakov and Kolia Krasotkin. But the *coup de grace* is certainly administered by the last of Ivan's "doubles," the Devil in the chapter entitled "The Devil: Ivan Fedorovich's Nightmare." Here the Grand Inquisitor is exposed as a mere front, and his creator, therefore, as a fraud. It would seem to me that this chapter not only is more than a set of variations on the "Legend," as Rozanov suggested,[3] but is actually its direct refutation. The Devil, too, is a product of Ivan's mind,[4] but he has deeper roots, is more organically a part of him, than the abstract and fictional Grand Inquisitor. It is the Devil who shows what the Russian atheist is *really* like.

What is the Devil like? Externally, he is a middle-aged gentleman with a full head of dark, graying hair and a Vandyke beard. His dress is decent,

3. V. V. Rozanov, *Legenda o velikom inkvizitore F. M. Dostoevskogo,* 3d ed. (St. Petersburg, 1906), p. 135.

4. "You are a hallucination of mine," says Ivan, "you are an incarnation of me, however, only of one side of me . . . of my thoughts and feelings, but only of the foulest and the most stupid" (*PSS* 15:72).

though slightly out of style and a little shabby. He has seen better days and may be a bit of a genteel hanger-on, living with wealthy relatives. His manners and behavior are most pleasant, exuding bonhomie, common sense, and good humor even in adversity, with a sympathetic appreciation of the "human" and all-too-human aspect of things, and a touch of sentimentality and sensitivity to the arts.[5] He has his human frailties: he is a great hypochondriac, is a little superstitious and gossipy. He tells bad jokes, and his witticisms are rather banal. But all in all he is, it seems, not such a bad sort.

His philosophy is rather what one would expect of a man of this description. He does not believe in God, but not because he is against religion. On the contrary, he would dearly like to become a believer—in fact, he would "give up all that translunar life, all those ranks and honors, just to be incarnated in the soul of a two-hundred-and-fifty-pound merchant's wife, attending Church and dedicating candles to the Lord."[6] Many a time he was within an inch of joining in the angels' "Hosanna!" But an innate skepticism and a sense of duty—who would be left to represent the necessary negative principle without which all life would inevitably come to a standstill?—has so far always prevented him from going through with it.[7] But he certainly won't exclude the possibility that some day he will! He, for his part, is perfectly willing, as soon as he has been told "the secret."[8] But in the meantime, he voices the Cartesian doubt, veers into Fichtean idealism,[9] and all along complains about the absurdity of his existence: "What about me? I suffer, and still I don't live. I am x in an indefinite equation. I am some sort of phantom of life, which has lost all ends and all beginnings, and I have actually myself forgotten, finally, what to call myself."[10]

Unmistakably, we are facing here a modern agnostic, trying rather sadly to make the most of an absurd world, where eternal, blind, senseless, and

5. "As you well know, I am very sensitive [the Russian word *chuvstvitel'nyi* means "sensitive" as well as "sentimental"] and receptive to art," says the Devil (*PSS* 15:82).

6. This particular image appears twice: 15:74, 77.

7. The Devil keeps reiterating this idea, then recapitulates it in a long tirade (15:82).

8. "The secret" is the one of which Father Zosima speaks in the passage quoted below (14:290).

9. He wonders "if all these worlds, God, and even the Devil himself . . . exist as such, or if they are perhaps merely an emanation of the *I*" (15:77).

10. Time and again, too, the Devil sadly observes that existence as he knows it is a "comedy." This squares with Turgenev's view as expressed in "Enough," where he quotes "Life's but a walking shadow." It may be mentioned that another quotation from Shakespeare that is similar in its worldview, Lear's "None does offend," is quoted by Ivan Karamazov (14:222) and in Turgenev's "Enough."

inexorable Nature is the only reality.[11] To be sure, the Devil has heard of the possible existence of an antiworld, that of God and His angels (the human world being a neutral zone, as it were, into which both parties make incursions), but this belongs to the realm of legend:[12] "No, as long as the secret remains a secret, there will exist for me two truths: one, belonging to that other world, theirs, of which so far I know nothing at all, and another, which is mine. And let me say this, as things stand now, who knows which truth is better" (*PSS* 15: 82).

And here, toward the conclusion of the interview, the Devil echoes the Grand Inquisitor's dream of a new golden age, without God. But unlike the Grand Inquisitor, he drops a hint that there may be a minor hitch: the golden age may be slow in coming. And so an impatient man may well anticipate it by adopting the principle of a godless world, "Everything is allowed," for his own private use (15: 79).

Having made this inventory, one cannot escape the impression that the figure of the Devil fits the image of a man who, in one way or another, accompanied Dostoevsky through virtually all of his adult life, Ivan Turgenev. It is safe to say that no other living man occupied as important a place in Dostoevsky's mind as did Turgenev.[13]

Turgenev's superficial bonhomie and affability, his genteel emphasis on good manners,[14] his frequent plaintive tone of hurt dignity,[15] his hypochondria and history of rheumatic complaints,[16] his sentimentality and aestheticism,[17] his cosmopolitanism and weakness for Germany,[18] his penchant

---

11.   Dostoevsky's most explicit and most powerful expression of this notion is found in Ippolit's confession in *The Idiot* (see Chapter 5 above).

12.   The notion of "antiworlds" is made quite explicit here: "So this is a strange legend, going back all the way to our Middle Ages—not yours, but ours—and no one believes it even among us, except for two-hundred-and-fifty-pound merchants' wives, meaning again not your merchants' wives, but ours" (15:78).

13.   This has been demonstrated by several scholars. See, for example, Iurii Nikol'skii, *Turgenev i Dostoevskii: Istoriia odnoi vrazhdy* (Sofia, 1921); A. S. Dolinin, "Turgenev v 'Besakh,'" in *Dostoevskii: Sbornik*, vol. 2 (Peterburg: Mysl', 1925); I. S. Zil'bershtein, ed., *F. M. Dostoevskii i I. S. Turgenev: Perepiska* (Leningrad: Academia, 1928).

14.   Though he pretends not to care, the Devil explicitly asks Ivan to, please, be more polite (15:73).

15.   For example: "My most positive feelings, such as gratitude, for instance, I am officially prohibited from expressing, solely on account of my social position" (15:82).

16.   The Devil tells his medical history at length (15:76).

17.   Cf. n. 5 above.

18.   He travels all over Europe (Vienna, Paris, Germany) seeking a cure for his rheumatism, and even writes to Count Mattei in Milan, all in vain, until finally a good German home remedy,

for the supernatural,[19] his occasional flippancy and indulgence in frivolous pastimes[20] — all these things we find in Ivan's "double." I see the only apparent difference in the Devil's exterior (he has dark hair; Turgenev, prematurely gray, was light-haired), and in the circumstance that he is described as a poor *prizhival'shchik,* a genteel sponger, whereas Turgenev was quite wealthy. But in a metaphorical sense, he was, in Dostoevsky's view, an aging hanger-on in Russian literature. If one chose to be nasty, one could have said that Turgenev was even literally a "hanger-on" of the Viardot family. However, all of the aforementioned are trivial, incidental traits. There are some serious ones, too.

The Devil's "truth" is depressingly trivial, unexciting, as he himself regretfully admits. "The truth, unfortunately, is almost always banal," he says (15: 75). Compare with this Turgenev's words from his famous lyric prose piece "Enough" (1865): "Alas! It is not ghosts, or the fantastic, or chthonic powers, that are terrible . . . what is terrible is that there is nothing terrible, that the very essence of life is petty and uninteresting, and shallow in a beggarly way."[21]

Turgenev's resigned surrender to all-powerful Nature, which he often hypostatized, appears in the Devil's *Weltanschauung* also. Specifically, one of Turgenev's favorite ideas, that of eternal palingenesis, also voiced in "Enough," appears in the Devil's notion that our very planet was born, evolved, and died billions of times, in eternally repeating cycles.[22]

The parallel is most instructive, also, with regard to the Devil's professed

---

"Hoffs Malz-Extrakt," cures him miraculously. Needless to say, the Devil knows Goethe's *Faust* well. It was, as we know, Turgenev's favorite work, from which he habitually quoted.

19. "For, like yourself, I suffer from the fantastic, which is why I like your terrestrial realism. . . . Down here I walk around, daydreaming. I like to daydream. Moreover, on earth I become superstitious — don't laugh, please: this is precisely what I like so much, being superstitious" (15:73). Turgenev has surprisingly many stories in which the supernatural plays a key role. See Eva Kagan-Kans, "Fate and Fantasy: A Study of Turgenev's Fantastic Stories," *Slavic Review* 28 (1969): 543–60. Turgenev's supernatural is always transcendent, while Dostoevsky's "fantastic" is immanent in human nature — an important difference.

20. "I am by nature kindhearted and gay, 'why, I do all kinds of vaudevilles, too' " (15:76). I have not been able to trace this quotation. It is known, however, that Turgenev wrote the text for several of Mme Viardot's vaudevilles.

21. I. S. Turgenev, *Sochineniia v piatnadtsati tomakh* (Moscow: AN SSSR, 1960–68), 9:118. The translation is my own.

22. Vol. 15:79. A little later, the Devil exclaims unctuously, after having told a dirty little anecdote: "Yes indeed, Nature, the truth of Nature, claimed what is rightfully hers!" (15:81). For the passage in "Enough," see Turgenev, *Sochineniia,* 9:120–21.

agnosticism. The point is that the Devil is not a rebel who proudly returns his ticket to God. On the contrary, he wishes he could believe, but cannot. In fact, he envies any man who has not altogether lost his faith — and seeks to corrupt him. Fifteen years before he wrote *The Brothers Karamazov,* Dostoevsky criticized Turgenev's story "Phantoms," which had just appeared in Dostoevsky's journal, *Epoch:* " 'Phantoms' — in my opinion, there is a great deal of trash in that piece: something pettily nasty, sickly, senile, *unbelieving* from weakness, in a word, the whole Turgenev and his convictions. (However, the poetry in it will redeem a great deal.)" [23]

We know that Turgenev considered his lack of faith a personal tragedy, but nevertheless persisted in his agnosticism.[24] Turgenev's pessimistic agnosticism found its most famous expression in "Enough," which Dostoevsky parodied, along with "Phantoms" and several other pieces, in *The Possessed.*[25] "Enough" presents the image of a man who, while more richly endowed by life than most, nevertheless despairs of life on account of its apparent transitoriness and senselessness. Ivan Karamazov is in the same condition. To this position the following words of Father Zosima apply:

> "Much of what is on Earth is concealed from us, but as a substitute we are given a secret mystical sensation of a living connection with another world, a lofty, higher world, and indeed, the roots of our thoughts and emotions are not here, but in other worlds. This is why philosophers say that we cannot grasp the essence of things here on Earth. God has taken the seeds of other worlds and sown them here on Earth and is growing His garden here. And all that could come up has come up, yet all that grows here lives and stays alive only through its feeling of being in touch with another, mysterious world. When this feeling weakens or is destroyed in you, that which has been growing in your soul also dies. Then you will become indifferent to life and you may actually begin to hate it. (14: 290)

There remains the question whether Dostoevsky was consciously aware of the coincidences between Ivan's double and Ivan Sergeevich Turgenev. It seems significant that Turgenev's "Enough" is explicitly mentioned in *The Brothers Karamazov:* "Enough, as said Turgenev," Mrs. Khokhlakova exclaims at one point (14:348). It seems significant, also, that the same Mrs. Khokhlakova, in a passage in which she states at some length precisely Ivan Karamazov's and his Devil's argument, again quotes Turgenev: "Well

23.   Letter to M. M. Dostoevsky, dated March 26, 1864 (*PSS* 28/II:73).
24.   See Nikol'skii, *Turgenev i Dostoevskii,* pp. 31–35.
25.   See n. 13 above.

then, I think, what if I've been a believer all my life, and then I die, and suddenly there is nothing there at all, except that 'the burdock will grow upon my grave,' as one writer put it" (14:52).

The passage in question is found in chapter 21 of *Fathers and Sons*, where Bazarov says: "All right, he will be living in a white cottage, and I'll be pushing up burdocks; well, and then what?" Mrs. Khokhlakova's quotation is fully appropriate in its context. Uncle Erosha says something similar in *The Cossacks*, but in a somewhat different context, and the verbatim correspondence with *Fathers and Sons* is closer.

Dostoevsky had introduced Turgenev in his fiction before: in *The Possessed*, of course, and perhaps also in "A Little Hero" (1857), as Konstantin Mochulsky has suggested.[26] In both instances, the image is a highly negative one. Ivan Karamazov is as close to being a projection of Dostoevsky himself as any of his characters are. We know that Turgenev was on his mind a great deal, for many years. It makes some sense that Dostoevsky would project his own loathing for Turgenev and everything he stood for upon his hero's lowest *alter ego*. It may be significant that the Devil at one point mockingly echoes Dostoevsky's very personal story of the "crucible of doubt" through which his "Hosanna" had passed. Surely Turgenev's version of agnosticism was not entirely alien to Dostoevsky.

Chapters iv and v of Book Five of *The Brothers Karamazov* have received a disproportionate amount of critical attention. To those opposed to Dostoevsky's idea, they have been the most worthwhile aspect of the novel; to those who are willing to accept *The Brothers Karamazov* as a Christian novel, they have been a serious stumbling block. M. A. Antonovich said that "the poem 'The Grand Inquisitor' provides the only poetic pages in the whole novel," a statement worthy of Rakitin.[27] On the other side, one senses wariness and outright disapproval in K. P. Pobedonostsev's reaction to "Pro and Contra." Western readers have tended to react similarly.

The foregrounding of these chapters has meant that "The Grand Inquisitor" has been read not as an integral part of the novel, but as an independent text. In fact, the position of the Legend in the structural configuration of the novel is complex. It has a contrapuntal relationship with a number of specific scenes in the novel, and specific phrases and images of the Legend are echoed in phrases and images throughout the novel. In many instances

26. Konstantin Mochulsky, *Dostoevsky: His Life and Works*, trans. Michael A. Minihan (Princeton: Princeton University Press, 1967), p. 139.
27. M. A. Antonovich, *Novoe obozrenie*, no. 3 (1883): 210–11.

a phrase in the Legend will sound familiar, and there are cases of mirroring in the opposite direction as well. For example, when Ivan suggests that the Grand Inquisitor "has joined . . . the clever people" (14:238), one immediately thinks of Fiodor Pavlovich's words when he declares himself a member of that group of "clever people sitting snug and enjoying their brandy" (14:123). In both instances "clever people" (*umnye liudi*) means "people who have discovered that there is no God" and are using this knowledge to their advantage. In the other direction, the phrase, of course, belongs to Smerdiakov: it appears in the heading of chapter vii of Book Five.

First and foremost, the Legend is a function of the character of Ivan Karamazov. As such it is an expression of Ivan's particular version of atheism, distinct from the atheism of Fiodor Pavlovich, Miusov, Rakitin, and Smerdiakov. The Legend's most important contrapuntal relationships are with chapters and passages belonging to Ivan: his synopsis of his article on Church and state in Book Two, the chapter preceding "The Grand Inquisitor," and Ivan's interview with the Devil.

It was Dostoevsky's professed intent to present Ivan's ideas merely in order to refute and to discredit them. In the process, he destroys Ivan Karamazov as a man and intellect by introducing a cleverly disguised subtext of derogatory detail. Ivan gets a proper buildup for his role: his precocious maturity, his intellectual brilliance, his early self-reliance and independence, are established even before we hear his voice. From the outset, all the positive things we hear about Ivan are undercut by a strategy that will become clear, even to the attentive reader, only much later. His intellectual ability is presented as unquestioned, but with a hint that it may be overestimated; his proud independence as praiseworthy, yet less admirable than Aliosha's humble way of accepting as well as giving kindness; his early fame as undoubted, but limited to narrow intellectual circles.

When we first hear Ivan's voice, it fully lives up to earlier advertisements: his synopsis of his controversial article makes a good impression. It takes an observer of Zosima's intuition to sense the dissonance under the smooth surface of Ivan's balanced presentation. At the conclusion of Book Two, the annoying but harmless Maksimov boards the Karamazov carriage at Fiodor Pavlovich's invitation. Ivan angrily pushes him off: a seemingly trivial incident that the reader is apt to forget. But it starts a pattern.

Over a glass of brandy, Ivan's few words and actions seem well controlled—until the ugly outburst: "One viper will devour the other, and good riddance!" Ivans smooths over the disturbance by suggesting that this was only a wish, and "as for my wishes, I reserve myself full latitude." Ironically, it is from this point on that Ivan begins to lose precisely what he defends so energetically: his "latitude" as a free individual. From here on, there will be more and more hints that Ivan's behavior is compulsive and that he is losing control of himself. In chapter v of Book Four, the scene with Katerina Ivanovna, he puts up a bold front, but we know that he will not be able to tear himself away from her.

Book Five shows Ivan at the summit of his role. His rebellion against God's world is fervently eloquent. His rejection of a God who allows innocent children to suffer has the ring of inspired invective. Ivan speaks like a prosecutor who is convinced of the guilt of the accused. He cheats a bit when he generously declares that he will limit his argument to the sufferings of children: "This will reduce the range of my argumentation about tenfold, but let it be about children only. It is so much less to my advantage, of course" (14:216). One feels that the speaker's loathing of the child abusers is stronger than his compassion for their victims, but this hardly reduces the power of his argument. The truth is, of course, that Ivan advances only his strongest evidence, leaving the more dubious aside. One has to read between the lines to realize how Dostoevsky undermines Ivan's position, as in this example:

> "And so they dragged Richard, all covered with his brothers' kisses, up on the scaffold, put him on the guillotine, and in good brotherly fashion zapped off his head after all, on account of God's grace having descended upon him, too." (14:219)

Dostoevsky does not have to say that Ivan, obsessed by his hatred of God's world and moved by his contempt for the pious citizens of Geneva, is blind to the obvious fact that God's grace had indeed descended upon the hapless Richard, who died in a state of grace.

At the end of the "Revolt" chapter, Aliosha advances the antithesis to Ivan's charges: the image and example of Christ. Ivan has anticipated this response and has prepared his counterargument: "The Grand Inquisitor." While the refutation of "Revolt" is left largely to later portions of the novel, the refutation of "The Grand Inquisitor" is largely implicit in the very ideas, structure, and style of the Legend as Ivan tells it. "The Grand Inquisitor" is an intricate web in which the unwary are caught all too easily—and Ivan is himself the first victim of Dostoevsky's stratagems. Dostoevsky once said:

> In an artistic presentation, idea and intent manifest themselves firmly, clearly, and comprehensibly. And whatever is clear and comprehensible is of course despised by the crowd. It is quite a different thing with something that is involved

and makes no sense. Why, "we don't understand this, and hence it must be profound." (*Notebooks* 1876–77, p. 610)

"The Grand Inquisitor" is composed according to this recipe: intricate, abstruse, and difficult to make sense of. However, Dostoevsky has taken care that a sensitive and attentive reader can see through Ivan's fabrication. He allows Ivan to build what appears to be an impressive argument that is, nevertheless, undermined and eventually destroyed by a counterpoint of false notes, dissonances, insinuations, and inadvertent revelations.

Ivan calls his piece a poem, but it is poetic only in those few passages that deal directly with Christ; the rest is rhetoric, in much the same style as the preceding chapter. Ivan juxtaposes his poem to the medieval Legend of the Virgin's Descent to Hell, of which he tells Aliosha with somewhat supercilious admiration. In the Virgin's forgiveness of the murderers and tormentors of her son is given a first response to Ivan's "Revolt." At the same time, the recollection of the genuine legend helps the reader to expose Ivan's pseudolegend for what it is: "A silly poem by a silly student who never wrote two lines of poetry in his life" (14:239).

The melodramatic appearance of the Grand Inquisitor, "tall and erect, with an emaciated face and sunken eyes, in which there gleams, however, a brilliance, like a fiery spark," shows up the unreal quality of this figure — one need only compare it with Father Zosima's modest and unassuming presence. Later, in Ivan's nightmare, the Devil will make fun of Ivan's penchant for romantic glamor (15:81). Anyway, the relationship between Ivan and his creation, the Grand Inquisitor, soon turns into one of romantic irony, as Ivan will alternately identify with the Grand Inquisitor and then detach himself from him and present him as a vehicle of his own ideas. He thus deprives his creation of its authoritative voice and its integrity, making it sound self-conscious, overly emphatic, defensive, and even shrill. The Grand Inquisitor's arguments, recognizably Ivan's own, are advanced intermittently and intertwiningly on several different levels.

On an anthropological level, the notion is advanced that there are two kinds of men: the superior few and the inferior many. The ideal condition for humanity is that the inferior be ruled by the superior. On a metaphysical level, it is established that there is no God. Therefore man is free. However, only the superior few know this. Inferior men have a need to believe in a higher power and are anxious to relinquish their freedom at the earliest occasion. The superior will oblige and rule them.

On a hermeneutic level, Christ's temptation by the Devil is reinterpreted as a fatal mistake on the part of Christ, who misjudged human nature when

He extended the privileges of superior men to all humans. Meanwhile, on a historical level, the Church has long since decided that Christ was wrong and the Devil right—and has acted accordingly. Finally, on an apocalyptic level, a terrible age of persecution of the Church by the frankly godless is predicted. But humanity's attempt to erect this second tower of Babel will fail, and mankind will return to the Church, which will then establish its own utopia on earth, based on miracle, mystery, and authority. The elect will know that these foundations of their rule are fraudulent, but they will bear the burden of this knowledge to make the masses of inferior humans happy.

Although these ideas are presented with great fervor, inserted into each and every one of them are details that will undermine and explode them. Ivan's anthropology is vitiated by the fact that it is self-serving, for he counts himself among the "clever people." The Grand Inquisitor has done nothing for suffering humanity. How is one to believe in a love for mankind whose only expression that we have been told of is the burning of numerous heretics?[28]

On a metaphysical level, Ivan is quite unaware of the words he himself said only minutes earlier: in the Virgin's descent to Hell, mention is made of certain sinners "whom God forgets." Ivan calls this "an expression of extraordinary depth and force." Could he be one of these sinners? Ivan credits himself, through the Grand Inquisitor, with a love of freedom, yet denounces similar feelings in others as a "mutiny" of "schoolboys"—while Aliosha's word "mutiny," applied to Ivan, still rings in his ears, and while Ivan refers to himself as "only a student." The Grand Inquisitor will not allow Christ to add an iota to what is said in Scriptures, "lest He deprive men of their freedom" (14:229), yet he is himself engaged in a conspiracy to do just that. Moreover, the Grand Inquisitor lets us know, inadvertently, that without God there is no real miracle, no real mystery, and no real authority, only a false promise and a false pretense of such. For if Christ had only made a move toward the edge of the tower, He would have naturally fallen to His death (14:233). So the Grand Inquisitor denies miracle, mystery, and authority, substituting for them magic, deception, and tyranny.[29] The whole secret of the Grand Inquisitor, says Aliosha, is that he does not

---

28.   Cf. Dostoevsky's own comment: "The Inquisitor is immoral even by virtue of the fact that in his heart, in his conscience, there could exist the idea of the necessity to burn people." *Notebooks,* 1880–1881, p. 675, first printed in *Biografiia,* 1883, p. 371.

29.   Pointed out by Roger L. Cox in his chapter on the Grand Inquisitor, in *Between Earth and Heaven: Shakespeare, Dostoevsky, and the Meaning of Christian Tragedy* (New York: Holt, Rinehart and Winston, 1969), pp. 192–214.

believe in God. In Ivan's interview with the Devil, we shall learn that such unbelief comes from weakness, not from strength.

The very words that introduce the Devil ought to be enough to put the reader on guard: "The awesome and wise spirit, the spirit of self-destruction and nonbeing" (14:229). Who wants any part of self-destruction and non-being? When the Grand Inquisitor advertises the Devil's temptation of Christ as something that "all the wisdom of the world could not equal in power and profundity," it must become clear to any reader who is not blind to the drift of Dostoevsky's argument that it leads *ad absurda*. Obviously there is nothing profound about the Devil's suggestions, for all three have occurred to everybody in one form or another. The wise man knows that the Devil, or any disciple of his, has not the power to fulfil his promises and that his disciples will likewise have to depend on fraud.

Ivan's claim that the Church has been for centuries in the hands of men like his Grand Inquisitor is based on mere speculation, as Ivan admits (14: 238–39). Aliosha indignantly rejects the assertion, even for the Catholic Church as a whole. Still, this might be one of Ivan's stronger points. Dostoevsky makes sure it remains a marginal one. Ivan's apocalyptic vision has him use the Book of Revelation to the extent that it suits his purposes. He predicts the collapse of the godless materialist utopia of "the Beast" (14:236), following Revelation 17:5, but ignores the exposure and disgrace of the Great Harlot (14:236). Ivan perverts the Book of Revelation, much as he perverts every other source he uses in "The Grand Inquisitor" (the Gospel, the Legend of the Virgin's Descent to Hell, Tiutchev, Pushkin).

All these details in the subtext of "The Grand Inquisitor" are not easily detected, but an attentive reader will catch enough along the way. Even a less careful reader will be impressed by a basic emotive undercurrent that is present in "The Grand Inquisitor" from beginning to end: the weak, lowly, wretched masses of humanity and the wise and mighty few. A steady stream of abuse is heaped upon the former, a steady flow of self-congratulatory adulation descends on the latter. The former are ultimately reduced to so much "cattle" and "geese," while the latter become "gods" (14:238), implying, "And whosoever shall exalt himself, shall be abased, and he that shall humble himself shall be exalted" (Matt. 23:12).

The physical details of the Grand Inquisitor's utopia are made to be very much like those of any socialist materialist utopia. The difference is that the socialist utopia is based on faith in a rational effort of an enlightened mankind (Rakitin's statement, 14:76), while the Grand Inquisitor's utopia is produced by an elite for the benefit of the ignorant masses and involves a sham religion:

"Receiving bread from us, they will of course see clearly that we take the bread made by their hands from them, to give it to them, without any miracle. They will see that we do not change any stones to bread, but in truth they will be more thankful for taking it from our hands than for the bread itself!" (14:235)

The suggestion that the Grand Inquisitor's utopia could survive after the socialist utopia has failed seems unconvincing. In competition with Rakitin's theory, Ivan's suffers the same fate as does his personal career: by discrediting Rakitin, he discredits himself.

When Ivan finally declares that even Christ "turned back and joined . . . the clever people," he forgets that only the day before Fiodor Pavlovich had declared himself to be precisely one of those "clever people" who have discovered that there is no God and take advantage of this circumstance. Soon Ivan will be welcomed to the circle of "clever people" by none other than the lackey Smerdiakov. In the chapters following "The Grand Inquisitor," Ivan keeps saying and doing things he did not mean to do or say. The reader suspects that he acts under a subconscious compulsion and that this compulsion is somehow linked with the person of Smerdiakov.

This pattern becomes quite pronounced in Book Eleven. We see clear indications of a split personality, as Ivan's conscious mind frantically tries to suppress the thought of Smerdiakov's and his own guilt, a thought that must be deeply implanted in Ivan's subconscious. Again, this is not made explicit, but must be gathered from between the lines. In Ivan's interview with the Devil, foreshadowed by earlier hints about a mysterious visitor, the disintegration of Ivan's personality becomes explicit and complete. From here on he is a raving madman. My point is that this pitiful condition of the once proud and self-assured atheist has been set up by an extensive subtext.

Furthermore, "an emotional atmosphere is prepared for what will be brought forth in the next book (The Russian Monk)," as A. S. Dolinin has observed.[30] If there is anything else that will strike the reader even without a careful scrutiny of the text, it is that freedom is an important and a precious thing. The Grand Inquisitor protests too loudly that men do not care for their freedom and will gladly hand it over to the elect few. By protesting too much, the Grand Inquisitor plants in the reader's mind the idea that freedom is, in spite of everything, man's greatest good. The opposite idea, that bread is the greatest good, is presented wrily, without much enthusiasm, and as even V. V. Rozanov observed, is soon undermined: the Grand

---

30. A. S. Dolinin, *F. M. Dostoevskii: materialy i issledovaniia* (Leningrad: Nauka, 1935), p. 75.

Inquisitor admits that man will abandon "even his bread and follow him who will seduce his conscience" (14:232).

Here the Grand Inquisitor's argument is truly balanced on a razor's edge. He admits the power of man's conscience only in a negative way (it may be seduced — *prel'stit'*), but he leaves the door open to a positive restatement: a man will abandon even his livelihood and follow Him who will win his conscience, Jesus Christ.

The major characters of *The Brothers Karamazov* are all theologians of sorts, not excluding even Fiodor Pavlovich and Smerdiakov. Those theologians who side with the Devil proclaim, in one way or another, that "all things are lawful," a quotation from 1 Corinthians 6:12. Those who are with God have several leitmotifs, all of which appear as a subtext more often than they are stated explicitly. The epigraph of the novel (John 12:24), quoted several times in the text, appears between the lines even more often. Father Zosima's oft-repeated principle of universal guilt and responsibility, and his joyous affirmation of life, likewise appear as a subtext throughout the novel, with many passages gravitating toward Father Zosima's words.

The theme of fatherhood and sonhood, clearly of focal importance, appears largely as a subtext related to biblical passages (Matt. 18:3, 19:14). The text of the novel features the sufferings of innocent children as *the* argument against God's fatherhood. But a concurrent subtext tells the reader that all men are really children: the vigorous and violent Dmitry is childlike, and even the old lecher Fiodor Pavlovich appears "like a child" to his murderer at the moment of his death.

The presence of the Devil as a subtext, first pointed out by Robert Belknap,[31] is reinforced by recurrent explicit references to Hell. Ivan Karamazov's behavior becomes understandable once one is aware of the Devil's presence. The fact that Ivan often uses the Devil's name in vain thus becomes meaningful, as do such details as Ivan's asking, "Am I my brother's keeper?" the words of Cain.

Other characters who are in the Devil's clutches are likewise marked by diabolic references. Fiodor Pavlovich jokes about devils who drag sinners down to hell with hooks: little does he know that the Devil's hooks already have a firm grip on him. It is significant that he puts his trust in Smerdiakov. Fiodor Pavlovich also declares to Father Zosima that he is possessed by a demon — "one of small caliber, to be sure."

Smerdiakov is the Devil's disciple all along, even as a child. He enacts black rites; he is the tempter not only of Ivan and Dmitry, but also of little

31. Robert L. Belknap, *The Structure of* The Brothers Karamazov (The Hague: Mouton, 1967), p. 105 and passim.

Iliusha. He lures Dmitry into a deadly trap, and even Fiodor Pavlovich is a pitiful figure as Smerdiakov uses the old man's lust for Grushenka to manipulate him. In the end there are some strong hints—note that all this is between the lines—that Smerdiakov may be himself the Devil. At his last interview with Ivan, he appears to the latter more like a phantom than a human being. When he begins to roll down his stocking to pull out the bundle of banknotes, Ivan is paralyzed by fear: we are not told of what. Is it fear of the cloven hoof that will show under the stocking? When the Devil finally appears in person, we will learn that he arrived precisely one minute after Smerdiakov hanged himself. No connection between these two events is indicated, but the reader cannot help sensing one. Smerdiakov remains present through Book Twelve: we hear his voice in the background of Ippolit Kirillovich's reconstruction of the murder, a circumstance that Fetiukovich registers. Ippolit Kirillovich, who believes that he is honestly performing his duty as attorney for the people, is in effect doing the Devil's bidding.

The workings of the Devil may be traced in many other scenes throughout the novel. In particular, scenes involving Father Ferapont, Rakitin, and Maksimov offer ample material. It is certainly significant that the Devil is not absent from the world of children either: Liza Khokhlakova and Kolia Krasotkin are both in grave danger, she because she is already tainted, and he because he is clearly a double of Ivan Karamazov. Could this be a part of Dostoevsky's strategy to diffuse the power of Ivan Karamazov's charge that God allows innocent children to suffer?

Needless to say, the above are only some of the instances in which the positions of the novel's characters are expressed in terms of a subtext based on religious beliefs or, more directly, in terms of biblical quotations or allusions to sacred texts. The repeated mention of the Book of Job suggests that *The Brothers Karamazov* is no more and no less than a modern version of the Old Testament theodicy. The temptation of Christ in the desert appears as a subtext throughout the novel, starting with Book One, where a good deal of attention is devoted to the question of "faith" and "miracle." As Ellis Sandoz has pointed out, the ultimate frame of reference of the Grand Inquisitor chapter and its many echoes throughout the novel is 2 Thessalonians 2:6–12, St. Paul's prophecy of the coming of the Antichrist.[32]

The main literary presence in *The Brothers Karamazov* is of course that of the Bible and religious literature at large. However, *The Brothers Karamazov* is after all a work of secular literature, and, accordingly, Russian and world

---

32. Ellis Sandoz, *Political Apocalypse: A Study of Dostoevsky's Grand Inquisitor* (Baton Rouge: Louisiana State University Press, 1971), p. 96.

literature have left deep imprints on the novel's thematics, structure, and texture.

Marcel Proust recognized in *The Brothers Karamazov* a version of the ancient myth of a crime born of hubris, and its atonement.[33] Fiodor Pavlovich's rape of Elizaveta, a ward of the community, is avenged by her son, and the innocent suffering of Dmitry finally expiates the crime. The high fence of the Karamazovs' courtyard is the physical symbol that closes the circle. Elizaveta is "lifted over the fence" as if by a demonic power to introduce her son, the avenger, into the Karamazov house. And on another night a generation later, Dmitry is caught on that very fence, trying to escape the curse of the Karamazovs.

Proust's conception squares with Viacheslav Ivanov's idea that a Dostoevskian novel is essentially a "novel-tragedy," with a tragic paradigm emerging, like a pattern in a rug, from the texture of what at first appears to be a modern social and psychological novel. Ivanov's conception implies that a certain primeval tragic theme is the nucleus of a Dostoevskian novel, that its details are, as it were, in orbit around this theme, and that the novel is structured so as to give full expression to this theme.[34]

More obvious is the paradigm of the father and his three sons, the youngest of whom is a simpleton who restores the family's fortunes. In *The Brothers Karamazov* this familiar paradigm of the folk tale is expanded into an allegory of the human condition: Fiodor Pavlovich, old Adam, carries in his lustfulness the seed of the personalities of his three sons: Ivan, whose passion is intellectual, Dmitry, whose passion is sensual, and Aliosha, whose passion is spiritual.[35] It is Aliosha's spirituality that will save the Karamazovs — that is, the human race.

Also obvious, though less important, is the allegory of the triumph of the simple soul over the "clever man," enacted in several variations in the course of the novel and ultimately valid for the whole.

Besides the dominant religious paradigms, the text also depends on some literary paradigms that support the biblical ones. Goethe's spirit of negation,

33. Marcel Proust, *A la recherche du temps perdu*, vol. 3, ed. Pierre Clarac and André Ferré (Paris: Librairie Plon, 1954), p. 378.

34. Vyacheslav Ivanov, *Freedom and the Tragic Life: A Study in Dostoevsky*, trans. Norman Cameron (New York: Noonday, 1952). See also my essay "The Metaphysics of the Novel-Tragedy: Dostoevsky and Viacheslav Ivanov," in *Russianness: Studies on a Nation's Identity* (Ann Arbor: Ardis, 1986), pp. 153–65.

35. See V. V. Zen'kovskii, "Fiodor Pavlovich Karamazov," in *O Dostoevskom: Sbornik Statei*, 3 vols., ed. A. L. Bem (Prague: Petropolis, 1929–36), 2:109.

"which always wishes evil and always does good," is sublated by an aging Devil who wishes to do good and does evil.[36] This dovetails into the paradigm of a Schillerian humanism,[37] sublated to a hymn to God by Dmitry, or deflated to a sorry egoism by other humanists, such as Miusov.

Dostoevsky took for granted that art is both a basic human need and a manifestation of the life force. Hence he also saw art as a key to understanding life's riddles. Throughout *The Brothers Karamazov*, aesthetic categories are applied to the phenomena of life — for instance, when Dmitry thus describes the story of his romance with Katerina Ivanovna: "You understand the first half: it is a drama, and it took place there. But the second half is a tragedy, and it will happen here" (14:106).

The Karamazovs' excursions into the realm of art and literature invariably lead to questions regarding the very essence of life. The antinomies and *aporiai* of the Good and the True encountered in the novel are paralleled by similar difficulties as regards the Beautiful and, in fact, emerge most clearly in the aesthetic realm. Fiodor Pavlovich's assertion that it is "not only pleasant, but even beautiful at times to be insulted," so that a man would "feel insulted for the sake of aesthetics" (14:41), Dmitry's discourse on the ideal of the Madonna and the ideal of Sodom (14:100), Ivan's anecdotes on the delights of child abuse, Liza Khokhlakova's pleasurable daydreams of crucified children and pineapple compote — all these examples from the aesthetic realm show up the problematic nature of man even more clearly than the respective examples regarding truth and justice, also present throughout the novel.

The Karamazovs are voluptuaries (*sladostrastniki,* the title of Book Three), aesthetes, and poets, whose true nature is revealed through the workings of their imagination. Fiodor Pavlovich's lubricious erotic fantasies, Dmitry's ardent declamations and "hymn of praise," Ivan's dreams of power, Aliosha's serene vision of "Cana of Galilee," and even Smerdiakov's utterly prosaic imagination reveal more about their nature than their actions. Their characters are determined aesthetically as much as morally, and perhaps more so.

What is true of the characters of the novel is true of the novel as a whole. Impressions created by hundreds of literary quotations and allusions are as

---

36. See A. L. Bem, "Faust *v tvorchestve Dostoevskogo,*" fasc. 5 of *Russkii Svobodnyi Universitet v Prage* (Prague, 1937), p. 132.

37. See D. Čyževs'kyj, "Schiller und die *Brüder Karamazov,*" *Zeitschrift für slavische Philologie* 6 (1932): 1–42.

important as plot line and philosophical argument.[38] The role of quotations from and allusions to Pushkin provides ample evidence to this effect.

The genesis of *The Brothers Karamazov* overlaps with that of Dostoevsky's most significant statement on Pushkin, his "Discourse on Pushkin." It is generally acknowledged that many motifs of *The Brothers Karamazov* can be identified in Dostoevsky's discursive prose of the period. The "Discourse on Pushkin" focuses on certain ideas that may be traced to Gogol, Belinsky, and Grigoriev: Pushkin is Russia's national poet, the first Russian to be conscious of what it meant to be Russian and thus completely at one with the Russian people, as well as the first to understand the meaning of Russian history:

> That Pushkin with his profoundly perspicacious and ingenious mind and purely Russian heart, was the first to detect and record the principal pathological phenomenon of our educated society, historically detached from, and priding itself on it, the people. He indicated and graphically set before us our negative type—the restless man, refusing to be reconciled, having no faith in his own soil and in the native forces, denying Russia and ultimately himself (i.e., his own society, his educated stratum which grew upon on our native soil), refusing to co-operate with others and sincerely suffering. (*The Diary of a Writer*, 2: 959) [39]

Furthermore, Pushkin was a prophetic genius who was the first to realize the ideal of Russia's national character, Russia's man of the future. Pushkin's poetic genius was the first manifestation of that "faculty of universal susceptibility" so peculiar to the Russian nation as a whole. The poet's intuition recreated the world, and the word, of each of the great nations of Europe, while remaining deeply Russian, an indication of Russia's role as the nation that would create a synthesis of European Christian civilization.

Like Gogol, Belinsky, and Grigoriev before him, Dostoevsky believed that great art is organically linked with a nation's historical evolution, being a manifestation of its national spirit. He saw in great poets bearers of important new ideas (*novoe slovo*). For example, Byronism is seen as an expression of "the dreadful anguish, disillusionment and almost despair" with which European man reacted to the failure of the ideas of the Enlightenment (*Diary of a Writer*, 2:939), and Pushkin is credited with having transcended Byron by finding a positive solution where Byron had seen only a void. That solution was, of course, "the truth of the Russian people."

38.   I owe a debt to Nina Perlina, "Quotation as an Element of the Poetics of *The Brothers Karamazov*" (Ph.D. diss., Brown University, 1977), for some of the material presented here.

39.   Trans. Boris Brasol (New York: Braziller, 1949).

Literary types created by great artists of the word are seen as social and historical universals in whom the destiny of a nation is highlighted and often anticipated. Dostoevsky follows Grigoriev in crediting Pushkin with a first incarnation of two types on whom both critics believe Russia's destiny to depend: Aleko, the "predatory" type, uprooted from the Russian soil, alienated from the people, yet desperately striving to rejoin them, is one. The "meek" type that finds its way back to the ideas and values of the Russian people is the other. Grigoriev often mentions Ivan Petrovich Belkin as the first incarnation of this type. In Dostoevsky's "Discourse on Pushkin," it is Tatiana, of course, who is assigned this role.

Dostoevsky's conception, while generally accepted in Russia, is open to criticism on two major points. The first is Dostoevsky's sweeping acceptance of social, national, and historical organicism. The second is his arbitrary interpretation of Pushkin, based on preconceived ideas. The deep meaning ascribed to the figure of Onegin by Belinsky, whose interpretation Grigoriev and Dostoevsky developed even further, was debunked quite properly by Pisarev. As for Aleko, he is a sketchy, vague character, and Dostoevsky's conception of him is superimposed upon Pushkin's text, rather than present in the text itself. Dostoevsky's image of Tatiana is also largely Dostoevsky's own, not Pushkin's.

Are any of these ideas reflected in the text of *The Brothers Karamazov*? Of course they are: Ivan Karamazov is the "predatory" type, alienated from the Russian people. Aliosha is the "meek" type, while Dmitry, through suffering, finds his way back to the people (his dream of "the babe"!). Aliosha stands for Russia's future. But what is Pushkin's direct role in the formulation of these ideas? *A priori* one should expect Pushkin's voice to ring out as the most authoritative in the novel's concert of voices. Actually, Pushkin *is* the most often quoted author by far, although the quotations from and allusions to Schiller and even Gogol are more massive and spectacular. Goethe or Shakespeare follows, then Victor Hugo, Tiutchev, Voltaire, Turgenev, Nekrasov, Apollon Maikov, Belinsky, Fet, and others. The various quotations and reminiscences from Pushkin draw the Karamazovs into the orbit of Dostoevsky's ideas about Russia and Russian man. Several reminiscences from Pushkin are gathered in the Grand Inquisitor chapter. Ivan's bittersweet confession that in spite of everything he still loves "those sticky little leaves" of springtime (14:210, 239) is a reminiscence of Pushkin's poem "Cold Winds Are Still Blowing" (1828). An outright quotation from Pushkin's "The Stone Guest" appears in the description of Seville at night: "The air is fragrant with laurel and with lemon blossoms" (14:227). An allusion to the Beast of Revelation 13 and 17 blends into a reminiscence of Pushkin's "The Covetous Knight":[40] "But then the Beast will crawl up to us, and lick our feet, and wet them with bloody tears from its eyes" (14:235). Scene 2 of Pushkin's play has: "Submissive, timid, bloodspattered crime / Comes crawling to my feet, licking my hand, / Looking me in the eye." The last line of the "Grand Inquisitor" has an explicit quotation from Pushkin: "And he releases him 'into the dark squares of the city'" (14:239). Like Pushkin and the "eternal Russian wanderer," Ivan loves and understands Europe, even though—with Herzen, and with Dostoevsky, of course—he perceives it as a graveyard. But being Russian, Ivan loves life, and it is Pushkin who gives him the proper words to express his feelings.

Dostoevsky finds a way to connect Aliosha to Pushkin, too. The letter that Aliosha receives from Liza Khokhlakova is obviously derived, perhaps simply cribbed, from Tatiana's letter to Onegin. Then, in Book Ten, Tatiana appears in person—through the back door, as is Dostoevsky's habit. Kolia Krasotkin, challenged by Aliosha as to whether he has actually read anything by "old Belinsky," says: "The bit about Tatiana, why she did not go with Onegin" (14:501). Kolia, who *has* read at least some of Belinsky, has not read Pushkin, however, and one senses Aliosha's pain as he establishes this fact. The implication is that Aliosha, who stands for Russia's future, has read Pushkin and reveres him.

Dmitry is initially dominated by Schiller and that poet's lofty humanism. But as Fate strikes him down in Book Eight, he moves into Pushkin's orbit. His surprising refusal to become jealous of his Polish rival is explained in terms of an aphorism from Pushkin's *Table Talk:* "Jealousy! 'Othello is not jealous, he is trustful,' Pushkin observed, and even this note is evidence of the extraordinary profundity of our great poet's mind. . . . When he saw Grushenka, Mitia would lose his jealousy, and for a moment he would become trustful and generous" (14:343–44). Then, at a crucial juncture of chapter iv, "In the Dark," a line from Pushkin's "Ruslan and Liudmila" flashes through his mind: "And naught but whispering silence" (14:353). Half an hour later he quotes Pimen's "One more last tale" (*Eshche odno poslednee skazan'e*) from *Boris Godunov*. Dmitry's eventual transfiguration into a Christian and a willing martyr is highlighted by a convict's hymn of praise, which rises heavenward from a Siberian underground mine, a reminiscence of Pushkin's "In the depth of Siberian mines" (*Vo glubine sibirskikh rud*).

As a whole, *The Brothers Karamazov* touches on themes found in Push-

---

40. See A. L. Bem, "*Skupoi rytsar'* v tvorchestve Dostoevskogo," in Bem, *O Dostoevskom,* 3:82–123.

kin's "Little Tragedies." Allusions to these are found frequently in the text. We have established that all three brothers love and quote Pushkin. What about Fiodor Pavlovich? Interestingly, Fiodor Pavlovich's contact with Pushkin coincides with an explicit quotation from Schiller (all four Karamazovs quote Schiller!). When Fiodor Pavlovich challenges Dmitry to a duel "through a handkerchief," he is quoting—perversely, to be sure—from Schiller's *Cabal and Love*. But at the same time, an elderly father's challenge to his son is a strong echo from Pushkin's "The Covetous Knight," a work to which Dostoevsky responded repeatedly (and explicitly in *A Raw Youth*). Fiodor Pavlovich is of course a travesty of Pushkin's hero, a "miser with an idea," being simply a tightfisted and selfish old man without any ideas.

Pushkin was in the 1860s and 1870s a symbol: rallying point or target of attack. To the radicals, he stood for hedonism, *l'art pour l'art*, the callous disregard of the upper class for the lot of the common people. To the radicals he was the bard of "little feet" (*nozhki*), who would begin a poem on an ostensibly civic note, only to return to those "little feet":

> *Gorod pyshnyi, gorod bednyi,*
> *Dukh nevoli, stroinyi vid,*
> *Svod nebes zeleno-blednyi,*
> *Skuka, kholod i granit—*
>
> *Vse zhe mne vas zhal' nemnozhko,*
> *Potomu chto zdes' poroi*
> *Khodit malen'kaia nozhka,*
> *V'etsia lokon zolotoi.*[41]

D. D. Minaev had parodied this poem, attacking what he saw as its mindless frivolity: *Ia ot nozhek sam v ugare / I za nikh-to noet grud': / Ved' na nashikh trotuarakh / Ikh legko sebe svernut'.* Dostoevsky comes up with a spirited antiparody, Rakitin's epigram occasioned by Mrs. Khokhlakova's sore foot:

> *Uzh kakaia zh eta nozhka,*
> *Nozhka, vspukhshaia nemnozhko!*
> *Doktora k nei ezdiat, lechat,*
> *I bintuiut i kalechat.*

41. "City luxurious, city poor, / Spirit of unfreedom, regular appearance, / Greenish-pale vault of heaven, / Tedium, cold and granite—// Still, I'm a bit sorry to have left you, / Because sometimes here / There walks a little foot, / A golden lock curls" (1828).

Ne po nozhkam ia toskuiu, —
Pust' ikh Pushkin vospevaet:
Po golovke ia toskuiu,
Chto idei ne ponimaet.

Ponimala uzh nemnozhko,
Da vot nozhka pomeshala!
Pust' zhe vylechitsia nozhka,
Chtob golovka ponimala. (15:30) [42]

What do we see? Pushkin is properly put down, a social message is introduced, and there is a touch of humor — seminarian style, of course. The
destruction of Rakitin and what he stands for is one of Dostoevsky's objec-
tives. Presenting him as utterly unworthy of Pushkin is one of the devices
by which the author makes Rakitin a hopeless vulgarian (*poshliak*). In the
semiotic system of *The Brothers Karamazov,* to be with Pushkin means to be
on the side of life, hope, and what is genuine and Russian. Anything that is
hostile to Pushkin is vulgar, shallow, lacking in life and vigor.

While Pushkin's voice is never ambiguous, the voice of Friedrich Schiller
is of focal importance to the novel's dialectic. It must be kept in mind that
Schiller was a living influence to whole generations of Russians, including
Dostoevsky, for whom he was an influence to be overcome, though not
without deep regret. When Dmitry quotes Schiller's "Ode to Joy" and "The
Eleusinian Festival," it appears that the message conveyed is unequivocally
positive. Dmitry appears to be living proof of the correctness of Schiller's
idea of the moral regeneration of mankind through the development of an
aesthetic sensibility. But, soon enough, Dmitry discovers that aesthetic sensibility is ambivalent: there is "the ideal of the Madonna," but there is also
"the ideal of Sodom" (14:100). Still, Dmitry's sensuous passion is less of an
obstacle to eventual salvation than Ivan's intellectual passion, likewise born
of Schiller's humanist ideal. When Ivan returns his entrance ticket to God's
world, he also quotes Schiller: "And so I hasten to give back my entrance
ticket. . . . It's not God that I don't accept, Aliosha, only I most respect-
fully return to Him the ticket" (14:223). Vasily Zhukovsky's translation of
the relevant passage in Schiller's poem "Resignation" reads: "The entrance

42.   "Oh, what a little foot, / A little foot a bit swollen! / Doctors go to see it, treat it, / Dress
and abuse it. // But I am not sad about the little feet, / Let Pushkin sing about them: / I am sad
about that little head, / because it does not understand ideas. // She was starting to understand
a bit, / But then that little foot spoiled it! / So let the little foot get better, / So the little head will
understand." Minaev's poem: "I am myself crazy about little feet / And it is for them that my
heart aches: / Why, on our sidewalks / It is easy to turn them."

letter to an earthly paradise / I return to Thee unopened," and the context is similar to that in Dostoevsky's passage.[43] The Grand Inquisitor in Schiller's drama *Don Carlos* is a character similar to Dostoevsky's, and he offers King Philip virtually the same alternative presented by Dostoevsky's Grand Inquisitor: freedom and personal responsibility for one's sins, or giving up freedom and ridding oneself of responsibility, which the Grand Inquisitor will assume. Many further quotations from and allusions to Schiller appear throughout the novel. At least a dozen of Schiller's works can be identified in *The Brothers Karamazov*, compared with two dozen of Pushkin's.

Goethe's presence in *The Brothers Karamazov* is less ubiquitous, but no less crucial. Ivan Karamazov's dialogue with the Devil is a response to Goethe's *Faust*, even in such details as the reversal of the meaning of "the spirit of negation," the Devil's insistence on Euclidean reasoning, and Dostoevsky's preference for the power of the Johannine Word, as against a Faustian "Am Anfang war die Tat."[44]

Thus Schiller's "aesthetic education of mankind," the romantic conception of the "negative principle" (Goethe's Mephistopheles and romantic Satanism), Gogol's famous "troika" passage, Victor Hugo's conceit of a meeting between Christ, returned to earth, and His vicar, the Pope ("La voix de Guernsey," 1867, and "Le Pape," 1878), and a multitude of other highlights of Russian and world literature are taken up, challenged, manipulated, transformed, and sublated or reversed. A literary discourse consisting of quotations, allusions, polemics, parody, paraphrases, and interpretation accompanies the plot, forming a subtext that complements the ideological message of the novel. With an erudite reader, it may in fact claim top attention. Dostoevsky's novels tend to have a literary quality, but none has it to the same degree as *The Brothesr Karamazov*. The one Russian novel that equals it in "literariness" is *Eugene Onegin*, surely no accident.

The world of a Dostoevskian novel develops in a dialectic of figures of fact and figures of fiction. It is a symbolic world for which Dostoevsky claims a higher degree of reality than outright facts possess when rationally perceived and analyzed.[45] Dostoevsky's preoccupation with details of fact is well known. The power of simple, concrete fact often becomes apparent. Dmitry, for one, struggles with the bare facts of life, which he calls *realizm*, from beginning to end. But then, too, the figure of fiction is just as impor-

---

43. The German original is not quite as close.
44. Zen'kovskii, "Fiodor Pavlovich Karamazov."
45. See n. 4 to Chapter 3.

tant, for Dmitry, as it is for everyone else in *The Brothers Karamazov*. The fiction of the open door combines with the fact of the brass pestle in the grass to convict Dmitry of a crime that he did not in fact commit, but for which he assumes responsibility in his mind.

A *quid pro quo* of fact and fiction runs through the whole novel. An imaginary 3,000 rubles are as potent a factor in the development of the plot as a real 3,000. In a display of ingenious novelistic craftsmanship, Dostoevsky introduces a whole series of details that implant in the minds of several witnesses the erroneous notion that Dmitry was in possession of 3,000 rubles the night of his father's murder. Yet nobody bothers to look for the real 3,000 rubles hidden in Smerdiakov's stocking. One wonders if Dostoevsky is not polemicizing with Immanuel Kant's famous disquisition on the difference between an imaginary 100 thalers and 100 real thalers.

This raises the question of what connection, if any, there is between truth on the one hand and "fact" or "fiction" on the other. Since Dostoevsky was convinced that art is an avenue to truth,[46] and art is part fact and part fiction, this question becomes directly relevant to Dostoevsky's philosophy of art. Early in the novel, the narrator develops a notion of what makes a man a "realist." It appears that a realist — that is, a person who sees the truth — is one who lives and thinks in terms of an immediately and intuitively given reality (14:24).[47] The opposite is, then, a "theoretician,"[48] who seeks to create and to realize a rational world of his own making. This makes Aliosha a realist and Rakitin a theoretician.

It is clear that those who pursue the truth rationally, trusting their human reason, are led into error. Truth will come to men through intuition and inspiration. The distance from the truth of each character in the novel is measured by the power and quality of his — or her — imagination.

Fiodor Pavlovich's perverse mind and amoral character would suggest that he is far from the truth. But Dostoevsky seems to have aimed at endowing him with an almost uncanny clairvoyance. Fiodor Pavlovich asks

46.   In a notebook passage Dostoevsky calls Shakespeare "a prophet sent by God" (*PSS* 11:157). He was equally convinced that Pushkin, Gogol, and he himself were prophets of the Russian nation. See, for example, *Notebooks for* A Raw Youth (*PSS* 16:329–30).

47.   Dostoevsky considered himself a "realist in a higher sense": "I have my own peculiar view of reality in art, and that which the majority calls almost fantastic and exceptional is sometimes for me the very essence of reality. The commonplaceness of events and a standard view of them is, in my opinion, not realism at all, but actually its opposite." Letter to N. N. Strakhov, February 26–March 10, 1896 (*PSS* 29/I:19).

48.   For Dostoevsky's disparaging view of theoreticians, see his 1862 article "Dva lageria teoretikov" (*PSS* 20:5–22).

Aliosha to leave the monastery only minutes after Father Zosima did. He speaks the mysterious and prophetic words, "*Da, Dmitriia Fiodorovicha eshche ne suschestvuet*" ("Yes, Dmitry Fiodorovich is not yet in existence," 14:34). As so often, his verbal clowning ("Dmitry Fiodorovich is not yet in existence," instead of "Dmitry Fiodorovich isn't here yet") leads to the utterance of a deep truth. His assessment of his son Ivan's personality is quite correct, also. He genuinely loves Aliosha and respects Father Zosima. The only person he misjudges is Smerdiakov, though he correctly recognizes the lackey's basic flaw: the man has no imagination, his sharp intelligence being entirely practical (14:115). Fiodor Pavlovich underestimates the Devil and will pay for it. He may be predicting his own fate when he projects the image of von Sohn, old lecher and victim of an obscene murder, on the "landowner" Maksimov, who is clearly his "double."

Dmitry, a man of the senses and, like his father, a raconteur and lover of women and beauty, though of a finer mold, is gifted with intuition, empathy, and imagination. His gift for language lets him utter his spontaneous impressions in palpable poetic form. He has a sense of humor and a keen ear for the false and insincere. He intuitively senses the sterility and ugliness of Rakitin's positivism. He also senses immediately when Aliosha falls into "Jesuit" casuistry, repeating in effect an argument of Smerdiakov's in trying to save his brother (15:186).

But this is not how Dmitry appears to most of those he meets. Dostoevsky does a marvelous job of presenting the discordant aspects of this character without ever making them explicit. The reader is never told that Dmitry's personality is, one might say, poorly orchestrated, or, to put it differently, that he is often out of tune. The contrast between his facial expression and his actual mood is a significant trait: "People who saw something pensive and sullen in his eyes were startled by his sudden laugh, which revealed light-hearted thoughts while his eyes seemed so gloomy" (14:63). Dmitry arrives at the monastery with the best of intentions and at first displays exemplary behavior and the appropriate volume as well as tone of voice. But within minutes he flies off the handle and produces a gamut of words and intonations that are quite unseemly in those surroundings.

Dmitry's behavior and speech just before he starts his "Confession of an Ardent Heart" are marked by effects that may well be described as "dissonant." With nobody within earshot, he insists on communicating with Aliosha in sign language: "Over the low garden fence he saw Dmitry waving violently, beckoning to him, obviously afraid to utter a word for fear of being overheard" (14:95). After the two brothers have come together, they both continue in a low whisper, until Aliosha asks: "There's no one here.

Why do you whisper?" Dmitry responds: " 'Why do I whisper? The Devil take it!' — now at the top of his voice" (14:95). Shouting secrets at the top of one's voice is not the right volume either. Dmitry has trouble finding the right volume, as he has trouble finding the right tone.

Dmitry's confession strikes our ear with a series of unexpected dissonances. We encounter the power of imaginative dissonance as Schiller's classicistic and rather tame verses are given a vigorous "change of accents" (*pereaktsentovka*). Then there is that wonderful dissonance of the sublime and the ludicrous in Dmitry's head-over-heels tumble, accompanied by a "hymn of praise" (14:99), and immediately thereafter the passage on the co-existence of the ideal of Sodom and the ideal of the Madonna — yet another dissonance.

Dmitry's confession "in anecdotes" shows his ability to imagine false notes:

> "I became spiteful. I wanted to play the nastiest swinish trick; to look at her with a sneer, and on the spot where she stood before me to stun her with a tone of voice that only a shopman could use. I wanted to say: 'Four thousand five hundred! What do you mean? I was joking. You've counted your chickens too carelessly. Two hundred, if you like, with all my heart. But four thousand five hundred is not a sum to throw away. You've gone to a lot of trouble for nothing, madam.' " (14:105)

The point is that Dmitry has a vivid enough imagination to create this "voice" in his mind, but that he also has decency enough to suppress it.

Dmitry goes on hitting false notes. He makes a big row at his father's house, with a lot of hysterical words and violent action, thinking that Grushenka is hiding in the old man's bedroom. But she was never there and never even thought of going there. All the sound and fury were for nothing.

Later, when Dmitry is waiting for Aliosha at the crossroads outside town, he decides, for some inexplicable reason, to play a prank on his brother:

> As soon as Aliosha reached the crossroads, the figure rushed at him, shouting savagely: "Your money or your life!"
> "It's you, Dmitry," cried Aliosha, surprised and startled.
> "Ha, ha, ha! You didn't expect me? I wondered where to wait for you. By her house? But I might have missed you. At last I thought of waiting here, because you had to pass here. There's no other way to the monastery. Come, tell me the truth. Crush me like a beetle. . . . But what's the matter?"
> "Nothing, Dmitry — it's just that you frightened me. Oh, Dmitry! Father's blood just now." (Aliosha began to cry. He had been on the verge of tears for

a long time, and now something seemed to snap in him.) "You almost killed him—cursed him and now—here—you cry: Your money or your life!"

"Well, what of it? It's not right—is that it? Not proper in my position?" (14:141)

Obviously Dmitry is guilty of having chosen a most inappropriate tone. He has been, so it seems, insensitive, rude, and tactless—to say the least. But once again Dostoevsky pulls him back from the brink. Dmitry goes on to explain what went through his mind just before he decided to play his prank, and we are reassured that he is a sensitive man who dearly loves his brother. A minute later there comes another example of Dmitry's "dissonant" behavior. Here is his reaction to Aliosha's report on the "duel" between Grushenka and Katerina Ivanovna:

> As the story went on, Dmitry's face became gloomy and threatening. He scowled, he clenched his teeth, and his fixed stare became still more rigid, more concentrated, more terrible. Then suddenly his savage face changed, and he broke into uncontrolled laughter. He literally shook with laughter. For a long time he could not speak. (14:142)

Dmitry goes from bad to worse in his desperate hunt for 3,000 rubles. He keeps hitting the wrong notes with predictable regularity. In his meetings with Mrs. Khokhlakova, with Samsonov, and with Gorstkov he literally plants all the clues (most of them false!) that will give the prosecutor an airtight case against him. Of these, his drunken letter to Katerina Ivanovna is the most flagrant one: it is all written on a single, drawn-out false note.

At Mokroe, especially after his arrest, Dmitry begins to hit the right notes more often. From here until the end of the novel, he says many things that are deep and heartfelt and true, and for which he has found the best possible form of expression. But his truthful words are not in concert with the best course of his defense, as to a perverted audience truth often sounds false. Moreover, Dmitry falls into a tone that must alienate his judges. It all contributes to the court's opinion of Dmitry as a negative character: a murderer and, since he denies his guilt, a liar.

But what about the reader's opinion of Dmitry? Some readers may finish the novel considering Dmitry a negative type. Of course this was not Dostoevsky's intent. Dostoevsky's presentation of Dmitry Karamazov is one of his many exercises in pushing the limit of ambiguity so far that readers are in danger of misinterpreting his intent. Dostoevsky presents a model of this risk in Ippolit Kirillovich's "reconstruction" of Dmitry's character and the circumstances that led to his crime. To be sure, Ippolit Kirillovich must operate without the many true notes that the reader is allowed to hear.

Dmitry Karamazov is thus presented as a positive type whose intuitions are basically correct and lead him to God's truth. But his character is deeply flawed. It may be said that Dmitry plays the right tune, but often plays it badly. Dmitry is a counterimage to his brother Ivan, whose intuitions are basically false and lead him away from God; but Ivan has many admirable traits. He delivers a false message, but does it extremely well. The point of Dostoevsky's painstaking efforts to bring the good and the bad in both brothers as close to a balance as possible is to show that what ultimately matters is a man's heart, while his deeds, his accomplishments, and his success in the world are irrelevant before God. The point is made indirectly, for the most part, through a subtext of false notes and inner contradictions that in Dmitry's case turn out to be minor, and in Ivan's case, decisive.

Ivan Karamazov, author of "The Grand Inquisitor," which he calls "a poem," and also of an earlier poem, "A Geological Cataclysm," and other works, is by far the most literate of the Karamazovs. His destruction as an author, which goes hand in hand with his downfall as a man, is one of Dostoevsky's main concerns. As a "poem," "The Grand Inquisitor" is undermined even from within through the introduction of false notes, melodrama, and inner contradictions, all of which together suggest that the Grand Inquisitor is no prince of the Church or glamorous Miltonic Satan, but "a silly student, who never wrote two lines of poetry" (14:239).

Aliosha is the author of Father Zosima's *Vita*. He also echoes his teacher's words and teachings throughout the novel. It is surely significant that he is susceptible to the temptations of reason, visited on him through his brother Ivan and his friend Rakitin. However, his teacher's example leads him back to the truth of God. Aliosha is a youth of delicate sensitivity, which he displays in his dealings with children. But he also has a vivid imagination, which shows in his response to Ivan's arguments. Aliosha has the rare gift of empathy with people of all characters and tempers.

Like the Karamazovs, many characters of lesser importance are determined very largely by the products of their respective imaginations: Grushenka by the story of her first love, clearly embellished by her, and by her tale of the onion, but also by the way in which she outduels her rival in the chapter "Both of Them Together"; Katerina Ivanovna by her perverse dream of a life devoted to saving Dmitry; Liza by her fantasies, alternately sweet and cruel. Some characters we know virtually from their fictions only: Maksimov and Father Ferapont, for instance.

We know Dmitry's prosecutor, Ippolit Kirillovich, and his defender,

Fetiukovich, almost exclusively through the products of their imagination. The former is an honest man and nobody's fool. But he is a positivist and a believer in psychology as an exact science and has an ordinary imagination. The prosecutor's version of what happened the night of the murder is, however, based on two fictions: Grigory's honest mistake about the open door, which was actually closed, and Smerdiakov's clever insinuations. The prosecutor also ignores a key fact that speaks in Dmitry's favor: the discrepancy between the amount of money found on Dmitry and the balance between the stolen 3,000 rubles and the money Dmitry spent.

Ippolit Kirillovich believes that he can expose each statement made by the accused as a clumsy fiction, and demolish it by the logic of his own version. In fact, though, everything Dmitry says is true, while the prosecutor's version is false. In particular, the prosecutor fails to see that the screw of psychological analysis can always be given another turn: Dmitry's fumbling may be evidence of his guilt, but it also may be evidence of his innocence, for an innocent man might blunder and fall into a trap that a guilty man, who would be on his guard, would see. In fact, Dmitry's vivid imagination creates evidence against him; for instance, he blurts out that the money was under his father's pillow—which he could not have known unless he was the murderer (14:416). Ippolit Kirillovich simply underestimates the complexity of human nature. He is satisfied when he has proved Dmitry's story to be absurd, forgetting that the truth is sometimes absurd (15:142).

The narrator's condescending attitude toward Ippolit Kirillovich suggests that the townspeople find him a nice enough, but somewhat limited, person. Yet, against all expectations, he triumphs over the redoubtable Fetiukovich. He never suspects that he has convicted an innocent man. It is a bit of a surprise that Ippolit Kirillovich expresses many ideas that we know were Dostoevsky's own. Dostoevsky was, like Ippolit Kirillovich, a believer in Holy Russia, "her principles, her family, everything she holds sacred" (15:150). Ironically, these principles are upheld by the conviction of an innocent man.

The defender Fetiukovich is the exact opposite of Ippolit Kirillovich. He has his facts right. He can see through Smerdiakov. With perspicacity and intuition, he reconstructs almost the entire course of events as they actually happened. He knows that he is skating on thin ice and skillfully slurs over the more dubious steps in his argument. Fetiukovich says outright that the prosecutor's version of the events is open to the very same charge he had made against Dmitry's version—namely, that it is a fiction: "What if you've been weaving a romance and about quite a different kind of man?" (15:158–59). Fetiukovich reminds his opponent that one's image of another person is necessarily a fiction, and that the real question is: how close is this fiction to the truth? He sarcastically calls the theory by which the prosecutor had tried to prove premeditation on Dmitry's part "an entire edifice of psychology" (15:161), and promptly demolishes it. But he will not deny that his own version is a fiction, too. In fact, he will boldly admit that it is just that (15:166–67). The fact of the matter is that Fetiukovich's version happens to be true.

Fetiukovich is called an "adulterer of thought." His liberalism is clearly odious to the narrator (and to Dostoevsky). Moreover, there is reason to believe that he thinks Dmitry is really guilty. When he swears "by all that is sacred" that he believes in his client's innocence (15:166), he is probably perjuring himself. And, last but not least, he loses his case, as the "jury of peasants" chooses to believe Ippolit Kirillovich.

In some ways the duel between Ippolit Kirillovich and Fetiukovich may be seen as an allegory of Dostoevsky's effort in *The Brothers Karamazov*. It was his swan song, much as Ippolit Kirillovich's oration was his. But then, too, like Fetiukovich, Dostoevsky pleads a difficult case in which the odds seem to be against the accused. The accused is God, and the charge is that He has created a world in which injustice and the suffering of the innocent are allowed to prevail. Like Fetiukovich, Dostoevsky pleads his case with skill and eloquence, and is not above an occasional *argumentum ad hominem,* slurring over inconvenient details, and discrediting the witnesses for the prosecution. Especially the latter: Dostoevsky makes sure that the reputation of every atheist in the novel is destroyed.

Could it be that Dostoevsky, like Fetiukovich, does not believe in the truth of his version of the case? This is immaterial, for all practical purposes. Fetiukovich does his best to save Dmitry. Nor is it his fault that the accused is found guilty: a conscientious and unbiased jury should have found him not guilty. Similarly, Dostoevsky certainly wants God to prevail and does his best to ensure that He does. Still, Dostoevsky will lose his case with most readers. Like Dmitry's jury, they are biased, biased against God. Or, better, like Dmitry's jury, they lack the imagination and empathy to follow Dostoevsky's intricate metaphysical argument.

At any rate, Dostoevsky assigns the voice of truth to the man with the greater imagination — that is, to the artist; and he does so regardless of the man's moral qualities. He also lets a jury of honest peasants reject the truth. The moral of the tale, then, is that an honest but pedestrian mind is prone to deep error and acts of grave injustice. It is Grigory, a righteous and devout but also obtusely unimaginative man, who gives the false evidence that convicts Dmitry. To attain truth requires imagination, empathy, and intuition.

Ippolit Kirillovich tries to put Dmitry down, saying: "To be sure, we are poets" (*PSS* 15:144). The irony backfires. Not only is Dmitry a poet, but he also knows, by now, more about the truth of life than the pedestrian prosecutor ever will. In the world of *The Brothers Karamazov,* everybody knows his or her measure of facts, and everybody must create his or her own fiction of the world. The poet's fiction is closest to the truth. The less a person is a poet, the farther he or she is from the truth. It is Smerdiakov, the devil's disciple, who advances the Russian nihilists' arguments against poetry (14:204). Rakitin's anti-Pushkin polemic serves the same purpose. All and sundry nonpoets and antipoets are hopelessly removed from the truth as Dostoevsky sees it, as well as blind to the truth in the Karamazov murder case.

This forces us to return to Fiodor Pavlovich, an atheist and an evil man, who is, however, by no means bereft of intuition, imagination, and aesthetic discrimination. A frank sensualist, Fiodor Pavlovich reverses Pascal's wager, suggesting that it is foolish to renounce life's sinful pleasures for the sake of a belief in a nonexistent God, an afterlife, and retribution (14:122–23). Where does this put him in Dostoevsky's strategic plan? Fiodor Pavlovich wins his bet if there is no afterlife or, as Fiodor Pavlovich puts it, no devils dragging sinners down to Hell with long hooks. Since the outcome of the wager is determined by faith, Dostoevsky does the one thing he can do to discredit Fiodor Pavlovich's position: he makes him a nasty person and lets him come to a bad end. Yet his artistic tact makes him give due respect to the inveterate sensualist's philosophy. Fiodor Pavlovich is not nearly as despicable a character as Rakitin, or even Miusov. He has a touch of the poet. He is allowed to die almost happy, expecting Grushenka. He will be remembered by the last words he may have written, or thought: "*I tsyplionochku*" ("and my little chick"), added as an afterthought to the note on the envelope with 3,000 rubles and the legend: "A treat of 3,000 rubles for my angel Grushenka, if she wants to come" (14:410).

Throughout *The Brothers Karamazov* we find comments on the art of fiction in general, on various pieces of fiction introduced in the text, and on the novel at hand. The narrator's prefatory statement suggests that "the main novel is the second," a novel yet to be written. While enough is said in the text of *The Brothers Karamazov* to indicate that Dostoevsky did in fact intend to write a sequel, this and other references to the "second novel" relate to an unknown and unknowable entity as far as the reader of *The Brothers Karamazov* is concerned. "The second novel" is a fiction yet to be created and hence as indeterminate as life itself.

It seems odd that the narrator identifies his work as a novel (*roman*), abandoning the veracity topos used, for example, by the chronicler of *The*

Possessed. In fact he occasionally presents himself to the reader as the author of a work of fiction and even discusses novelistic strategy. His chapter titles, in particular, remind the reader that he is reading a piece of fiction. The narrator also provides the reader with bits and pieces of an internal commentary regarding the style of narrative passages he has introduced. Aliosha's summary of Father Zosima's last discourses to his disciples is said to be "incomplete and fragmentary" (14:293). Dmitry's pathetic or funny effusions are accompanied by a continuous ironic commentary. When the prosecutor says: "Perhaps I am exaggerating, but it seems to me that certain basic features of our educated class are reflected in this family picture" (15:125), this is implicitly a comment on the whole novel. When Ippolit Kirillovich exclaims: "But we, so far, only have our Karamazovs!" this may be read as a coded self-apotheosis of the novel, its message, and its author.

With all the false leads, backtracking, falsehoods that are revealed to be true and vice versa, as well as the fact that we leave the novel with the fate of all three brothers still undecided, the notion emerges that any form of human truth (legal, psychological, empirical) is irrelevant to the absolute truth, which is God's. A flagrant miscarriage of justice reveals God's truth to Dmitry. In the Epilogue, if only for a brief moment, "a lie becomes the truth" for Katerina Ivanovna, the person who, of all the characters in the novel, is the least gifted in seeing the truth. Yet the fact remains that some men and women are closer to God's truth than others.

Granted, then, that every human effort to reach the truth is a work of fiction based on highly insecure facts, which is more important in this effort: realistic detail or "grand invention as a whole," as Ippolit Kirillovich puts it (15:149)? Fetiukovich states the dilemma in his summation: "What troubles me and makes me indignant is that of all the mass of facts heaped up by the prosecution against the defendant, there is not a single one that is certain and irrefutable" (15:162). The answer to this question, implicit in the entire text of the novel, is that both elements are inseparably linked. The whole is always more than the sum of its parts, and it takes intuition to grasp it. The flawed details of the prosecutor's fiction destroy his whole conception. Fetiukovich's intuitive grasp of every detail produces the truth of the whole.

The inevitable corollary of all this is that in his search for truth, man needs to be not only sincere, but also gifted with an artist's intuition and imagination. The malodorous sinner Fiodor Pavlovich Karamazov has imagination and is therefore potentially closer to the truth of God than the pedestrian Miusov, a man of proper conduct and undoubted honesty. What makes Rakitin such a contemptible and worthless person is first and foremost the fact that he has absolutely no imagination and cannot even understand a joke, as Dmitry observes. Katerina Ivanovna stumbles from one falsehood to another, betrayed by a total absence of real intuition. It also seems that the power of a person's imagination is proportional to his or her capacity for love, erotic or spiritual. But this is a different question.

Appendix

Bibliography

Index

APPENDIX: HOW MUCH DOES DOSTOEVSKY LOSE IN ENGLISH TRANSLATION?

Poetry has been defined as that which gets lost in translation. Substituting "verbal art" for "poetry," as in German *Dichtung,* one faces the same challenge in a prose work. Certainly the elements of poetry—mythos, logos, pathos, ethos, and melos—are applicable to many works of prose fiction as well as to poetry. However, their relative importance is hardly the same. Melos, in particular, is vastly more important in poetry, though it may play a major subsidiary role in a prose work.[1] It is almost impossible to duplicate it in translation.

Both poetry and prose fiction have a syntagmatic and a paradigmatic dimension. The latter tends to appear more clearly in poetry. The various forms of repetition, parallelism, contrast, gradation, and climax are more readily detected in a poem, but also tend to pose greater difficulties to the translator of prose fiction, as they are easily overlooked in a long text. In a poem, every word and every sound are, at least presumably, significant. In a prose work, a certain randomness is taken for granted, though any given work, or even any given phonic or rhythmic element, may be significant.[2] It is the translator's task to identify such instances.

A translation, like its original, is addressed to a reader. The reader of a translation is, as a rule, different from the reader of the original. Faithfulness to the original may very well clash with considerations regarding the readers of a translation. The translator, of course, is a reader before he (or

1. "The Overcoat" in Boris Eichenbaum's interpretation is a case in point.
2. Anybody familiar with classical rhetoric will attest to this.

she) becomes a translator. A conscientious translator will not start his work before having read the whole work, perhaps repeatedly. His reading of the text is informed by insights into the work's syntagmatic and paradigmatic structure. In some instances the translator may have an advantage over the author, since he starts his work with a conscious understanding of its significance and structure, which may not have been the case with the author. Furthermore, the translator is often assisted by the interpreters, commentators, and critics who have preceded him as readers of the text.

This chapter pursues a dual purpose. It tries to establish what is retained and what is lost in a good translation of *The Brothers Karamazov*. It also tries to assess the importance of elements lost in translation and to find in them a measure of Dostoevsky's art: the untranslatable "poetry" of his work. I compare two translations, both excellent: a relatively free one and one that is as close to the original as seems possible. The former is the Constance Garnett translation, revised by the late Ralph E. Matlaw (New York: W. W. Norton, 1976), and the latter is by Richard Pevear and Larissa Volokhonsky (San Francisco: North Point Press, 1990). A comparison of these translations raises some semiotic and aesthetic questions.

The Brothers Karamazov is a text apparently more complex than most. It has a personalized narrator, clearly distinct from the implied author, and a large number of long sections composed in other voices: "The Grand Inquisitor" chapter, "From the Life of the Hieromonk and Elder Zosima," Grushenka's "The Tale of the Onion," and many others. Dialogue involving socially and individually distinct voices dominates the text. A religious, philosophical, and moral argument is developed alongside the novel's plot. It involves an intertextual polemic with Dostoevsky's ideological opponents. A symbolic religious subtext accompanies the entire text. A very large number of biblical and literary quotations, references, and allusions will be recognized by a well-read reader. Intratextual patterns of repetition, parallelism, and symbolic correspondences appear throughout the text.

The mimetic aspect of the text poses some serious problems to the translator. Because of the differences between the society in which the action is set and the translation's readers, some terms may distort the original's meaning if translated literally.[3] Similarly, the mythology that Dostoevsky

3. All references to the Russian text are to *PSS* 14 and 15 of the Academy edition (Leningrad, 1976). Some examples: *iurodivyi* (14:20, l.27): "religious eccentric" (Garnett), "holy fool" (Pevear); *seminarist:* "divinity student" (Garnett), "seminarian" (Pevear); *prostoi narod* (14:299, l.45): "peasants" (Garnett), "simple people" (Pevear); *meshchanka* (15:90, l.44): "common woman" (Garnett), "tradeswoman" (Pevear).

assumes his readers are familiar with is at times wholly unknown to the reader of the translation, and something comprehensible must be substituted.[4] More serious are the problems involved in the social, psychological, and moral delineation of the novel's characters. There are characters who belong to the educated class: intellectuals (Ivan Karamazov), government officials, middle-class landowners, genteel ladies, and the semieducated Dmitry Karamazov. A German doctor's strangely fractured Russian, schoolboy jargon, and the broken Russian of two Polish characters provide a further challenge. Other characters belong to the uneducated classes and speak their language: merchants, peasants, the semiliterate peasant Trifon Borisych, Grushenka and other women of the people, the semiliterate servants Grigory and Smerdiakov, some semiliterate monks. Ecclesiastical speech plays a major role. The monks in the novel may be educated (Father Zosima and some others), semieducated,[5] or uneducated.[6] A perversion of ecclesiastical diction appears in the language of the seminarian Rakitin.

The language of the narrator, an educated local resident with roots in the community, and that of the other members of his class (Fiodor Pavlovich Karamazov, the "landowner" Maksimov, various government officials, lawyers, etc.) poses few problems, for it has an equivalent in English. (Individual traits will be discussed later.) The same is true of the language of the intellectuals: Ivan Karamazov, Miusov,[7] even Aliosha Karamazov, a well-educated young man. The schoolboy slang of Kolia Krasotkin, Dr. Herzenstube's grammatically correct but wooden Russian, and the Russo-Polish of Musiałowicz and Wróblewski are difficult to translate, but are of minor importance.[8]

The ecclesiastical strain in the novel's language poses a huge problem, largely due to the fact that Church Slavonic coexists with the Russian vernacular, though distinct from it, allowing subtle discriminations: *zhitie,* "*vita,* sacred life": *zhizn',* "life"; *lik,* "God's, man's spiritual face": *litso,* "face"; *perst,* "finger" (in its sacred function): *palets,* "finger"; *lobyzanie,* "kiss"

---

4.   The legend that has a *iurodivyi* throwing rocks at the church, because the devils are outside, unable to get in, but crossing himself in front of the pothouse, where he sees all the guardian angels anxious to protect their charges (14:73, ll.21–22), familiar to a Russian reader, has to be changed in translation.

5.   The young monk who escorts the party to the hermitage in Book Two.

6.   Father Ferapont and the visitor from Obdorsk.

7.   Miusov's Frenchified verbiage is made fun of: he pursues a lawsuit with the local "clericals" (14:10, l.46).

8.   For example, 15:102, l.44 (Dr. Herzenstube), 14:463, ll.16–17 (the Poles).

(in its ritual function): *potselui*, "kiss"; *izreki*, "say" (a word of sacred import): *skazhi*, "say"; *slovesa*, "sacred words": *slova*, "words"; *pokrov*, "divine assistance": *pokrovitel'stvo* "protection"; *uspenie*, "dormition, passing on": *smert'*, "death"; and many others. The English translation inevitably misses these nuances. A Slavonic phrase will directly mark itself as belonging to the sphere of religion, or give the occasion an air of solemnity.[9] It may also signal irony or blasphemy, when coming from the mouth of Rakitin or Fiodor Pavlovich.[10] In some sections of the novel it has a mimetic function, as when the action moves to the monastery.[11]

The Slavonic strain appears in different combinations. In Father Zosima's speech it combines with the somewhat archaic Russian of the late eighteenth or early nineteenth century, the age of Sentimentalism. In Father Ferapont it combines with the earthy language of a peasant.[12] In Rakitin, it is travestied by being mixed with seminarian slang and progressive jargon.[13]

9. The fifth chapter of Book Two is entitled *Búdi, búdi!*—"So be it! So be it!" The accent mark identifies the verb as a Slavonic imperative (the Russian form is *bud'*, and *budí* means "awaken"). *Búdi, búdi* are the words with which Father Zosima concludes his discourse on the role of the Church in leading humanity to the Millennium (14:61, ll.35–36).

10. Such as when Fiodor Pavlovich introduces Slavonic words into a description of an obscene murder in a brothel (14:81, ll.44–46), or when Rakitin, a godless blasphemer, turns out to be the author of a vita of Father Zosima, with a title in Slavonic, of course (15:100, l.11).

11. As in chapter i of Book Seven.

12. Peasant vernacular will appear side by side with Slavonic, even in the same sentence: *Blagoslovliaia da blagoslovishisia, sadis' podle. Otkuleva zaneslo?* (14:152, ll.29–30).

13. Clearly, Dostoevsky is out to show how "progressives" like Rakitin destroy the Russian language. Rakitin's speech is an ugly mixture of intellectual clichés, progressive jargon, seminarian slang, vulgarisms, intentional catachresis, and journalese. Some examples: *vsegdashnie blagogluposti* (14:73, l.7), where *blagogluposti* is a seminarian's combination of a Slavonic *blago* and a Russian *gluposti;* Garnett translates "the usual holy mummery," Pevear "the usual blessed nonsense." Rakitin predicts that Ivan *Katerinu Ivanovnu priobretiot* (14:75, l.34), which Garnett translates "will carry off Katerina Ivanovna," Pevear "will acquire Katerina Ivanovna," the latter being accurate—Rakitin makes a point of abusing words. Rakitin calls Grushenka (who happens to be his first cousin) a *publichnaia devka* (14:77, l.44), which is not only a gratuitous insult, but also vulgar and bad style: *publichnaia zhenshchina* (literally "public woman") was the legal term for "prostitute," *devka* is a vulgarism meaning "wench." Rakitin succeeds in combining the vulgar with the official. Garnett's "common harlot" and Pevear's "loose woman" are both off the mark. Dmitry, sensitive to language, notices that Rakitin uses the verb *lakomstvovat'* as a euphemism for *p'ianstvovat'*, "to carouse"—"relishing" instead of "drinking" (Pevear), "indulging" (Garnett); the point, however, is that Rakitin's creation is a hideous abortion. Rakitin likes to show off his sophistication by using foreign words: he says *profit* (14, 319:38), a needless Germanism, when a good Russian word is available. Rakitin has a way of perverting a good word. "Man of God" is Aliosha's epithet, after his patron saint. Rakitin calls

The language of the uneducated appears in several variations: the merchant Samsonov's,[14] the peasant entrepreneur Trifon Borisych's,[15] the pious old servant Grigory's,[16] the lackey Smerdiakov's,[17] and Grushenka's, the last being the most interesting and the most difficult to translate. Grushenka, a woman of the people, observes the proprieties when entering the sexual sphere: her euphemisms belong to the folk culture.[18] She is close to the world of folk culture, using words that immediately mark her as "of the people."[19] When she is coarse, it is also in the manner of the uneducated.[20] She likes her diminutives, a trait of "substandard" speech.[21] All this, together with the fact that Grushenka tells a folk tale ("The Onion"), is significant: the novel's heroine and positive image of Russian womanhood belongs to the people, not to the educated class. In contrast to Grushenka's vigorous folksiness, Katerina Ivanovna's finishing school Russian seems bookish and awkward, while Mrs. Khokhlakova's mannered and somewhat Frenchified

---

him *Alioshen'ka, bozhii chelovechek* (14:321, l.30), "little man of God." These examples are easily multiplied. Most of the points Dostoevsky makes are lost in translation.

14. For example, 15:71, ll.8–9.

15. For example, 14:450, ll.34ff.

16. For example, 14:86, ll.10–13, 14:129, l.36.

17. For example, 14:247, l.12, 14:118, ll.24ff., 14:120, l.24, 14:204, l.27, 15:59, ll.32ff.

18. In her encounter with Katerina Ivanovna, Grushenka threatens: *A vdrug domoi pridu i pozhaleiu ego — togda chto?* (14:139, ll.27–28). Garnett translates, "I feel sorry for him," and Pevear, "I take pity on him," which is literally correct, but misses the formulaic *double entendre* of *pozhaleiu.* A woman of the people, Grushenka vacillates between sexual levity, as in the preceding example, and outright rejection of erotic love as shameful. She wishes that someone would love her *ne za odin tol'ko sram* (14, 323:32), which Pevear translates "not only for my shame," trying to stay close to the original, and Garnett "not only with a shameful love," neither quite catching her euphemism. When speaking of sex, Grushenka calls it *za khudym etim delom priiti* (14, 320:24), which Pevear again translates literally, "come for that bad thing," and Garnett as "coming with any evil purpose" (badly off the mark).

19. For example, she addresses her rival as *dostoinaia baryshnia* (14:138, l.3) — neither "excellent young lady" (Garnett) nor "worthy young lady" (Pevear) places Grushenka as clearly with the people as the Russian expression does. Elsewhere, Grushenka comes up with a cute folk etymology: *kapital kopit'* (14:320, l.43), as if *kapital* were derived from *kopit'*, "to save."

20. To insult Katerina Ivanovna, she says: *Sami vy devitsei k kavaleram za den'gami v sumerki khazhivali* (14:140, ll.25–26) — "You yourself as a young girl used to go to your gentlemen at dusk to get money." (Pevear tries to catch the coarse *k kavaleram* by adding a "your" to "gentlemen.") Also, "as a young girl" fails to get the venom of *devitsei*, which is "young girl," but also "virgin," suggesting that she no longer is one.

21. For example, *liubila ego chasochek* (14:329, l.13), "loved him for one little hour," where *chasochek* is a double diminutive from *chas*, "hour."

speech (with a pretense of intellectual sophistication) veers on the silly. Both are captured reasonably well in both translations. Grushenka's speech, however, poses serious difficulties.

The most difficult of all characters for the translator is Dmitry Karamazov. He is not wholly uneducated, but his vocabulary is behind the times: he says *efika* instead of *etika* (*PSS* 15:27, l.39) and uses foreign words such as *privilegiia* (15:31, l.20) or *shef* (15:32, l.4), where a contemporary educated Russian would have chosen a native word. He often has to find his own words to express an idea.[22] Dmitry is also a poet, who often comes up with puns and witticisms.[23] His lyric effusions have a certain rhythmic quality that is difficult to capture in translation.

The number of biblical and literary quotations and allusions in *The Brothers Karamazov* is very large. While the former are readily captured in translation, the latter, being mostly Russian, will be lost to the English reader, who will have to be told of the echoes from Pushkin, Gogol, Turgenev, Herzen, Saltykov, Nekrasov, Maikov, and others in footnotes.[24] Some of these allusions have an intratextual dimension: the repeated association of the frivolous Mrs. Khokhlakova with progressive writers (Turgenev, Saltykov) or the allusions to progressive writers and ideas by Ivan Karamazov and their travesty in remarks by Kolia Krasotkin, a precocious thirteen-year-old.

Labels and leitmotifs play a certain role in the novel. Aliosha is "man of God," epithet of the hero of a spiritual rime, or "angel." Maksimov is the "landowner" (ironic, since he has not owned any land in some time): Garnett uses "gentleman" instead of "landowner" on occasion, Pevear stays with "landowner" throughout. Grushenka's label is her link with the folk culture, but so is the word *tvar'*, "creature," applied to her repeatedly by others and finally by herself,[25] a fact Garnett misses, while Pevear observes it

22. He calls Grushenka an *infernal'nitsa* (14:143, l.1). He calls his brother Ivan a *sfinks* (15:32, l.1). When he expounds his philosophy to Aliosha (15:31, ll.45ff.), he does so vigorously, but entirely in his own words.

23. For example: *Silen—silen* (14:98, l.16), which Pevear tries to duplicate by "Silenus—silent"; *podlyi—podlaidak* (14:398, l.9)—quite untranslatable; *ne to chto zhdal, a zhazhdal* (15:27, ll.18-19), "I wasn't merely expecting you, I've been thirsting for you" (Pevear). The pun (*zhazhdal,* "thirsted" is made into a derivative of *zhdal,* "waited") is quite untranslatable.

24. Some examples: Tiutchev (14:423, ll.3-14); Turgenev (14:348, ll.38, 14:52, l.14); Saltykov (14:350, ll.12-26); Gogol (14:381, ll.16-24), Pushkin (14:74, l.23). There are many more.

25. See 14:68, l.30, 14:140, l.23, 14:320, l.13 (here Garnett translates "wretch," while Pevear stays with "creature"). An intratextual echo may be observed between *sozdanie,* "(heavenly) creature," used by Katerina Ivanovna early in her meeting with Grushenka (14:136, l.13), and *tvar',* when the rivals clash. Here, Garnett stays with "creature," while Pevear translates "being."

consistently. Rakitin is labeled by his ugly, graceless, and styleless language. By and large, these "labels" pose no insurmountable problem to the translator, once recognized as such.

Some leitmotifs pose difficulties. Father Zosima's *za vse i vsia,* "for all and for everyone," expressing the universal and mutual responsibility of man for all creation, is echoed throughout the text. In the Russian text it stands out and is remembered because of its Slavonic grammar (in the vernacular, "for everyone" is *za vsekh,* actually used by Dmitry, 14:372, l.19). Another leitmotif, *nadryv,* with its verbal equivalents *nadorvat'* (past passive participle *nadorvannyi*), also poses a problem. Garnett's "laceration" does not pursue it consistently, losing it as a leitmotif. Pevear uses "strain" consistently, but "strain" is less expressive than *nadryv,* derived from *rvat',* "to tear," with the prefix *nad-,* "over." [26] *Umnye liudi,* a persistent leitmotif introduced by Fiodor Pavlovich and then repeated by Smerdiakov, Ivan Karamazov, and Rakitin, is recognized as such by both translators, Garnett translating "clever people," Pevear "intelligent people." [27] Dmitry's *ditio* is translated as "the babe" by Garnett, as "the wee one" by Pevear, the latter perhaps more effective (*ditio* is a striking and memorable dialect expression, as is "the wee one"). The Devil's presence is a leitmotif that emerges clearly as the novel moves along. Having failed to recognize this, Garnett has translated some occurrences of "the Devil!" with other expletives. [28] Pevear has kept the Devil in the text throughout. Some other leitmotifs are less striking, but still must be observed: *zemlia,* "earth"; *vor,* "thief" (Dmitry's preoccupation!); Grushenka's *chasok,* "short hour."

The Brothers Karamazov has a personalized narrator. Duplicating his idiosyncratic style is not easy. To begin with, there are those "word-tics," words used with extraordinary frequency and often pleonastically or even somewhat beyond their dictionary meaning. Such are *dazhe, slishkom,* and *vdrug.* [29] They are not always picked up by the translator. Another striking trait of narrative modality is a clearly excessive use of indefinite pronouns and adverbs. [30] Other traits that make for a show of homespun amateurish-

26. For example: *No est' gore i nadorvannoe* (14:45, l.11) — "But there is grief also that is strained" (Pevear), and "But there is also a grief that breaks out" (Garnett), where the former pursues the leitmotif, the latter the exact meaning.

27. See, for example: 14:123, ll.19–20, 14:238, ll.18–19, 14:254, l.36, 15:29, l.10.

28. For example: *E, chort* (14:247, l.32), "Confound it!"

29. See Gleb Struve, "Notes on the Language and Style of Dostoevsky," *Bulletin of the International Dostoevsky Society,* no. 7 (1977): 76.

30. One example will illustrate this point: *No vsio-zhe kak by luch kakoi-to svetloi nadezhdy blesnul emu vo t'me* (14:394, ll.46–47). Garnett: "Yet a ray of bright hope shone to him in his

ness are occasional overstatements, pleonasms, awkward syntax or choice of words, unexpected noun-adjective combinations, and quirky phraseology.[31] All of these traits tempt the translator to improve on the original. Garnett often yields to this temptation; Pevear tends to be more literal.

The homespun quality of the narrator's language is underscored by the use of many idiomatic and proverbial expressions.[32] The use of idiomatic expressions enhances certain traits of the characters, too: Grushenka's closeness to the folk culture,[33] Dmitry Karamazov's "touch of the poet,"[34] and Fiodor Pavlovich's clowning.[35]

Russian diminuitives and hypocoristics are important for the ethos of both narrative and dialogue. In the narrative, they may have a descrip-

---

darkness"; Pevear: "Yet it was as if a ray of some bright hope shone on him in the darkness." The Russian phrase has three words that express the fragility of Dmitry's hope: *vsio-zhe,* "(and) still"; *kak by,* "as though"; and *kakoi-to,* "some kind of."

31.   For example: *No vsio-taki ogromnoe bol'shinstvo derzhalo uzhe nesomnenno storonu startsa Zosimy* (14:28, ll.34–35). "However, the vast majority were already undoubtedly on the elder Zosima's side" (Pevear). "But the majority were on Father Zosima's side" (Garnett). Of course the narrator overstates his point, as we will see in Book Seven, so, in a way, Garnett is right in reducing the narrator's emphasis. The narrator, at least occasionally, seems at a loss for a word: *liudi spetsial'nye i kompetentnye* (14, 26:8). Garnett has "authorities on the subject" (which is of course what he means); "special and competent people" (Pevear) is true to the original.

32.   For example: *samodurka* (14:13, l.4) — "tyrant" (Garnett), "crank" (Pevear), neither being close; *kazionshchina* (14:37, l.21) — "conventional" surroundings (Garnett), all this "officialism" (Pevear), the latter being closer; *v ezhovykh rukavitsakh i v chornom tele* (14:311, l.45) — "strictly and in humble surroundings 'on Lenten fare'" (Garnett), "in an iron grip, on a short leash" (Pevear), the latter being much better (perhaps "on lenten fare and on a short leash" would be closer). At the beginning of Book Two, we hear that the party arrived at the monastery *k shapochnomu razboru,* literally, "to the picking up of hats" (14:32, ll.8–9). Garnett translates "immediately after late mass," Pevear "just as the show was over," neither catching the humor of the formulaic Russian phrase. These examples may be easily multiplied.

33.   Grushenka's welcome to Aliosha (14:314, ll.30–40) provides some good examples: she calls Aliosha a "prince" (*kniaz'*) and "my young moon" (*mesiats ty moi molodoi*). She greets him with a formulaic *ne zhdala ne gadala* (Pevear tries: "I never dreamed, I never expected," which does not come close).

34.   For example: *Kamen' v ogorod!* (14:428, l.35), a formulaic expression, which Garnett translates by "That's a thrust!" and Pevear by "A rock through my own window!" More difficult is *a vy seichas lyko v stroku* (14:432, l.32) — "you pounce on it" (Garnett), "you pick up every stitch" (Pevear).

35.   For example: *V chuzhoi monastyr' so svoim ustavom ne khodiat* (14:35, l.1), literally, "One does not go to someone else's monastery with one's own rules," which both translators render by "In Rome do as the Romans do," losing the monastic flavor.

tive function,[36] but may also introduce a deprecatory or ironic nuance.[37] Fiodor Pavlovich is apt to use diminutives in various nuances: mock self-deprecation,[38] a hypocritical show of pious respect,[39] lechery,[40] imprecation,[41] scornful rudeness.[42] Captain Snegiriov speaks of his *borodenka* ("little beard," 14:185, l.44), expressing hurt and self-pity, a nuance impossible to translate. Both translators simply say "beard." When speaking of his beloved son Iliusha, Snegiriov uses a slew of tender diminutives: *ruchka ego v moei ruke, po obyknoveniiu; makhon'kaia u nego ruchka, pal'chicki tonen'kie, kholodnen'kie, — grudkoi ved' on u menia stradaet* (14:188, ll.30–32, literally: "his little hand is in my hand, as usual, he has such a wee little hand, thin little fingers, such cold little fingers — for he is ill in his little chest") — quite untranslatable. Pevear uses "little" twice, while the Russian text has seven diminutives. When Ivan Karamazov refers to the legend he will relate as *odna monastyrskaia poemka* (14:225, l.13), he suggests that he is intellectually above it and, in a way, apologizes for even bringing it up. Garnett translates simply "poem"; Pevear has "little poem," which still does not catch the nuance entirely.

The narrator directs irony and sly innuendo at the characters whom he dislikes: Fiodor Pavlovich, of course, but also his son Ivan, as well as other intellectuals, like Miusov and Ippolit Kirillovich, the public prosecutor. He lets Fiodor Pavlovich earn the "rank" (*chin*) of a sponger (14:8, l.24) and cuckold (14:9, l.27), which neither translator is able to duplicate effectively.

---

36.   The description of Father Zosima's face (14:37, ll.31–39) has as many as ten diminutives, creating an effect of physical debility and spiritual intensity that is quite impossible to translate.

37.   The title of Book One, *Istoriia odnoi semeiki* is a good example. Garnett misses the irony and translates "The History of a Certain Family." Pevear translates "A Nice Little Family."

38.   *Priezzhaiu let sem' nazad v odin gorodishko, byli tam delishki, a ia s koi kakimi kupchishkami zaviazal bylo kompan'ishku* (14:38, ll.12–14). Pevear tries: "I came to a little town seven years ago, I had a little business there, and went around with some of their merchants." This misses the diminutives in *kupchishkami* ("merchants") and *kompan'ishku* ("company"), the former belittling the merchants and the latter casting a shade on the company he kept.

39.   When he asks to kiss Father Zosima's "little hand" (*ruchku*, 14:41, l.31). Both translators have simply "hand."

40.   Speaking of his second wife: *eti nevinnye glazki* (14:13, l.19), literally: "those innocent little eyes." Both translators have simply "those innocent eyes."

41.   When begging for help: *Vanechka, Leshechka* (14:128, l.20). Both translators use the Russian form, there being no English equivalent.

42.   When angry at his sons, he calls Ivan a disrespectful *Van'ka* ("Johnny-boy"), and Dmitry *Mit'ka* (14:159, ll.15ff.).

He makes him the "founder" of many taverns (14:21, l.34); Garnett misses the irony, but Pevear properly translates *osnovatel'* as "founder." When Fiodor Pavlovich and his son Ivan arrive at the monastery, Fiodor is said to be *s synkom svoim* (14:32, l.31; literally, "with his sonny"), though Ivan is twenty-four and a university graduate. The whole party, which includes Miusov and Kalganov, is said "not to have graced Mass with their presence" (*k obedne, odnako, ne pozhalovali,* 14:32, l.4). The translators miss the irony, as they also do in some other references to the westernizer Miusov.[43]

The following example shows how wary a translator must be of Dostoevsky's irony. As Ivan Karamazov takes leave of his father, the latter, rather uncharacteristically, commends him, first to God (twice), and then to Christ (14:254, ll.23–25). Garnett translates *S Bogom* as "Good luck to you," thus missing the irony: the godless Ivan has tacitly consented to his father's murder. Pevear properly translates, "God be with you."

Nuances of meaning require the translator's attention and ingenuity. Thus, when Fiodor Pavlovich is referred to as a *sub'ekt* (14:22, ll.26–27), both translators miss the negative connotation of this word, Garnett translating "subject" and Pevear "individual." Russian in this case follows German by using "subject" to refer to a shady character — a person accused of a crime, for example. When the narrator calls Fiodor Pavlovich a *sramnik* (14:24, l.2, from *sram,* "shame"), Garnett translates "blackguard" and Pevear "stinker," both missing the nuance. The following example is more subtle. The narrator reports, in a tone of apparent approval, that Ivan Karamazov became known "in some literary circles" (*stal v literaturnykh kruzhkakh izvesten,* 14:16, ll.1–2). Both translators have "circles" for *v kruzhkakh,* whereas *kruzhok,* a diminuitive of *krug,* is literally a "small circle," as opposed to "wide circles." This point is actually developed a few lines further in the text; it is in fact a term signifying a small group of people with a common interest. The narrator also reports that Ivan developed "some sort of unusual and brilliant faculties for learning" (*kakie-to neobyknovennye i blestiaschie sposobnosti k ucheniiu,* 14:15, l.12). Garnett omits the indefinite pronoun (*kakie-to*), while Pevear translates "some sort of" — correctly, for the expression falls in line with the narrator's subtle putdown of Ivan Karamazov, which starts almost immediately.

When Grigory, Fiodor Pavlovich's servant, accepts a slap from Mme Vorokhova *kak predannyi rab* (14:14, l.19), both translators translate "like a devoted slave," missing the biblical flavor intended by the narrator — "ser-

43. Speaking of Miusov: *pozhalovav iz Parizha* (14, 16:43), close to "who favored us with a visit from Paris." Both translators have "who happened to be in the neighborhood."

vant" would have been better. Fiodor Pavlovich himself meets that formidable lady while *p'ianen'kii* (diminutive of *p'ianyi*, "drunk"), which Garnett translates as "drunk," and Pevear by "tipsy," the latter being closer. Ivan Karamazov's Devil is identified as a *russkii dzhentl'men* (15:70, ll.27–28). The translators have no choice but to translate "a Russian gentleman," thus missing the nuance of the foreign and mannered that the Russian phrase conveys: a real Russian gentleman would have been a *russkii barin.*

In some instances the language itself provides nuances that the translator is powerless to render. When Ivan Karamazov appears in court, his face has *chto-to kak by tronutoe zemlioi* (15:115, l.38), literally, "something as though touched by earth." Garnett translates "an earthy look," Pevear "touched with clay." The point is that Dostoevsky does not mean "earth-colored, sallow" (there is a word for that: *zemlistyi*), but actually "touched by the earth, the grave, or the nether world," Russian *zemlia* having broader mythical connotations than English "earth." Russian *pravda,* a key term in the novel, has a built-in ambiguity, since it means both "truth" and "justice." It is translated by "truth" throughout, which loses the important dimension of divine justice.[44] When Dmitry hears of Smerdiakov's suicide, he shouts: *Sobake sobach'ia smert'!* (15:94, l.18), which both translators render more or less literally (Pevear: "The dog died like a dog!"). However, the Russian phrase is formulaic, which the English is not. Dmitry Karamazov thanks the good Dr. Herzenstube by exclaiming: *Bravo, lekar'!* (15:105, l.33). Garnett translates "apothecary," Pevear "leach," both catching the condescension, but missing the nuance: *lekar'* is an army surgeon, and Dmitry, a military man, cannot think of a better term (there is a tinge of condescension in it, too, since an officer looked down on mere surgeons). I suggest "sawbones."

Two examples of a nuance missed and caught follow. Katerina Ivanovna tells Aliosha that Captain Snegiriov was "expelled" from the army (*ego vykliuchili,* 14:176, l.40). Garnett misses the nuance (Katerina Ivanovna's finishing school diction) and translates "he was discharged"; Pevear has it correctly. When Smerdiakov brings up the possibility that a crime may be committed at the Karamazov residence, he says: "If he [Dmitry Karamazov] will choose to commit something, why, then let him" (*Zakhotiat oni chto uchinit'* —*uchiniat-s,* 14:248, l.14). Garnett translates *uchinit'* by a neutral "to do," whereas Pevear catches the ominous subtext and translates "to commit."

Great difficulties await the translator when the prose text assumes a lyrical quality. (Inserted poetry, of which there is a good deal, is another

44. For example, 14:25, l.16.

problem.) Again, Grushenka and Dmitry provide the best examples. Grushenka's drunken monologue (14:397, ll. 15–37) is a poem in prose, made up of previously established motifs. It has to lose some of its flavor in translation. Some other passages belonging to her have a similar quality (e.g., 14:395, ll.24ff.). Dmitry is a born poet. Not only does he quote poetry, but he produces it himself, quite involuntarily. This trait, along with the fondness that it elicits in the narrator, is difficult to render.[45] Pevear tries to give a poetic quality to Dmitry's prayer on the road to Mokroe (14:372, ll.25–35), with some success. Father Zosima's exhortations have a certain rhythmic quality that approaches poetic prose of an old-fashioned kind. This effect does not come through in either translation, but the general tone of religious edification does.

Dostoevsky's prose is not above introducing blatantly poetic devices such as anaphora, parallelism, and alliteration. These effects almost invariably get lost in translation.[46]

The syntax of both narrative and dialogue is often an icon of the content. For example, a single sentence (14:16, ll.31–39), nearly ten lines long, expresses the narrator's well-founded perplexity at Ivan's seemingly harmonious coexistence with his father. It contrasts with a much shorter sentence that establishes the actual fact. The whole passage has a decidedly Tolstoian flavor, which both translators have retained.

The cumbersome yet disciplined syntax of Father Paisy's reaction to "the odor of corruption" (14:296, ll.10ff.) projects a well-schooled theologian's thought. Garnett does not quite stay with it; Pevear follows it faithfully.

The rapturous lyric passage bringing Dmitry's departure from Mokroe is orchestrated staccato and with obvious poetic devices, including alliteration (14:461, ll.18–24).[47] Pevear sees this and actually introduces a rhyme of his own: "But the cart started, and their hands were parted."

Syntax can create drama. The lengthy passage at the beginning of Book Twelve (15:89, ll.32–40) describing the carnival atmosphere at Dmitry's trial

45.   Dmitry's suicide note is a two-line poem (14:364, l.12), which neither translator can quite duplicate. As Dmitry takes leave of Piotr Il'ich, he says: *Tebe posledniaia sleza!* (14:368, l.23) — a perfect iambic tetrameter, which Pevear duplicates: "For you, for you is my last tear!"

46.   For example: *vymogatel'stvami i vymalivaniiami* (14:9, ll.9–10; *so vzvizgivaniiami i vskrikivaniiami* (14:18, ll.17–18); *besnuiushcheisia i b'iushcheisia zhenshchiny* (14:44, ll.27–28); *besporiadok, bunt i bezzakonie* (14:463, l.13); *vskinulas' i vzmolilas'* (15:11, l.48); *gorestno i goriacho* (15:38, l.41); *shevelenie i shopot* (15:94, l.13). All these instances have iconic significance, which the translations fail to convey.

47.   Note the alliterations: *No telega tronulas', i ruki ikh raznialis'. Zazvenel kolokol' chik — uvezli Mitiu.*

is a case in point. In eight lines, the Russian word *vsio* and its plural *vse* ("all, everybody") occur eight times; in addition, its synonyms *tselyi*, "all," and *kazhdyi*, "each," as well as other words that create a similar impression, such as *chrezvychaino*, "exceedingly," all contribute to create an iconic sign of crowds, noise, and hysteria.

The language of *The Brothers Karamazov* is rich in various forms of linguistic extravagance: sayings, puns, slang, etymologism, and the like.[48] In his confession to Aliosha, Dmitry says that he is *to gol, no sokol*, literally "though penniless, but a falcon" (14:109, ll.37–38), a pun on the proverbial *gol kak sokol*, "penniless (literally "bare") like a falcon." Pevear's "broke, but a hero" gets the meaning, of course, but misses the pun. During his interrogation by the examining magistrate, Dmitry facetiously takes the magistrate's words "you have failed to mention him" to refer to his expletive of a moment earlier, "Eh, the Devil," rather than to the brass pestle brought up by the magistrate (14:423, ll. 37–38). Both translations miss the point.

Etymological connotation is usually impossible to translate: *prizhival'-shchik* (15, 72:66) is "sponger," of course, but the English word does not imply that the sponger lives with his patron, as the Russian word does. The noun *izuver* (14, 203:28–29) means "fanatic," but "fanatic" does not indicate that the obsession has something to do with "faith" (*vera*); *izverg* is one of Dmitry's labels, which Garnett correctly translates as "monster"; but when Dmitry says *kak izverga sebia izvergaiu* (14:282, ll.2–3), a nuance is lost when the translator gives up on the paronomasia. Pevear tries to retain it by translating "as an outcast, I cast myself out," but sacrifices the force of *izverg*. Russian *proshchai/prosti* means "forgive," but is also routinely used as "farewell." When Dmitry takes leave of the good people of Mokroe, he says: *Proshchaite, bozh'i liudi!* They respond: *I nas prosti* (14:460, l.29). Pevear solves the problem by translating: "Farewell and forgive, God's people!" — "And you forgive us."

What conclusions may one draw from these observations? Certainly that the text of *The Brothers Karamazov* possesses a great deal of energy, derived from various forms of connotation, which a translation can duplicate only imperfectly, if at all. It may be the energy of live creative speech. It may be the energy generated by estrangement, by being "different" in a social, national, or personal way. It may be the energy of a literary subtext. It may be the energy of a Russian phrase that has no equivalent in English. It may

---

48. This includes even funny tongue-twisters, like Fiodor Pavlovich's *voznepshchevakhu!* (14:84, l.7), mock Slavonic.

be the energy of "the other voice" in irony, parody, innuendo, or inner dialogue. It may be the energy generated by a foregrounding of language *per se,*
its phonic, syntactic, or semantic form.

The two translations have followed different methods of coping with
these difficulties. Garnett has created an eminently readable text, staying
close to the original but often ignoring the original text's multiple connotations. Pevear, ever alert to the various subtexts of the original, has tried,
often successfully, to introduce them into the English text.

What is inevitably lost in both translations? I am afraid that it is the
vibrant poetic quality of Dostoevsky's language, energized by multiple connotations, its "polyphonic quality," to use Bakhtin's term. The inevitable
question, "which is the better translation?" must, I believe, be qualified by
introducing the factor of the reader. Pevear's translation serves the scholarly
reader better, as it brings him or her closer to Dostoevsky's craftsmanship.
Garnett's somewhat old-fashioned English has great charm and is close to
the ethos of Dostoevsky's Victorian narrator. It is not quite Dostoevsky,
falling short of the prodigious energy of his dialogue, but the general reader
may find it preferable to Pevear's.

BIBLIOGRAPHY

Works, Letters, and Notebooks of F. M. Dostoevsky

Polnoe sobranie sochinenii v tridtsati tomakh. [*PSS*]. 30 vols. Leningrad: Nauka, 1972–90.

The Short Novels of Dostoevsky. Trans. Constance Garnett. New York: Dial Press, 1945.

Notes from Underground. Trans. Ralph E. Matlaw. New York: Dutton, 1960.

Crime and Punishment. Trans. J. Coulson. Oxford: Oxford University Press, 1980.

The Idiot. Trans. D. Magarshack. Harmondsworth: Penguin, 1955.

Devils. Trans. and ed. Michael Katz. Oxford: Oxford University Press, 1992.

A Raw Youth. Trans. Constance Garnett. London: Heinemann, 1964.

The Brothers Karamazov. Trans. Constance Garnett. Rev. and ed. Ralph E. Matlaw. New York: W. W. Norton, 1976.

The Brothers Karamazov. Trans. Richard Pevear and Larissa Volokhonsky. San Francisco: North Point Press, 1990.

Complete Letters. 5 vols. Trans. David Lowe and Ronald Meyer. Ann Arbor: Ardis, 1988.

The Diary of a Writer. Trans. Boris Brasol. New York: Octagon Books, 1973.

A Writer's Diary. Trans. Kenneth Lantz. 2 vols. Evanston: Northwestern University Press, 1993–94.

The Notebooks for Crime and Punishment. Trans. and ed. Edward Wasiolek. Chicago: University of Chicago Press, 1976.

The Notebooks for The Idiot. Trans. Katharine Strelsky. Ed. Edward Wasiolek. Chicago: University of Chicago Press, 1967.

The Notebooks for The Possessed. Trans. Victor Terras. Ed. Edward Wasiolek. Chicago: University of Chicago Press, 1968.

The Notebooks for A Raw Youth. Trans. Victor Terras. Ed. Edward Wasiolek. Chicago: University of Chicago Press, 1969.

The Notebooks for The Brothers Karamazov. Trans. and ed. Edward Wasiolek. Chicago: University of Chicago Press, 1971.

The Unpublished Dostoevsky: Diaries and Notebooks, 1860–81. Ed. Carl R. Proffer. 3 vols. Ann Arbor: Ardis, 1973–76.

Secondary Literature

Anderson, Roger B. *Dostoevsky: Myths of Duality.* Gainesville: University of Florida Press, 1986.

Antonovich, M. A. "Mistiko-asketicheskii roman," *Novoe obozrenie,* no. 3 (1881): 192–243.

Bakhtin, M. M. *Problems of Dostoevsky's Poetics.* Trans. and ed. Caryl Emerson. Minneapolis: University of Minnesota Press, 1984.

Bakhtin, M. M. *Problemy poetiki Dostoevskogo.* Moscow: Sovetskii pisatel', 1963.

Belinskii, V. G. *Polnoe sobranie sochinenii.* 13 vols. Moscow: Izdatel'stvo Akademii Nauk, 1953–59.

Belknap, Robert L. "Shakespeare and *The Possessed,*" *Dostoevsky Studies* 5 (1984): 63–69.

Belknap, Robert L. "The Sources of Mitja Karamazov." In *American Contributions to the Seventh International Congress of Slavists,* Warsaw, August 21–27, 1973, vol. 2: 39–51. The Hague: Mouton, 1973.

Belknap, Robert L. *The Structure of* The Brothers Karamazov. The Hague: Mouton, 1967.

Bem, A. L., ed. *O Dostoevskom: Sbornik statei.* 3 vols. Prague: Petropolis, 1929–36.

Berdiaev, Nikolai. *Mirosozertsanie Dostoevskogo.* Prague, YMCA, 1923.

Berlin, Isaiah. *The Hedgehog and the Fox.* London: Weidenfeld & Nicolson, 1953.

Blagoi, D. D. *Dusha v zavetnoi lire: Ocherki zhizni i tvorchestva Pushkina.* Moscow, Sovetskii pisatel', 1977.

Braun, Maximilian. *Dostojewskij: Das Gesamtwerk als Vielfalt und Einheit.* Göttingen, Vandenhoeck & Ruprecht, 1976.

Camus, Albert. *The Rebel: An Essay on Man in Revolt.* Trans. Anthony Bower. New York, Knopf, 1956.

Chicherin, A. V. "Poeticheskii stroi iazyka v romanakh Dostoevskogo," in *Tvorchestvo F. M. Dostoevskogo* (Moscow: AN SSSR, 1959), pp. 417–44.

Chirkov, N. M. *O stile Dostoevskogo.* Moscow: AN SSSR, 1963.

Chizhevskii, Dmitrii. "K probleme dvoinika: Iz knigi o formalizme v etike." In *O Dostoevskom,* ed. A. L. Bem, vol. 1: 9–38. Prague: Petro polis, 1929.

Cox, Roger L. *Between Earth and Heaven: Shakespeare, Dostoevsky, and the Meaning of Christian Tragedy.* New York: Holt, Rinehart and Winston, 1969.

Dalton, Elizabeth. *Unconscious Structure in* The Idiot: *A Study in Literature and Psychoanalysis.* Princeton: Princeton University Press, 1978.

Danow, David K. "A Note on the Internal Dynamics of the Dostoevskian Conclave," *Dostoevsky Studies* 2 (1981): 61–68.

Danow, David K. "Stavrogin's Teachings: Reported Speech in *The Possessed,*" *Slavic and East European Journal* 32 (1988): 213–24.

Dobroliubov, N. A. *Sobranie sochinenii v deviati tomakh.* Leningrad, Khudozhestvennaia literatura, 1963.

Dolinin, A. S. *Poslednie romany Dostoevskogo: Kak sozdavalis'* Podrostok *i* Brat'ia Karamazovy. Moscow and Leningrad, Sovetskii pisatel', 1963.

Engel'gardt, B. M. "Ideologicheskii roman Dostoevskogo." In *F. M. Dostoevskii: Stat'i i materialy,* ed. A. S. Dolinin, vol. 2:79–109. Moscow and Leningrad, 1924.

Fanger, Donald. *Dostoevsky and Romantic Realism: A Study of Dostoevsky in Relation to Balzac, Dickens and Gogol.* Cambridge: Harvard University Press, 1965.

Frank, Joseph. *Dostoevsky.* 5 vols. Princeton: Princeton University Press, 1976–95. [4 vols. have appeared.]

Fuchs, Ina. "Homo Apostata," *die Entfremdung des Menschen: Philosophische Analysen zur Geistmetaphysik F. M. Dostojewskijs.* Munich: Otto Sagner, 1987.

Gibian, George. "Traditional Symbolism in *Crime and Punishment,*" *PMLA* 70 (1955): 979–96.

Gide, André. *Dostoïevsky (articles et causeries).* Paris: Librairie Plon, 1923.

Grigor'ev, Apollon. *Sochineniia.* St. Petersburg, 1876.

Grossman, L. P. *Dostoevskii: Put', poetika, tvorchestvo.* Moscow, Sovremennye problemy, 1928.

Grossman, L. P. "Dostoevskii—khudozhnik." In *Tvorchestvo F. M. Dostoevskogo,* pp. 330–416. Moscow: AN SSSR, 1959.

Grossman, L. P. *Poetika Dostoevskogo.* Moscow: Gosudarstvennaia Akademiia khudozhestvennyk nauk, 1925.

Ivanov, Vyacheslav. *Freedom and the Tragic Life: A Study in Dostoevsky.* Trans. Norman Cameron. New York: Noonday, 1952.

Jackson, Robert L. *The Art of Dostoevsky: Deliriums and Nocturnes.* Princeton: Princeton University Press, 1981.

Jackson, Robert L. *Dialogues with Dostoevsky: The Overwhelming Questions.* Stanford: Stanford University Press, 1993.

Jackson, Robert L. *Dostoevsky's Quest for Form: A Study of His Philosophy of Art.* New Haven: Yale University Press, 1966.

Jones, Malcolm V. *Dostoevsky after Bakhtin: Readings in Dostoevsky's Fantastic Realism.* Cambridge: Cambridge University Press, 1990.

Komarowitsch, W., ed. *Die Urgestalt der "Brüder Karamasoff": Dostojewskis Quellen, Entwürfe und Fragmente.* Intro. Sigmund Freud. Munich: Piper, 1928.

Lachmann, Renate. *Memory and Literature: Intertextuality in Russian Modernism.* Trans. Roy Sellars and Anthony Wall. Theory and History of Literature, vol. 87. Minneapolis: University of Minnesota Press, 1997.

Leatherbarrow, W. J. "Idealism and Utopian Socialism in Dostoyevsky's *Gospodin Prokharchin* and *Slaboe serdtse,*" *Slavonic and East European Review* 58:524–40.

Leont'ev, K. N. *Sobranie sochinenii.* 9 vols. Moscow, lzd. M. V. Sablina, 1912.

Linnér, Sven. *Dostoevsky on Realism.* Stockholm: Almqvist and Wiksell, 1967.

Maikov, V. N. *Sochineniia.* 2 vols. Kiev, 1901.

Matlaw, Ralph E. *"The Brothers Karamazov": Novelistic Technique.* The Hague: Mouton, 1957.

Matlaw, Ralph E. "Recurrent Imagery in Dostoevskij," *Harvard Slavic Studies* 3: 201–25.

Meier-Graefe, Julius. *Dostojewski der Dichter.* Berlin: Rowohlt, 1926.

Merezhkovskii, D. S. *L. Tolstoi i Dostoevskii.* St. Petersburg: Mir iskusstva, 1901.

Merezhkovskii, D. S. *Prorok russkoi revoliutsii.* St. Petersburg, Pirozhkov, 1906.

Mikhailovskii, N. K. *Literaturno-kriticheskie stat'i.* Moscow: Gosizdat, 1957.

Mochulsky, Konstantin. *Dostoevsky: His Life and Works.* Trans. Michael A. Minihan. Princeton: Princeton University Press, 1967.

Nabokov, Vladimir. *Lectures on Literature.* Ed. F. Bowers. New York: Harcourt, Brace, Jovanovich, 1980.

Neuhäuser, Rudolf. *Das Frühwerk Dostoevskijs: Literarische Tradition und gesell-schaftlicher Anspruch.* Heidelberg: Winter, 1979.

Nigg, Walter. *Der christliche Narr.* Stuttgart and Zurich: Artemis, 1956.

Nikol'skii, Iurii. *Turgenev i Dostoevskii: Istoriia odnoi vrazhdy.* Sofia, 1921.

Passage, Charles E. *Dostoevski the Adapter: A Study in Dostoevski's Use of the Tales of Hoffmann.* University of North Carolina Studies in Comparative Literature, vol. 10. Chapel Hill: University of North Carolina Press, 1954.

Perlina, Nina. *Varieties of Poetic Utterance: Quotation in* The Brothers Karamazov. Lanham, Md.: University Presses of America, 1985.

Pisarev, D. I. *Sochineniia.* Ed. Iu. S. Sorokin. 4 vols. Moscow, Khudozhestvennaia literatura, 1955–56.

Proust, Marcel. *A la recherche du temps perdu.* Vol. 3. Ed. Pierre Clarac and André Ferré. Paris: Librairie Plon, 1954.

Rosenshield, Gary. "*The Bronze Horseman* and *The Double:* The Depoeticization of the Myth of Petersburg in the Young Dostoevskii," *Slavic Review* 55 (1996): 399–428.

Rosenshield, Gary. *Crime and Punishment: The Techniques of the Omniscient Narrator.* Lisse: Peter de Ridder, 1978.

Rozanov, V. V. *Dostoevsky and the Legend of the Grand Inquisitor.* Trans. Spencer E. Roberts. Ithaca: Cornell University Press, 1972.

Saltykov-Shchedrin, M. E. *Sobranie sochinenii.* 20 vols. Moscow, Khudozhestvennaia literatura, 1965–77.

Sandoz, Ellis. *Political Apocalypse: A Study of Dostoevsky's Grand Inquisitor.* Baton Rouge: Louisiana State University Press, 1971.

Seduro, Vladimir. *Dostoyevski in Russian Literary Criticism 1846–1956.* New York: Columbia University Press, 1957.

Shestov, Lev. *Afiny i Ierusalim.* Paris: YMCA, 1951.

Shklovskii, Viktor. *Za i protiv: Zametki o Dostoevskom.* Moscow: Sovetskii pisatel', 1957.

Solov'ev, S. M. *Izobrazitel'nye sredstva v tvorchestve F. M. Dostoevskogo: Ocherki.* Moscow: Sovetskii pisatel', 1979.

Solov'ev, V. S. *Sobranie sochinenii.* 12 vols. 2d ed. St. Petersburg: Prosveshchenie, 1911–14.

Strelsky, Katharine. "Dostoevsky's Early Tale 'A Faint Heart.'" *Russian Review* 30 (1971): 146–53.

Struve, Gleb. "Notes on the Language and Style of Dostoevsky," *Bulletin of the International Dostoevsky Society*, no. 7 (1977): 76.

Terras, Victor. *The Young Dostoevsky (1846–1849): A Critical Study*. The Hague: Mouton, 1969.

Tkachev, P. N. *Izbrannye sochineniia*. Ed. B. P. Kozmin. 6 vols. Moscow: Gosudarstvennoe sotsial'no-ekonomicheskoe izdatel'stvo, 1932–37.

Tolstoi, L. N. *Polnoe sobranie sochinenii*. Ed. V. Chertkov *et al.* 90 vols. Moscow: AN SSSR, 1928–58.

Torop, Peeter. *Dostoevskii: Istoriia i ideologiia*. Tartu: Tartu Ülikooli Kirjastus, 1997.

Tunimanov, V. A. "The Narrator in *The Devils*." In *Dostoevsky: New Perspectives*, ed. Robert L. Jackson, pp. 145–75. Englewood Cliffs, N.J.: Prentice-Hall, 1984.

Turgenev, I. S. *Polnoe sobranie sochinenii i pisem*. 28 vols. Ed. M. P. Alekseev. Moscow: AN SSSR, 1960–68.

Tynianov, Iu. N. *Dostoevskii i Gogol': K teorii parodii*. Petrograd: Opoiaz, 1921.

Vinogradov, V. V. *Evoliutsiia russkogo naturalizma: Gogol' i Dostoevskii*. Moscow: Academia, 1929.

Wasiolek, Edward. *Dostoevsky: The Major Fiction*. Cambridge: MIT Press, 1964.

Zen'kovskii, V. V. "Dostoevsky's Religious and Philosophical Views." In *Dostoevsky: A Collection of Critical Essays*, ed. René Wellek, pp. 130–45. Englewood Cliffs, N.J.: Prentice-Hall, 1962.

Zen'kovskii, V. V. "Fiodor Pavlovich Karamazov." In *O Dostoevskom*, ed. A. L. Bem, vol. 2:93–114. Prague, Petropolis, 1929–36.

INDEX